The United States and Persian Gulf Security

The Foundations of the War on Terror

The United States and Persian Gulf Security

The Foundations of the War on Terror

Steven Wright

DURHAM MIDDLE EAST MONOGRAPHS

THE UNITED STATES AND PERSIAN GULF SECURITY
The Foundations of the War on Terror

Published by
Ithaca Press
8 Southern Court
South Street
Reading
Berkshire
RG1 4QS
UK
www.ithacapress.co.uk

Ithaca Press is an imprint of Garnet Publishing Limited

First Edition

ISBN 13: 978-0-86372-321-6

British Library Cataloguing-in-Publication Data
A catalogue record for this book is available from the British Library

Typeset by PHi, India
Jacket design by David Rose
Cover photo used with permission of Ali Jasim/Reuters/Corbis

Printed in Lebanon

Contents

1

Introduction

---

*"The Middle East is an area in which the United States has a vital interest.
The maintenance of peace in that area, which has so frequently seen
disturbances in the past, is of significance to the world as a whole."*

Franklin D. Roosevelt
March 1944

The foreign policy response of George W. Bush's administration in the
wake of the trauma of the 11 September 2001 terrorist attacks on New
York and Washington D.C. signified a complete redefinition of US
grand strategy.[1] Whilst the collapse of the Soviet Union marked the end
of the Cold War, resulting in the post-Cold War era, the 9/11 attacks
marked the onset of the era of the War on Terror. This gave rise to the
most fundamental redefinition of US grand strategy since the presidency
of Franklin D. Roosevelt.[2] Yet the nature of Bush's post-9/11 foreign
policy agenda has emerged as the most ambitious since Woodrow
Wilson articulated his vision for a new international order following
the end of the First World War.[3] Understanding the origins, strategic
direction and application of this change is thus of great importance for
the field of international relations and policymakers in general.

The purpose of this book is to provide an examination of US foreign
policy and its success in achieving geopolitical security in the Persian Gulf
region from the post-Cold War era to the era of the War on Terror. Given
the fundamental revision in US grand strategy following the 9/11 attacks,
this study will analyse how this new grand strategic era has heralded a
redefinition of security for the Persian Gulf. This redefinition will be
shown to be a complete break from the long-standing historical position
of the United States in this regard. Crucially, it will be demonstrated that
this redefinition carries with it the prospect for geopolitical upheaval in
the region as a necessary part of achieving the long-term strategic objectives of the War on Terror and the regional needs for security. For scholars
of US foreign policy and strategic studies of the Middle East, the manner

in which this transition unfolds is likely to dominate the agenda for the foreseeable future. Nevertheless, only through a detailed understanding of where we have come from and how the current strategy and tactics differ from the past can a thorough exposition be achieved. In essence therefore, this volume is an examination of Bill Clinton's and George W. Bush's foreign and strategic policies vis-à-vis Persian Gulf security in the post-Cold War and War on Terror era.

The Historical Context: American Policy towards Persian Gulf Security

The contemporary national interests of the United States in the Persian Gulf region have their historical origins rooted in the circumstances of the First World War. Although the United States has had long-standing commercial interests in the Maghreb region dating back to 1784,[4] it was the inherent requirements of the modern era of mechanised warfare, in addition to the dynamics of Western industrialisation at the time, that led oil to become a key economic and strategic interest of the United States.[5] It is important to recognise from the outset that the paramount national security interest of the United States in the region has historically been in "[an] unhindered flow of oil from the Persian Gulf to the world market at a stable price".[6] With upwards of 60% of proven global oil reserves held within Middle Eastern countries surrounding the Persian Gulf, its strategic importance is unrivalled. Moreover, it is also a strategic linchpin as upwards of 90% of oil exported travels through the Strait of Hormuz. Given that Iran has the second highest natural gas reserves and is closely followed by Qatar, the importance of this region for global energy is likely to be long-standing.

During the Cold War, the containment of communism was the over-arching, global strategic consideration that characterised US foreign policy, and this was consequently reflected in its policy towards the Persian Gulf. The reasons why the Persian Gulf was a key strategic interest for the United States during the Cold War era are usefully summarised by Michael Hudson:

> [T]he entrenchment of Soviet power in that strategic region would [have been] a decisive shift in the world balance, outflanking NATO; Soviet control of Middle Eastern oil could disrupt the

economy of the free world; and triumph throughout Asia, Africa, and Europe.[7]

With Britain having decided to withdraw its presence east of Suez in the 1960s, Richard Nixon was prompted into developing a 'twin-pillar' security strategy of promoting Iran, and to a lesser extent Saudi Arabia, as guardians of regional security and as bulwarks against Soviet expansionism.[8] This policy involved the provision of military armaments to these two key allies with the aim of achieving regional security.[9] With Saudi Arabia leading the Arab oil embargo as a result of US support for Israel in the 1973 Arab–Israeli war, oil prices increased from around $3.00 per barrel to upwards of $12.00. The resulting recession and Saudi Arabia's involvement did not however cause the unravelling of the twin-pillars strategy. If anything, the strategic value of oil increased the desire of the US to maintain its geopolitical presence in the region and this ironically served to strengthen further the commitment of the US towards Persian Gulf security.

However, this twin-pillar strategy became defunct when Iran, the key pillar of the US security policy, experienced an Islamic revolution in 1979 that resulted in Muhammad Shah Reza Pahlevi being overthrown. The dramatic overthrow of the Shah ushered in a fundamentally new era for regional politics and US strategic policy towards the region. The subsequent seizure of the US embassy in Tehran in November 1979 and the ensuing hostage crisis was crucial in affirming the perception of the Islamic Republic as inimical to US interests. It was as a result of the anti-American position of the successor Islamic regime in Tehran that the revolution necessarily ushered in a reassessment of Iran's role in US policy towards Persian Gulf security. A further key factor was that Iran became equated with an asymmetric threat to Israel – a key long-term US interest – through its support for Hezbollah and its destabilising influence on the internal affairs of Lebanon. President Carter's response, known as the Carter Doctrine, was to commit the United States to preventing any hostile power from gaining control over this vital strategic area.

With the onset of the Reagan administration in 1981, US policy towards the Persian Gulf was essentially formulated within the context of the Iran–Iraq War and also through perceived Iranian links to international terrorist attacks against both the United States and Israel. Although the US professed neutrality towards the conflict, Reagan's policy was essentially characterised by a strategic balancing in which it provided intelligence assistance, 'dual use' technologies and export credits to Iraq.[10] But compounding this, the Reagan administration adopted Carter's ambitious plans for a 'Central Command' in the region and began to have increased military cooperation with the Arabian Peninsula states. Here it is worthy of note that Saudi Arabia was sold advanced military technology, an example being the sale of Airborne Warning and Control System Aircraft (AWACS) in 1981.

With the end of the Iran–Iraq War and the emergence of a post-Cold War international environment, the dynamics of US foreign policy had entered a new phase. However, this was complicated by the Iraqi invasion of Kuwait in 1990. With Saudi Arabia perceiving a clear threat from Iraq, it welcomed the deployment of US forces on its territory. This was to become the key factor behind a close relationship between several of the Arabian Peninsula states and the United States. Moreover, it was to be a fateful act which fanned the flames of radical Islamism that ultimately promoted a redefinition of US grand strategy in the post-9/11 environment. Whilst prior to the invasion the US presence had been mainly unseen and on the outskirts of the region, the new situation involved an active strategic deployment. America's Gulf naval force was renamed the Fifth Fleet and was stationed onshore in Bahrain. Military cooperation with Oman increased along with the UAE. Whilst the liberation of Kuwait was achieved, the military footprint of the United States remained. As both Iran and Iraq were considered as potential threats to the United States' interests in geopolitical security in the Persian Gulf subregion, the administration of George H. W. Bush laid the foundations for a containment of both countries. This was to be later codified into a clear strategy under the Clinton administration and formed the essence of post-Cold War security strategy towards this geopolitical area.

Post-Cold War Persian Gulf Security

Unveiled in May 1993 by Martin Indyk, Special Assistant to the President for Near East and South Asian Affairs, US foreign policy became officially lodged on the premise of containing and deterring both Iran and Iraq from challenging the security of the key oil producing Gulf States, in addition to undermining the peace process and threatening Israel.[11] Indyk portrayed the Clinton administration's approach to the Middle East as a

[4]

non-compartmentalised strategy which was premised on dual containment. The definitive outline of dual containment was made, however, by national security adviser Anthony Lake in a 1994 article in the journal *Foreign Affairs*.[12] Lake clarified the conception of the strategy as entailing a multilateral containment of Iraq as a means of forcing compliance with UN resolutions; and a unilateral containment of Iran until it altered its internal and external policies. The fact that these policies provided for Persian Gulf security was merely seen as a *by-product* as they were premised on other criteria.[13] Indeed, Lake's argument afforded Iraq under Saddam Hussein the prospect of having sanctions lifted over a period of time, once compliance had been recognised by the UN Security Council and confidence had been restored within the international community.[14] Iran received a similar prescription in that the United States sought a moderation of Iran's policies in order for a rapprochement to occur, but would maintain sanctions as a means of controlling Iran until it moderated policies deemed provocative by the United States. There was thus a degree of analytical conflict between these objectives and the conception of it as a containment strategy which one can equate with maintenance of the status quo.[15]

Although Lake presented the dual containment strategy as a prudent policy undertaking, debate exists on its origins and nature which contrasts with the official position. It is therefore prudent to examine these varying interpretations. One of the first assessments of dual containment was undertaken by Gregory Gause who interpreted it as a strategy geared towards achieving the wider regional strategic objective of Persian Gulf security.[16] He recognised that Iran and, to a lesser extent, Iraq were seen to pose a threat towards Israel and the peace process, but interpreted the overall dual containment strategy as being ultimately geared towards securing US geostrategic interests in the Persian Gulf. Whilst Gause maintained that the Clinton administration's dual containment policy was premised on geostrategic concerns towards the Persian Gulf, he argued that this was subservient to the long-term objective of making neighbouring states a "sufficient counterweight to both Iran and Iraq".[17] Therefore, containment was designed to weaken both countries to a degree sufficient to usher in a balance of power: through the application of containment, the status quo would be enforced and would thus cater for Persian Gulf security.

Anthony Cordesman also argued that the adoption of dual

containment was a necessity given the inability of the Gulf countries to offer a credible defence against their aggressive neighbours. Cordesman comments that "[it] is not solely a function of what Iran can do or Iraq can do, it is a function of what the nations in the region can do, and it is basically a function of American ability to contain Iranian and Iraqi military power."[18] He recognised that such an approach was required in order to safeguard vital US political and economic interests. Nevertheless, he conceded that, in the case of Iraq, containment would ultimately not be able to prevent an Iraqi production of unconventional weapons as it merely slows their development.[19] Gause, however, went even further by arguing that sanctions neither weakened Saddam's hold on power nor stopped his development of unconventional weapons.[20] Nevertheless, both shared the premise that dual containment was based on geostrategic interests in the Persian Gulf. Kissinger lends weight to this prescription by echoing the argument that dual containment was a thoroughly geostrategic response to the threat both countries posed to US interests in the Persian Gulf.[21]

In contrast, Gary Sick contended that the adoption of a containment policy towards Iran was primarily based on serving the strategic priority of the Arab–Israeli peace process.[22] He highlighted the fact that it was a policy undertaking that virtually mirrored a policy paper authored by Martin Indyk in 1993, prior to his taking office in the National Security Council, which called for a containment of the threats Iran and Iraq posed to Israel and the peace process itself. Therefore, US bilateral foreign policy towards Iran and Iraq was arguably subordinate to US interests in the peace process. Sick conversely saw US policy towards Iraq under the dual containment rubric as being premised on a compliance with UN resolutions: increased Persian Gulf security was thus seen by him as a by-product rather than an objective.[23] Indeed, Sick suggested that this resulted in the United States emerging as a *regional player* rather than an external actor, and was thus able to ensure these objectives were achieved.[24]

In what several scholars recognise as a seminal article on this subject, Zbigniew Brzezinski, Brent Scowcroft and Richard Murphy refined these interpretations. They suggested that the Clinton administration's bilateral policies towards Iran and Iraq were part of the mutually reinforcing strategic objectives of supporting the peace process and providing for Persian Gulf security.[25] Thus a mutually compatible dual track US geostrategic policy towards the Middle East was applied, and the 'dual containment strategy' was a mere slogan with little conceptual worth.

Even with the onset of the administration of George W. Bush, there is little dispute that foreign policy towards the Middle East actually retained consistency from the Clinton administration up until the watershed of the 11 September 2001 terrorist attacks. Indeed, Robert Kagan and William Kristol critically remarked that prior to the 9/11 attacks, Bush's policy seemed "content to continue walking down dangerous paths in foreign and defense policy laid out over the past eight years by Bill Clinton".[26] The views of other scholars, such as Kenneth Pollack, were more moderate but still identified US foreign policy towards Iran and Iraq as showing continuity from the preceding Clinton administration until the War on Terror actually began.[27]

As a result of the 9/11 terrorist attacks, Islamic terrorism emerged as the accepted primary strategic threat faced by the United States. However, understanding the intellectual context in which the Bush administration interpreted this threat is key to understanding its strategic response. The new grand strategy on how to counter the causes of Islamic terrorism in the long term will be shown to be completely linked to the redefinition of Persian Gulf security. Suffice it to say at this stage that the new intellectual context of the War on Terror subordinated long-standing US geostrategic interests in the Persian Gulf to the maxims of grand strategy in the War on Terror. Therefore, as with the Cold War era where Persian Gulf security was defined under the strategy geared towards countering the communist threat, so too in the War on Terror has Persian Gulf security been redefined. However, the redefinition will be shown to be far more sweeping – the achievement of security for this region is now conceived as premised not on a military enforcement through geopolitical power relationships, but rather as hinging on the domestic political form of the states within this subregion. In essence, the new definition of Persian Gulf security rests on the belief that insecurity is simply a product of the nature of the internal power structure within the region's states. Therefore, only through civil society having power to control the political elite, as in Western liberal democracies, can states' action be steered away from hostility and insecurity.

This book will aim to provide a detailed examination of this change by conducting an analysis of US foreign policy within the context of

Persian Gulf security. The following two chapters will provide the reader with an analysis of the intellectual context of US foreign policy, firstly, by showing its relationship with political Islam and terrorism, and secondly, by framing US foreign policy within a historical context to underscore the forces at play in shaping it. The chapter on political Islam is particularly important as it will show what the intellectual understanding of the root causes of Islamic radicalism are and thus will explain the essence of what US grand strategy is in the War on Terror. This is crucial to understanding the strategic change in Persian Gulf security post-9/11. The other sections of the book will analyse US foreign policy towards Iran and Iraq but will separate the analysis on US policy towards these countries before and after 9/11 in order to underline the redefinition that Persian Gulf security underwent.

NOTES

1 Grand strategy is defined as the over-arching strategic purpose or direction which takes precedence over regional geostrategic foreign policy calculations and bilateral foreign policies. It typically involves the application of all areas of national power to achieve a long-term national objective geared towards combating an over-arching strategic threat. For example, during the Cold War era the grand strategic purpose was commonly defined as the containment and deterrence of the ideological spread of Communism.

2 John L. Gaddis, "Grand Strategy in the Second Term", *Foreign Affairs* 84.1 (2005): 2.

3 Henry Kissinger, *Diplomacy* (New York: Touchstone, 1995) 218–45.

4 Thomas A. Bryson, *American Diplomatic Relations with the Middle East, 1784–1975 : A Survey* (Metuchen: Scarecrow Press, 1977) 1–57.

5 John A. DeNovo, *American Interests and Policies in the Middle East, 1900–1939* (Minneapolis: University of Minnesota Press, 1963) 167–69.

6 United States, "United States Security Strategy for the Middle East", ed. Department of Defence (GPO, 1995).

7 Michael C. Hudson, "To Play the Hegemon: Fifty Years of US Policy Towards the Middle East", *Middle East Journal* 50.3 (1996): 334.

8 Henry Kissinger, *The White House Years* (London: Weidenfeld & Nicolson, 1979) 1262–65.

9 F. Gregory Gause III, "British and American Policies in the Persian Gulf 1968–1973", *Journal of International Affairs* 45.2 (1985).

10 Anthony H. Cordesman, *The Iran–Iraq War and Western Security 1984–87: Strategic Implications and Policy Options* (London: Jane's Publishing, 1987) 157–63.

11 Martin Indyk, "The Clinton Administration's Approach to the Middle East", *Address to the Soref Symposium* (Washington, D.C.: Washington Institute for Near East Policy, 1993).

12 Anthony Lake, "Confronting Backlash States", *Foreign Affairs* 73.2 (1994).

13 Indyk, "The Clinton Administration's Approach to the Middle East".

14 Lake, "Confronting Backlash States" 45–50.

15 F. Gregory Gause III, *US Policy toward Iraq*, Emirates Lecture Series, vol. 39 (Abu Dhabi: The Emirates Center for Strategic Studies and Research, 2002) 12.

16 F. Gregory Gause III, "The Illogic of Dual Containment", *Foreign Affairs* 73.2 (1994): 56–58.

17 Gause III, *US Policy toward Iraq* 12.

18 Martin Indyk, Graham Fuller, Anthony H. Cordesman and Phebe Marr, "Symposium on Dual Containment: US Policy toward Iran and Iraq", *Middle East Policy* 3.1 (1994): 13.

19 Indyk, Fuller, Cordesman and Marr, "Symposium on Dual Containment: US Policy toward Iran and Iraq" 13.

20 F. Gregory Gause III, "Getting It Back on Iraq", *Foreign Affairs* 78.3 (1999): 62.

21 Henry Kissinger, *Does America Need a Foreign Policy?: Toward a Diplomacy for the 21st Century*, rev. ed. (London: Free Press, 2002) 191.

22 Gary Sick, "The United States and Iran: Truth and Consequences", *Contention* 5.2 (1996): 59–78.

23 Gary Sick, "Rethinking Dual Containment", *Survival* 40.1 (1998): 5–32.

24 Gary Sick, "US Policy in the Gulf: Objectives and Purpose", *Managing New Developments in the Gulf*, ed. Rosemary Hollis (London: Royal Institute for International Affairs, 2000) 14.

25 Zbigniew Brzezinski, Brent Scowcroft and Richard Murphy, "Differentiated Containment", *Foreign Affairs* 76.3 (1997): 20–30.

26 Robert Kagan and William Kristol, "Clinton's Foreign Policy Cont.", *Weekly Standard* 12 Mar. 2001: 11.

27 Kenneth Pollack, "Next Stop Baghdad?", *Foreign Affairs Editors' Choice: The Middle East Crisis*, ed. Gideon Rose (New York: Council on Foreign Relations, 2002) 116–32.

PART 1

SETTING THE CONTEXT OF CHANGE IN US FOREIGN POLICY

2

The Architecture of US Foreign Policy under Bill Clinton and George W. Bush

"The presidency has many problems, but boredom is the least of them."
Richard M. Nixon
January 1973

The most distinguishing feature of US foreign policy is the varying level of continuity and change that stems from each successive administration. Each President brings a new outlook, interpretation and agenda for US policy. The President's choice of staff disseminates change on a bureaucratic level which in turn has an impact on policy. The importance of recognising such factors is necessary for a comprehensive foreign policy analysis and interpretation to be achieved.

Here, comparative observations of Bill Clinton's and George W. Bush's administrations allow for a clearer understanding of the factors which contributed towards foreign policy formation. Such foreign policy analysis[1] will consider the drivers of policy within the administrations and will act as a useful precursor to the subsequent chapter which will analyse the intellectual context of US policy and political Islam in order to show the essence of strategy in the War on Terror and thus the motives behind the post-9/11 redefinition of Persian Gulf security.

The following analysis will provide an examination of the idiosyncratic differences between Clinton and Bush in order to highlight how their background, outlook, and character would have had an impact on foreign policy. A second area which will be examined is that of the ideological influences on the elite decision makers. This will highlight the idiosyncratic differences of key staff members from both presidencies whose background and beliefs are important factors that allow for a deeper understanding of the origins of foreign policy. The final section will examine how this foreign policy manifested itself and contrasted under each presidency with particular attention paid to the nature of President Bush's post-9/11 strategy. In the first instance however, the historical context of change in US foreign policy needs to be appreciated in order to show the relationship between pragmatic *realpolitik* calculations and moralism. This is important in order for the reader to fully conceptualise the nature of change that the terrorist attacks of 11 September 2001 effected in US foreign policy.

The Historical Competition in US Foreign Policy: Moralism vs. *Realpolitik*

To be sure, the United States has, since the early days of the republic, been heralded as a nation that is motivated by the dictates of enlightened rationalism, its very destiny tied to serving as a beacon of freedom, hope and advancement. In its isolationist years of the nineteenth century, two central themes came to dominate US diplomacy: the values on which the republic was founded were viewed to be universal moral maxims, and their global adoption was seen to become yet more certain once the United States had refined them at home and properly conceived a 'shining city on the hill' for others to emulate – symbolic of the views articulated by Thomas Jefferson. Such moral maxims did, however, have to operate under observance of the accepted Westphalian doctrines of sovereignty and non-intervention and so did not successfully emerge as integral parts of US foreign policy. With Secretary of State John Quincy Adams famously stating in 1821 that the United States' role was "the well-wisher to the freedom and independence of all" but not a nation that "goes in search of monsters to destroy", the promotion of such moral virtues was largely to be a missionary affair with foreign policy confining itself with *realpolitik* statecraft. However, a fundamental break from this occurred under the fateful Presidency of Woodrow Wilson, the legacy of which has had a defining resonance within contemporary US foreign policy.

After a century of feeling inhibited by the Westphalian order, the First World War presented an opportunity for Wilson to remake the international order based on the underlying political moral maxims that captured the essence of enlightened American rationalism. Indeed, Wilson explicitly justified America's involvement as premised on the objective of reordering the international system in its own image. This was a clear departure from the long-standing US foreign policy practice of conducting its diplomacy based on practical rather than ethical considerations. The pursuit of a national interest was thus rejected as selfishness and substituted with the broader doctrine of seeking the advancement of values which could benefit all of mankind; such an objective was thus in clear tension with long-standing Westphalian notions on a nation's sovereignty over its internal polity.

Wilson left a defining impression on all subsequent US foreign policy through three interrelated themes. Firstly, he held the progressive view that the natural state of the international system was harmonious cooperation – the Hobbsian world view was largely rejected. Secondly, the use of force to achieve change was similarly abandoned in favour of international law and arbitration. Moreover, such normative values were extended to the sub-state level which upheld that people had an innate right to determine their own future; the principles of self-determination and democracy were therefore seen as the pillars on which a nation should be based.

Finally, and most importantly, Wilson upheld the view that nations that are built on such criteria would not only be stable internally – therefore ending the risk of carnage through civil war – but also that such nations would never opt for external war. Achieving a global adoption of such values was therefore upheld as not only a moral imperative but also a practical means of reducing the risk of war which could embroil the United States. Nevertheless, the driver was firmly seen as for the benefit of all mankind. Wilsonian doctrine therefore challenged the purely amoral *realpolitik* conception of statecraft by taking the founding values of the republic and applying them within a cogent foreign policy package.

The legacy of the Wilsonian world view on US foreign policy cannot be underestimated; it has served to challenge the very essence of an enlightened pragmatic or *realpolitik* conception of foreign policy. Although this thought has been an integral part of US diplomatic thinking since Wilson, the failure of the League of Nations showed that in the absence of a clear external threat to US national security, the political stomach for such crusading morally grounded diplomacy was limited. It was only with the onset of the Second World War that such Wilsonian values came to be merged with a clear conception of threat to US security. Indeed, America's appetite for entry into the Second World War was largely wanting until Pearl Harbour. This teaches us that in circumstances where US national security is challenged, a common cause emerges between those who seek to pragmatically safeguard the US and those who shape its objectives on a moral plateau. This affords wider support but also errs towards John Quincy Adams's[2] caution to the US should it be seeking a crusading foreign policy.

The onset of the Cold War allowed the continuance of this alliance between Wilsonian values and what Walter Russell Mead[3] describes as "Jacksonians" who are primarily concerned with defending the US from an external enemy. The Soviet Union was an ideal enemy that posed not only a military threat but also an ideological one which allowed this synergy of streams of thought to mutually reinforce each other. Nevertheless, the danger posed to US foreign policy from the Wilsonian school is that within contexts where national security is challenged, a crusading messianic globalism is a genuine risk. Vietnam was a prime example of where, within the Cold War strategic context, Wilsonian values, most notably under Johnson, ultimately triumphed over a *realpolitik* assessment of the geopolitical situation and thus propelled the United States into a misguided conflict that was hugely wasteful of life, and of financial resources, and detrimental to the standing of the US in the international system. The unfolding failure of the Wilsonian mission in South East Asia ultimately heralded a short-lived return to a sophisticated *realpolitik* diplomacy under Nixon and Kissinger which not only saw them manage the US withdrawal from the conflict, but also achieve other notable successes through a revolutionary triangular diplomacy. Whilst this episode was a golden era for US diplomacy, the ensuing Watergate scandal and ending of the Vietnam conflict once again brought about a revival in Wilsonian forces on foreign policy with *realpolitik* strategy merely dismissed as amoral and too power-centric. Given this, the key lesson of the tragedy of US involvement in Vietnam had not been learned: a rejection of the pursuit of national interest in favour of an unselfish and universalistic Wilsonian mission, driven by American exceptionalism, may ultimately lead to costly adventurism – increased suffering, death and a rejection of US values as being alien rather than universalistic.

Under Ford and Carter, the Wilsonian vigour that had brought about Vietnam began to resurface – this occurred most significantly within Congress and amongst disillusioned left-wing intellectuals. For Congress, a watershed occurred in 1974 when, for the first time, legislation was passed that directly concerned the domestic policy of another state. Here, Congress's concern was the immigration of Jews from the

Soviet Union. Within the framework of the universal human rights agenda which coincided with this, the concept of a Westphalian system was clearly on the wane as the formerly sacred cow of a nation's internal affairs was increasingly seen as fair game. Moreover, this struck a chord with several of the key principles on which the republic was founded and thus provided a second coming for Wilsonians.

Compounding this, a new intellectual movement, neoconservatism, emerged from the controversy of the Vietnam antiwar context and struck a chord with the human rights activism that gained momentum initially under President Ford. As an intellectual movement, neoconservatism provided a synthesis between the universalistic Wilsonian morals and the Jacksonian need to safeguard US national security. In essence, neoconservatism advocated the pursuit of Wilsonian values as being in the national interest in the long term as only through their global adoption could the United States achieve the security it so yearned for. During the Cold War, it bridged the divide between both those who wanted to combat the Soviet military threats and those who wanted to free its people enslaved by a hostile ideology. Neoconservatism advocated the objective of achieving freedom and human rights, as the adoption of such values would not only free an enslaved people, but would also nullify the risks posed to US national security. Democratic states were, at the end of the day, more likely to resolve their disputes through international law and arbitration rather than war so the global adoption of such values thus provided for US national security. In essence, neoconservatism had given Wilsonianism the new character of being a crusading messianic globalism whilst also serving the selfish national interests of US security.

Under Reagan, this neoconservatism began to define a presidency as Reagan adopted the Wilsonian rhetoric of a crusading moralism against an 'evil empire' intent on challenging the very existence of the United States. Traditional *realpolitik* statecraft was thus deemed to be an unworkable concept unless guided by this crusading moralism. Amoral *realpolitik* statecraft was thus relegated from defining the national interest to helping achieve the neoconservative strategic objectives by providing the basis of a sophisticated tactical foreign policy towards this end. But with the ending of the Cold War, the loss of a clear external threat to the United States resulted in the demise of neoconservatism as a guiding ideology that fused a clear moralism with a security-based conception of Cold War grand strategy.

Victory over the Soviet threat saw the post-Cold War strategic environment characterised by a 'New World Order' without a clear threat to US national security. For neoconservatism, this translated into the loss of an essential pillar which made it largely redundant in the post-Cold War strategic context. With this onset of American hegemony and the lack of a clear external competitor, a clear-sighted political strategy did not emerge. The Clinton era maintained the Wilsonian theme by engaging in several humanitarian causes, but given the lack of a political strategy, its diplomacy was ad hoc and not geared towards a clear conception of the national interest along *realpolitik* lines. The foreign policy of the United States thus retained its Wilsonianism but lost its crusading zest that characterised previous eras. With the absence of a clear political strategy, foreign policy during the Clinton era largely gave way to a promotion of global economic integration as the cornerstone of day-to-day US diplomacy. This largely accounts for the unparalleled economic success that the 1990s bore for America. Nevertheless, the promotion of economic globalism is not a satisfactory substitute for a coherent political strategy as it lends itself to an ad hoc and, crucially, a reactive foreign policy that is absent of any recognition of the national interest and the statecraft involved in preventing geopolitical threats from emerging.

The trauma caused by the 11 September 2001 terrorist attacks fundamentally changed this post-Cold War conception of the 'New World Order'. The devastation and shock caused by a small number of Islamic fundamentalists to the US homeland was reminiscent of the Japanese attack on Pearl Harbour. The threat posed by Islamic extremism was viewed as akin to communism during the Cold War and thus the new grand strategic era of the War on Terror had begun.

With the Bush administration including a number of key decision makers who had clear neoconservative idiosyncrasies, the establishment of a comparable foreign policy was understandable; however, extremist political Islam constituted a threat unlike communism and thus produced a more nuanced Reaganite political strategy. Unlike the Cold War where the Soviet Union posed a clear ideological and military threat, radical political Islam was recognised to be an unintended offshoot of the social and political structure within autocratic Middle Eastern nations. Specifically, the lack of fundamental freedoms were seen as resulting in Islam serving as the sole political mobilising agent which, although Muslim politics had many faces, resulted in extremism directed internationally against the United States and the West in general. So unlike the Communist threat which was clearly state-centric, radical political Islam was simply viewed as an unintended by-product of the state structure having failed to adopt the universalistic pillars that captured the essence of the American republic: freedom of speech, equity and self-determination. Moreover, the failure of Middle Eastern countries to adopt such values was recognised as being initially a product of colonialism and later a result of the United States seeking maintenance of the status quo in order to ensure a secure flow of hydrocarbon resources from the region.

With the threat being an unintended by-product of the state structure, the manner in which neoconservatism approached this quag-mire differed in important ways to the Cold War Reaganite strategy. Specifically, it meant that whilst at a state level the United States could have friendly relations with a given Middle East regime, the problem at hand was their political structure and practices rather than the rulers themselves – the strategic objective for the neoconservatives was there-fore to elicit political change through the regimes' adoption of some of the universalistic standards on which the American republic was based. Whilst a risk of this was that a hostile power could gain control over the given friendly regime, it would, nonetheless, serve US strategic interests providing it upheld the key values that were deemed to be an antidote to political extremism.

In a historical context, with the George W. Bush administration adopting a nuanced Reaganite approach, or indeed neo-Reaganite strategy, the purpose of military force was relegated in importance: only in circum-stances where a state was an overt supporter of terrorism would a military, or Jacksonian, state-centric approach apply, otherwise the strategic focus was on achieving Wilsonian ends at a sub-state level. That is not to say that Bush's approach discounted *realpolitik* statecraft; as with Reagan, Bush saw such calculations as a tactical means of fulfilling the crusading Wilsonian strategic objective. So therefore the character of the threat had resulted in the adoption of a more nuanced approach when compared with Reagan's Cold War strategy: in essence the strategy took on a much greater Wilsonian character. Crucially, with the diagnosis of the Islamic terrorist threat being a result of Muslim nations having largely failed to adopt universalistic values on which the American republic was seen to be based, the scope for variance in US foreign policy, whilst geared towards this strategic endgame, was limited to how the US should effect change within Muslim nations. Nonetheless, the US conception of threat and its strategy towards countering it became firmly premised on an abandonment of the Westphalian concept of sovereignty.

With the approach of the Bush administration in the War on Terror being firmly grounded in a global messianic Wilsonianism, historical observations can be made on the risks pertaining thereto. As the tragedy of Vietnam had shown, a preponderance of Wilsonian values, as a determinist force in foreign policy, risked adventurism and miscalculation in the application of military power. The dilemma facing US foreign policy was whether a sophisticated *realpolitik* strategy, which could convincingly deal with the threats posed by Islamic extremism, could be developed which would determine the national interest over a currently preponderant and vigorous Wilsonianism.

With this historical character in mind, the following section will provide a foreign policy analysis of the Clinton and Bush presidencies in order to show the internal forces at play in their administrations. This will allow for a greater conceptualisation of US foreign policy towards Iran and Iraq in subsequent chapters.

The Clinton and Bush Presidencies: Idiosyncrasies

One of the key elements in foreign policy formation is that of the individual level which can lend itself to more psychological prescriptions.[4] How political decision makers construct a view of the world in their minds is an essential component in understanding foreign policy.[5] Such ontological factors have an impact on how foreign policy issues are perceived, interpreted and acted upon.[6]

The idiosyncratic differences between Bill Clinton and George W. Bush were significant in that their style of leadership, political ethos and vision differed markedly. In terms of their background, the differences are stark. Whilst Bush followed in the path of John Quincy Adams who also succeeded his father as President in 1825, Clinton grew up in a modest household at the hands of a drunken and physically abusive stepfather.

Clinton enrolled for his bachelor's degree in Foreign Service from Georgetown University. He subsequently attended Oxford University as a

Rhodes Scholar for two years. Bush went to Yale where he graduated with a bachelor's degree in History. Whilst Clinton subsequently went to Yale Law School, Bush opted for Harvard Business School. This academic and professional background had an impact on decision-making style: whilst Clinton approached issues in a lawyerly, systematic manner, Bush's style was characterised by the demonstration of leadership through decisive action.

The most important difference about their activities at university level, however, was that they took different positions during the anti-Vietnam War movement. Clinton was actively and vocally supportive of the movement during his undergraduate studies at Georgetown, and his subsequent move as a Rhodes Scholar to University College, Oxford was something that his political opponents would later seize on as evidence of his avoidance of the draft. In comparison, Bush's reputation at university was more apolitical and hedonistic. In contrast to Clinton, Bush enrolled with the Texas Air National Guard. The importance of their differing political outlooks at the time of the anti-Vietnam War movement is significant: the Clintonian administration was, according to Henry Kissinger, "the first staffed by many individuals who came out of the Vietnam protest".[7] Bush's senior staff by comparison consisted of more politically seasoned individuals: many had served in previous Republican administrations dating back to Richard Nixon.[8] Indeed, Kissinger is correct to highlight that generational forces are significant factors in how policy issues are perceived and acted upon.

Their route to the White House was also different. Clinton's first attempt at a political career began in the wake of Nixon's resignation in 1974, when he ran unsuccessfully for a Congressional seat in Arkansas. Clinton subsequently ran for the State Attorney General which he then used as a platform for the Governorship in 1978. Elected as the youngest Governor in the United States, he held the position until 1982, but was then re-elected in 1984 and ultimately used this as a platform for the presidency. Bush also unsuccessfully contested a Congressional seat, but his political career really began in 1994 when he won the Texas governorship by capitalising on the political dissatisfaction with Clinton's "political ineptitude by pressing for and failing to achieve major health care reform".[9] Bush also capitalised on the breaking Lewinski scandal in 1998 to discredit his Democrat opponent and achieve re-election.

Whilst Clinton clearly had more political experience in office before winning the presidency, Bush had a wealth of experience from an inside exposure to his father's and the Reagan presidency. But even more importantly, their differential political backgrounds had an impact on their political ethos in general: Clinton's political ability was fostered through domestic politics, whilst Bush had a more rounded exposure but clearly lacked the level of experience in office that Clinton had accumulated. Either way, neither could be described as foreign policy-orientated before taking office in the way that George H. W. Bush had been.

In terms of their religious outlook, Clinton was a Baptist whilst Bush was a born-again evangelical Christian.[10] Whilst there is no question that Clinton was a devout Baptist, there is little indication that this had a bearing on his policy during office. Indeed, Clinton frequently spoke of the need to maintain a clear separation between the church and state.[11] But for George W. Bush religion was much more significant in that he regarded it as having shaped his world view, outlook and purpose in life.[12] Bush's religious outlook was significant in that, although several Presidents have been noted Christians – Ronald Reagan, Jimmy Carter and Richard Nixon – the Bush presidency appeared to be the *most* 'faith-based' to hold the White House.[13] But crucially, Bush appeared more than any of his predecessors to draw a policy guide from his spiritualism,[14] and it seems reasonable to conclude that his beliefs have complemented the outlook of key members of his administration on the basis of their similarity.

The differences were significant even with their election to the presidency. Clinton's November 1992 election victory saw him inaugurated on 20 January 1993, as the forty-second President of the United States and also as the first Democrat President since Jimmy Carter. Clinton won by a comfortable majority over the incumbent George H. W. Bush by wisely recognising that the key issue for the electorate was the economy. An often quoted phrase, "it's the economy, stupid," typified Clinton's highly successful 1992 presidential electoral campaign. He also entered office with the 103rd Congress (1992–1994) being Democrat controlled. Although the US economy was experiencing recession and required immediate attention, Clinton undoubtedly took office in a secure domestic, political position. Nevertheless, the Democrats' control of Congress was short-lived as control was lost in 1994 and was not regained during his two terms of office.[15]

In comparison, Bush became the first President since Benjamin Harrison in 1888, and only the fourth since independence, to win the Electoral College vote but lose the popular vote. The controversy surrounding the vote count in Florida, where the Supreme Court had to rule on the outcome, tainted Bush's first term on the grounds of legitimacy. Nevertheless, Bush entered office with a firm Republican majority in Congress and a strong economic environment which was only beginning to show signs of slowdown.

Although both experienced very different electoral victories, the most important factor was their contrasting style of leadership. It is generally accepted that Clinton treated issues in a highly systematic and unstructured manner in order to explore them to their full potential.[16] His propensity for lengthy meetings may have been a good means of fully exploring policy issues, but it also highlighted Clinton's lack of focus and decisiveness as a leader. The important point is that Clinton's approach favoured decision making on an ad hoc level, whilst trying to accommodate as many different positions as possible. In other words, Clinton sought wide-ranging consent and approval rather than being driven by an objective or ideology. Whilst such a style has the merit of allowing for informed decisions which are more utilitarian, it is also an inherently weak style in that clarity of purpose and direction can be lacking. Either way, it appears reasonable to conclude from the available evidence that Clinton had an aversion to foreign policy risk taking. Stephen Graubard appropriately asks:

> Why, then, was [Clinton] unable to address the problems that surfaced abroad, that recommended a major reconsideration of policies pursued by his two Republican predecessors? The short answer is that Clinton, like Bush and Reagan, feared any engagement that carried substantial risk, defined as the return of American body bags.[17]

By comparison, Bush saw his position as the Commander in Chief who did not get immersed in finer details in the way that Clinton had so typically done.[18] The focus was, therefore, on taking decisions once recommendations had been formulated, whilst giving general direction for policy.[19] The limitation of such an approach was that the President became more dependent on the advice of senior staff, but it does have its own merit in that there is clarity of purpose through decisiveness.

Indeed, this allows for a style of leadership epitomised by Ronald Reagan. But in comparison to Reagan and Clinton, George W. Bush appears to have been more comfortable in using American power in general. This was especially the case following the terrorist attacks of 11 September 2001.

In terms of a world view, both candidates did premise themselves on a platform that the United States should play an active role in world affairs: this is hardly surprising as this is a common trait that every major presidential candidate has positioned themselves on since the end of the Second World War.[20] For Bush, the promotion of American values was clearly *commensurate with US interests*. Indeed, he notably held in high esteem Natan Sharansky's arguments that democracy and freedom were the *universal remedies to tyranny and extremism*.[21] But as early as 1999, Bush commented that:

> [T]he basic principles of human freedom and dignity *are* universal . . . Some have tried to pose a choice between American ideals and American interests – between who we are and how we act. But the choice is false. America, by decision and destiny, promotes political freedom – and gains the most when democracy advances. America believes in free markets and free trade – and benefits most when markets are opened. America is a peaceful power – and gains the greatest dividend from democratic stability.[22]

Bush saw his position as being directly comparable to Clinton, whose foreign policy he alluded to as being "action without vision, activity without priority, and missions without end".[23] As for Bush's vision, Robert Kagan characterised it as having "no hint of a pseudo-realist notion that American principles have to be set aside in favor of exclusive concentration on America's vital national interests".[24] Interestingly this is a world view which is notably similar to Ronald Reagan's outlook.[25] Nevertheless, Bush's perception of American values as being universal and their promotion being in US national interests, underscores the point that he had a *neo-Reaganite* vision of international affairs.[26]

When Clinton is compared to Bush, there are surprising similarities in that Clinton also saw the promotion of democracy and freedom as being in US national interests. According to Clinton, "[t]he defense of freedom and the promotion of democracy around the world aren't merely a reflection of our deepest values; they are vital to our national interests. Global democracy means nations at peace with one another, open to one another's ideas and one another's commerce".[27] This vision, articulated by Clinton prior to taking office, was maintained throughout his two terms of office; however, he also saw geoeconomics as a key additional component. Clinton remarked "[o]ur economic strength must become a central defining element of our national security policy".[28] Indeed, this was commensurate with his domestic platform of defining the economy as his primary policy concern. Clinton's vision was, therefore, premised on dual strategic objectives. The importance of this for foreign policy analysis is, however, that in certain circumstances such objectives could be contradictory: the promotion of democratic reform could unbalance the status quo and thus be detrimental to geo-economics. Therefore, the key issue is the extent to which such strategies were applied in practice and served as a strategic guide for foreign policy.

Overall, there are noticeable differences in the background, outlook and leadership style of Bush and Clinton. But more importantly, such factors highlight a differential approach to how America's role in the world was perceived, and the difference in leadership styles was bound to have a bearing on policy formation. Nevertheless, it is also important to recognise the general bureaucratic differences which played a key role, so the following section will draw attention to the idiosyncratic differences of senior staff.

Ideological Influences on Elite Decision Makers

Whilst Clinton and Bush did have clear idiosyncratic differences, it is also of significance that this extended to the very essence of their admin-istrations. Clinton's choice of staff was telling as they closely mirrored his own style and outlook. The important characteristic of Clinton's choice of staff for foreign policy was that they shared his general lack of vision and caution in American foreign policy. This contributed to the administration's lack of strategic clarity and purpose in foreign policy matters.

In the first Clinton administration, the appointment of Warren Christopher as Secretary of State was viewed by many as a safe bet. Christopher was a distinguished lawyer who had been the Deputy Secretary of State in the Carter administration, However, although he was widely regarded as an efficient and capable bureaucrat, he was also seen as "lacking originality and beliefs of his own".[29] Given Clinton's lawyerly and at times indecisive character, the reluctance of Christopher to press for his own beliefs would have resulted in a relatively low-key input from the State department in foreign policy formation. Moreover, this contributed towards a reactive foreign policy rather than one that was striving for clearly defined objectives.

A similar appointment was made in the form of Anthony Lake as National Security Advisor. Unlike Christopher, Lake was far from afraid to voice his own opinions: he was notably critical of the Vietnam policy whilst he was on Kissinger's national security staff during the Nixon administration and resigned over the covert bombing of Cambodia. But in Lake, Clinton had an individual who shared his sentiments over Vietnam and took an equally cautious approach to the application of US military power. "Lake was a Wilsonian figure in an era that was less and less Wilsonian",[30] David Halberstam writes. In many respects, Kissinger is correct that key members of Clinton's staff were opposed to Vietnam and thus had a particular generational outlook on the international environment.[31] But although Lake was influential in devising strategy, his relationship with Clinton has been described as formal, and thus it is unlikely that he was able to exert the level of influence that some of his more notable predecessors had done.[32]

However across the board, it is striking that the first Clinton administration was devoid of individuals who had an inclination towards making use of US power projection capability. This was underscored by Les Aspin at Defense, and James Woolsey at the CIA, who found that they did not enjoy open access to Clinton.[33] With Aspin, Clinton's choice was poor as he was ill qualified to run a bureaucracy as large and complex as the Pentagon, even though he had an excellent command of defence issues.[34] When compared to Robert McNamara, Aspin was a relatively weak Secretary of Defense. Given Clinton's unstructured style of leadership and focus on domestic and, in particular, economic affairs, foreign policy was given less attention when compared to previous administrations and this was compounded by the idiosyncrasies of the key people he appointed.[35]

Few changes occurred, however, with the onset of the second Clinton administration. Madeleine Albright was appointed Secretary of State and this was a notable change which gave the State Department a higher profile. Albright was a highly talented and articulate diplomat, who was more charismatic than Christopher, but she was not noted for having a particular ideology: "no one associated her with any particular view or wing of the party".[36] Therefore, as with Clinton's previous senior level appointments, Albright was a highly capable individual but one who did not articulate a sense of purpose in foreign policy which would have filled the void created by Clinton's lack of decisiveness and weak vision of US foreign relations.

At the National Security Council, Sandy Berger replaced Tony Lake. Berger was a long-time friend of Clinton and had been Lake's deputy since 1993. Berger immediately confined himself to pursuing what had become the defining strategy of the Clintonian presidency: geoeconomics. According to Berger, he saw his purpose as promoting "a new international economic architecture for expanding trade and creating American jobs in the global economy".[37] Whilst this underscored the strategic outlook of the administration, it also was more indicative of the lack of clarity with which foreign policy was treated: geoeconomics is not a substitute for geostrategy.[38]

Overall, on a bureaucratic level the Clintonian presidency was marked by a cautious approach towards international affairs that generally seems to have resonated throughout both administrations. Indeed, Clinton's choice of candidates appears to have mirrored his own idiosyncrasies.

In direct comparison, George W. Bush's administration notably comprised strong-willed characters who had a clear world view before taking office. Bush's foreign policy team was "mostly drawn from people who had served in the third and fourth tiers of his father's administration".[39] Most importantly, several held a common outlook on international affairs that can be likened to the neoconservativism originally spawned by Leo Strauss.[40] Indeed, Condoleezza Rice famously coined the term 'Vulcans' to describe Bush's foreign policy team.[41] It is, therefore, pertinent to provide a more detailed discussion of neoconservatism in the following section with specific regard to how this characterised the Bush administration.

The Development of the Neoconservative School
As a school of thought, neoconservatism grew from the left-wing radicalisation of the 1960s which was primarily a product of the anti-Vietnam War movement. A number of left-wing liberal intellectuals

became disillusioned with the anti-Americanism of the period and began to reassert themselves against this counterculture. Norman Podhoretz writes:

> Neoconservatism came into the world to combat the dangerous lies that were being spread by the radicalism of the 1960s and that were being accepted as truth by the established liberal institutions of the day. More passionately and more effectively than any other group, the neoconservatives exposed those lies for what they were: an expression of hatred, rooted in utopian greed, for the life lived in this country, and the major weapon in a campaign to deprive it of the will to defend itself against its enemies in the world outside. [42]

Although neoconservative intellectuals were of left-wing origin themselves, their critique of the 'radicalised' left of the 1960s proved to be the key divide which saw a new intellectual school emerge. This became more pronounced as a neoconservative perspective on the welfare state developed into a critique of the expansionist policy epitomised by the New Deal. Through this reaction to left-wing ideology, neoconservatism gradually became more identifiable with traditional right-wing conservatism.

A further key pillar of neoconservatism is anticommunism. This can be broadened out into the desire for the promotion of Wilsonian ideals. Although traditional conservatives were also noted for their anticommunist zeal, their focus was primarily on the risks from internal subversion. Senator Joe McCarthy's zealous anticommunism within American society epitomised this approach. Neoconservative elites approached the issue from a much wider perspective, focusing primarily on the external risk of communist aggression against liberal democracies. President Reagan's ardent anticommunism meshed well with the views being articulated by neoconservative intellectuals and his view of a clear pursuit of freedom, liberty, justice and equality as universal ideals was wholly commensurate with this agenda. Indeed, such values are also seen as fostering peaceful relations as they are viewed as the norm amongst like-minded democratic countries. With this overriding belief in the moral supremacy of liberal democratic values, neoconservatives see other competing ideological or religious beliefs as a direct threat. Therefore foreign policy is seen as a means of both safeguarding and promoting their morally-based values for the national interest. This is an interesting combination of Wilsonianism/idealism premised on realist calculations.

[28]

Although it is clear why neoconservatives desire the spread of liberal democratic values, there is, however, no uniform acceptance within neoconservatism itself of the role the United States could feasibly play in achieving the goal of democratisation. In the seminal article "Dictatorships and Double Standards" (1979), Jeane Kirkpatrick, a leading neoconservative, argued that while the United States should uniformly promote the spread of democracy on moral grounds, it should recognise that country-specific factors may preclude the transformation to democracy occurring in a stable manner.[43] She argued that although the United States should promote democracy, it must recognise that premature reforms may result in a backlash which could allow communists to gain power: the support of non-communist dictatorships was therefore justified. Indeed, Kirkpatrick recognised that in many instances in the third world, a successful and stable democratisation process would likely be a *long-term* process, and went as far as advising against policies which would lead to a premature democratisation. The essence, therefore, of what has been widely described as the Kirkpatrick Doctrine, is the use of selective measures to promote democracy in order to combat the spread of communism. Kirkpatrick's argument, however, posed the key challenge to neoconservatives in terms of defining the strategic objective: democratisation versus challenging the Soviet Union whilst refraining from policies that could destabilise friendly regimes on a geopolitical level.[44]

Importantly, it was with this mainstream promotion of neoconservative values by President Reagan that its ideological division with traditional conservatism began to break down. But with the fall of the Soviet Union, and the 'defeat' of communism as an ideology, the neoconservative school of thought had lost its *raison d'être*. Intellectually its scholars generally became embroiled in mainstream conservatism and some of its more high profile advocates, such as Irving Kristol, indicated that the fall of the Soviet Union marked the culminating success of neoconservatism's key objective over tyranny.[45]

But with the fall of the Soviet Union, George H. W. Bush reverted, in line with his own beliefs, to a more realist foreign policy strategy reminiscent of the Nixon–Kissinger era.[46] Consequently, the most notable neoconservatives such as Paul Wolfowitz, Richard Perle, William Kristol, Robert Kagan, and Max Boot, were critical of Bush's realist policy which they generally equated with appeasement. Therefore, the end of the

Reagan administration and the implosion of the Soviet Union may have signalled the neoconservatives' loss of direct influence over the foreign policy reins of power, but it was a period which reinforced their optimism that democratic values have universal applicability.[47] Nevertheless, this also marked the evolution of the neoconservatives' 'Cold War ideology' into *new post-Cold War strategy*. It is this revision which later had a direct bearing on the presidency of George W. Bush.

A key event which galvanised neoconservative intellectuals in this new post-Cold War environment was the failure of George H. W. Bush's administration to take decisive action and topple Saddam Hussein after the liberation of Kuwait. Following the experience of the fall of the Soviet Union, neoconservatives saw every reason for the overthrow of Saddam and also saw the United States' new undisputed hegemonic primacy as the reason for believing it could be carried out. Against a background of the longevity of Saddam Hussein and failure of the Clinton administration to formulate an effective and coherent policy towards Iraq, neoconservative political groups such as the Project for the New American Century (PNAC) were founded. The PNAC was founded by William Kristol and its membership included many high profile members of the Reagan administration. Its core principle states:

> As the 20th century draws to a close, the United States stands as the world's pre-eminent power. Having led the West to victory in the Cold War, America faces an opportunity and a challenge: does the United States have the vision to build upon the achievements of past decades? Does the United States have the resolve to shape a new century favorable to American principles and interests?[48]

A further area of interest for neoconservatives was the issue of a rising China that could threaten the pre-eminence of the United States. It was, however, with the election of George W. Bush as President that many of those considered to be neoconservative intellectuals were able to return to positions of power after an 'exile' during the Clintonian era. This included Donald Rumsfeld as Secretary of Defense, Paul Wolfowitz as his deputy and also Dick Cheney as the Vice President. Given this, it therefore seems appropriate to examine the specific role of neoconservatism in the Bush administration and how this post-Cold War ideology evolved into a new one which characterised the outlook of the War on Terror.

Neoconservatism and the Bush Administration

Bush's national security advisor, Condoleezza Rice, had an outlook on international affairs that was more that of a traditional realist, and she thus shared the outlook of Brent Scowcroft and Kissinger.[49] However, Rice did hold some neoconservative views on the universalism of freedom and democracy which became more apparent after 11 September 2001.[50] In terms of her background, she gained her doctorate on a comparison of the Soviet and Czechoslovakian militaries, under the tutelage of Josef Korbel who was Madeleine Albright's father. She was thus more of a European specialist. But her relationship with George W. Bush was particularly strong as they both shared a love of sports and exercise and, as she was a devout Presbyterian, they also shared a similar outlook on life. Although Bush did not appoint her to Cabinet level as Clinton had done with Lake and Berger, it is generally accepted that she enjoyed excellent access to Bush and was instrumental in foreign policy formation.

Other senior level staff, however, held more ideological beliefs. Unlike Rice, Wolfowitz upheld many of the ideals espoused by Leo Strauss. James Mann describes Wolfowitz's outlook as being premised on "stopping tyranny and condemning evil; the notion that dictatorships operate in fundamentally different ways from democracies; the belief that liberal democracies and their intelligence agencies can be fooled by a dictator's elaborate deceptions".[51] Wolfowitz undertook his doctorate on the risks of proliferation from nuclear desalination plants at the University of Chicago under Albert Wohlstetter, who was a noted opponent of proliferation. Wolfowitz initially gained experience in the Nixon administration in the US Arms Control and Disarmament Agency and later under the Carter administration as the Deputy Assistant Secretary of Defense for the Middle East and Persian Gulf. It was in this capacity that Wolfowitz's views on the strategic importance of the Persian Gulf were developed.

In the final year of the George H. W. Bush administration, Wolfowitz, as Under Secretary of Defense, was charged with the task of formulating the Pentagon's first post-Cold War Defense Planning Guidance for 1992.[52] The purpose of the document was to develop an overall military strategy and develop future defence budgets from it. The person who actually wrote this classified document was Zalmay Khalilzad, the Assistant Deputy Under Secretary of Defense for Policy Planning. Khalilzad built on Wolfowitz's ideas to develop a coherent post-Cold War neoconservative military strategy. However, Khalilzad's 1992 draft was leaked to the press and was subject to a wave of criticism, both domestically and overseas. Although the draft was rewritten in a more diplomatic tone to alleviate the concerns of allies overseas,[53] its over-arching themes remained reasonably consistent in the revision. The primary themes within the reports were:

1. The United States should work actively to retain its pre-eminence in the world by preventing a rival power from emerging.
2. Future military coalitions would be ad hoc, and specific to the cause.
3. The United States would act unilaterally if it defined such action as being in its national interests.
4. The United States should aim to actively promote its values and interests on a global basis.[54]

Unlike the neoconservative vision during the Cold War, this revision had to alter according to, as Leo Strauss argues, the definition of threat facing liberal democracies.[55] Although during the Cold War the threat was clearly seen as Communism, the post-Cold War revision saw the new threat to be *potential challengers to American hegemony*. Nevertheless, with the onset of the Clinton administration the neoconservatives were essentially confined to an opposition role as they lost their positions in government. According to James Mann, however, despite using a different rhetorical vision, the Clinton administration did not substantively depart from this post-Cold War neoconservative strategy:

> Overall, the Democrats failed to come up with any clear alternative vision of American strategy that would forswear the 1992 vision of the United States as a sole superpower. When the Clinton administration sought to articulate its own view of America's role in the world, it stressed the importance of globalization, open markets and democracy. Those themes did not contradict the 1992 strategy, but rather described the economic and political basis of the new international system the United States intended to dominate.[56]

Although the Clinton administration was indirectly pursuing this aspect of the post-Cold War neoconservative vision, those neoconservatives who had lost their positions of power when Clinton took office developed their opposition to the Democrats through organisations such as the PNAC and also through influential publications such as the *Weekly Standard, National Interest* and the *Daily Star*. Indeed, during the Clinton years, Wolfowitz was particularly critical of the administration's policy towards Iraq; he, and many others, saw this as an incoherent and unworkable policy. The issue of Iraq was, along with China and Taiwan, the main moral and security issue they saw the United States facing. Accordingly, these issues, in particular Iraq, served as the key mobilising agents for the neoconservatives when they were not in office throughout the Clinton era. By 1997 Wolfowitz and other neoconservatives had openly begun to call for regime change against Saddam Hussein, and were actively lobbying Congress, through the Project for a New American Century, for an official change in Clinton's policy towards Iraq.[57] Moreover, this effective opposition to Clinton's policy toward Iraq played a key role in prompting Congress to legislate, and subsequently Clinton signing into law, the Iraq Liberation Act of 1998. This ultimately saw the neoconservative policy towards Iraq being *overtly* adopted as a foreign policy objective.

It was only following the 2000 election of George W. Bush as President that the neoconservatives were able to return to a variety of positions of power within government.[58] During the Clinton years they had remained as an opposition movement in exile. Although Bush's foreign policy team retained its hawkish views towards Iraq and its neoconservative outlook on international affairs in the months prior to 11 September 2001, its Straussian external threat remained premised on countries which could challenge the pre-eminent position of the United States. The 9/11 terrorist attacks, however, changed this perception of external threat. With the attacks, terrorism had become a readily identifiable threat by the American public which was capable of striking against them within the United States.

Others, such as Secretary of Defense Rumsfeld, Vice President Cheney and his Chief of Staff 'Scooter' Libby, were more concerned with maintenance of the qualitative edge the United States had over any strategic competitors, but did nonetheless share many of the idealistic views advocated by Wolfowitz. As has been highlighted earlier, the Pentagon's Defense Policy Guidance 1992, which was officially authored by Cheney, was later rewritten by Libby in diplomatic language without changing the underlying theme of maintenance of US hegemony.

Rumsfeld's political views also echoed this position as he had established himself as a leading hawk opposed to a reduction of the military capability of the United States whilst he was Defense Secretary during the Ford administration.[59] The findings of the 1997 Congressional commission to assess the ballistic missile threat to the United States, which he chaired, further cemented this reputation.[60] In essence, some members of the Bush administration held strong views prior to taking office for the need to maintain hegemony by preventing the rise of a strategic competitor to American military superiority.

In a similar fashion, Colin Powell and Richard Armitage both had strong views on the need for maintenance of the qualitative military edge of the United States. They slightly differed from Rumsfeld, Cheney and Libby by generally being more pragmatic and more willing to see value in multilateralism. In many respects, they were ideally suited for the top two positions in the Department of State. Nevertheless, they were not as political as the other members of Bush's senior staff and both had a disdain for idealism or ideology in foreign policy, which placed them in conflict with Wolfowitz and Condoleezza Rice.

The Bush administration did have a more religious character in comparison to the Clinton administration which cannot be ignored: it has been widely reported that religious practices such as Bible readings and group prayers before official meetings have been held in the Bush White House. But these were not just symbolic gestures as such beliefs translated into policy. Indeed, one of Bush's first domestic policies was the Faith-Based Initiative which sought to "unite conservative evangelicals, urban Catholics, minority pastors, and traditional *noblesse oblige* Republicans in a grand religious inspired approach to social problems".[61] But in terms of US foreign policy, the attacks of 11 September 2001 played a more telling role. The attacks served to reinforce Bush's existing convictions of the universality of the values that have grounded his own Christian faith: freedom, liberty and democracy. Indeed, as with many other fellow Americans, Bush categorised those who perpetuated the terrorist attacks as the embodiment of evil and, consequently, a direct challenge to the good values seen to be epitomised by the United States. Indeed, some commentators have gone as far as describing Bush as feeling that he has been called upon by God in the form of a religiously justified cause against evil.[62]

In his 2002 State of the Union Address, Bush illustrated his belief that such values are universal and enshrined in the Christian faith by saying that "the liberty we prize is not America's gift to the world, it is God's gift to humanity".[63] The importance of this is clear: Bush's own religious values and beliefs, which were shared by many within his administration, were a factor that shaped his outlook and, specifically, the desire to spread freedom, liberty and democracy as part of his foreign policy. This strikes a chord with the crusading moralism streak that has historical currency in US foreign policy as shown at the onset of this chapter.

All things considered, it seems possible to recognise several important characteristics on a bureaucratic level during the first Bush administration. There were two key complementary idiosyncrasies that resonated in the administration: a desire for maintenance of US hegemony and a firm belief in the desirability of spreading Wilsonian ideals. Indeed, prior to the 9/11 terrorist attacks, the general foreign policy focus of the administration was more geared towards the issue of China, which was seen as a possible strategic competitor. In the post-9/11 environment, however, these idiosyncrasies were reflected in US foreign policy, which saw a need to maintain US hegemony, in addition to combating the root causes of terrorism through the promotion of Wilsonian ideals. When compared with the Clinton presidency, it is noticeable that there were clear differences on a bureaucratic level which had a bearing on the perception, interpretation and decisions in US foreign policy during the time frame of this study. Therefore, on an idiosyncratic level the differences formed a near dichotomy.

The Strategic Maxims of Foreign Policy

From the preceding observations, it is possible to draw some initial comparisons of the foreign policies of Bill Clinton and George W. Bush. With the onset of the Clinton administration, the over-arching strategy underpinning US foreign relations was articulated as being premised on the dual objectives of a global promotion of democracy and a further-ance of global economic capitalism. The Clinton administration saw these two strategic objectives as mutually reinforcing. Whilst the promotion of liberal democracy and market capitalism has a strong vintage in US foreign policy history, the key issue for scholars has been whether the end of the Cold War truly marked the demise of a grand strategic era in

US foreign policy. Whilst some scholars such as John Ikenberry equate US grand strategy since the end of the Second World War as premised on the Jeffersonian pursuit of democracy, one cannot deny that the fall of the Berlin Wall and the implosion of the Soviet Union marked the end of an era where a clearly identifiable external threat was perceived by Washington, which served as a strategic guide for US foreign policy during the Cold War era. Therefore, despite the Clinton administration maintaining what can be described as the quintessential American goal of promoting liberty, freedom and democracy, there is justification for taking the position that the Clinton presidency occurred within a different grand strategic era to that of the Cold War.

Despite the Clinton presidency articulating a grand strategy based on the promotion of democracy and global capitalism, there is good reason to conclude that geoeconomics alone served as the strategic point of reference for Clintonian foreign policy. The problem with this approach, according to Kissinger, is that geoeconomics "is not a substitute for global order, though it can be an important part of it".[64]

In the case of US foreign policy towards Persian Gulf security and political Islam, the promotion of democracy was subjugated at the expense of regional geostrategic interests. Indeed, the very nature of Clinton's geostrategy was premised on maintenance of the status quo through containment and deterrence. Despite the administration's position towards political Islam being premised on widening democracy and civil liberties throughout the Middle East, this conflicted with Clinton's policy on a regional level. Therefore, at least in the case of the Middle East, it seems justified to conclude that Clinton's objective of pursuing democracy was more rhetorical than substantive.

But on a more general level, the Clinton administration failed to provide a coherent strategic guide for foreign policy: this was reinforced by the idiosyncrasies of Clinton and the senior personnel that he appointed. In terms of the Middle East, and the Arab–Israeli conflict in particular, it is fair to characterise Clinton's foreign policy as reactive and applied on an ad hoc level.

Nevertheless, Clinton's use of geoeconomics as a strategic guide for foreign policy and his ad hoc response to political developments was conducive to garnering multilateral support. Although Iraq proved to be a key point of contention with US allies in Europe in particular, Clinton's foreign policy did allow for a greater degree of multilateralism within the international system. Through his emphasis on geoeconomics, Clinton was better able to conduct his foreign policy and the cooperation it delivered would have fostered the spectacular global economic performance of the late 1990s. From this, one can interpret Clintonian foreign policy as being Jeffersonian on a rhetorical level, but overall, distinctly Hamiltonian in character.[65]

Although Clinton's foreign policy was inherently weak through its general reactive nature stemming from its geoeconomic basis, George W. Bush's foreign policy marked a clear departure from this trajectory. As has already been discussed, the idiosyncratic outlook, perception and vision of the Bush administration was based on wholly different criteria. On a bureaucratic level, the primary concern for many of Bush's senior foreign policy staff was the maintenance of a qualitative superiority of the United States relative to potential strategic competitors. A second underlying tenet was the neoconservatism which sought the promotion of democracy and freedom on a moral basis, in addition to seeing it providing for the national security of the United States.

When the Bush administration policy towards the Middle East is examined prior to the 9/11 attacks, there appears to have been a general level of continuity from the Clinton administration. The discernible difference towards the Arab–Israeli dispute appears to have been a product of the geopolitical environment and, importantly, this case study will indicate that a change in regional geostrategy did not occur at that time. Therefore, despite the administration having different idiosyncratic attributes from the Clinton presidency, foreign policy trajectory remained fairly constant. But it should not be forgotten that a policy review was still being conducted during this period of time and thus it is not possible to say whether these different attributes would, by themselves, have translated into a radical departure from Clinton's geostrategy. On the other hand, the Bush administration's initial policy, towards China in particular, indicates a change commensurate with the idiosyncrasies discussed.[66]

The attacks of 11 September 2001, however, do appear to have resulted in the onset of a new grand strategic era that one can equate in certain respects with the Cold War.[67] Given the importance of the Bush administration's foreign policy strategy post-9/11, the following section will analyse the nature of the Bush Doctrine in order to underscore that a new grand strategic approach was adopted in the wake of the trauma of the 9/11 attacks.

The Bush Doctrine

The Bush administration's response to the attacks was wholly commensurate with the idiosyncratic characteristics that have been defined above, and has been likened by Bob Woodward to a fundamentally new foreign policy doctrine.[68] The Bush Doctrine had three identifiable pillars which were originally outlined in the National Security Strategy of 2002.[69] These three pillars can be summarised as:

1. Prevent hostile states from acquiring unconventional weapons with unilateralism if necessary;
2. Promote democracy and freedom on a global basis;
3. Maintain the pre-eminence of the United States in the international system.

The nature of the Bush Doctrine was ambitious, optimistic and long-sighted. Clear comparisons could be drawn with Woodrow Wilson's vision in the aftermath of the First World War but, for the Bush administration, it was seen not only in moral terms, but also through a clear definition of what the national security threats to the United States were.[70] The nature of its pillars reflected this as it included both immediate security concerns from states intent on producing unconventional weapons, to the more long-term goal of combating the root causes of extremist political Islam and politically motivated extremism with global reach in general. Given this, the following section will provide an analysis of the more immediate concerns of the doctrine, whilst the subsequent section will look at its more long-term aspects.

The Preventative Use of Force

The first pillar of the Bush Doctrine emerged as a direct response to the realisation that if terrorists armed with box cutters could use aeroplanes as a weapon to cause mass casualties, what would the scenario be if an unconventional weapon was used?

The response to this possible scenario saw the Bush Doctrine draw a linkage between terrorism and hostile states with the intent to produce unconventional weapons. It also rejected in no uncertain terms Kenneth Waltz's argument that proliferation can be equated with international stability.[71] This aspect of the Bush Doctrine was controversial as it called for such threats to be dealt with preventatively. This linkage went beyond the separate issues of states harbouring and supporting terrorist groups which the Afghanistan campaign underscored.[72]

Vice President Cheney argued that the casualties threatened by terrorist groups using unconventional weapons to their greatest potential dwarfed those of 11 September 2001.[73] Given the difficulties in manufacturing and deploying such weapons, Cheney was correct in stating that the most logical means for terrorists acquiring such weapons would ultimately stem from 'rogue state' producers.[74] Indeed, this point was underlined by Bush:

> The gravest danger our Nation faces lies at the crossroads of radicalism and technology. Our enemies have openly declared that they are seeking weapons of mass destruction, and evidence indicates that they are doing so with determination. The United States will not allow these efforts to succeed. . . . [H]istory will judge harshly those who saw this coming danger but failed to act. In the new world we have entered, the only path to peace and security is the path of action.[75]

The significance of this pillar in the overall strategy was that it vastly broadened the target list from "terrorist organizations of global reach" to include "any terrorist or state sponsor of terrorism which attempts to gain or use weapons of mass destruction (WMD) or their precursors".[76] The scope was thus widened to include countries *defined by* the United States as hostile which were viewed as procuring, or *attempting* to procure, unconventional weapons. This was in spite of whether they were legally entitled to produce such weapons under international law. The reason why this potential form of terrorism was placed onto the national security agenda was not only attributable to a logical projection in the nature of terrorist attacks, but also to the anthrax attacks which took place in the immediate aftermath of the 9/11 terrorist attacks. Although it is unclear what impact the anthrax attacks had on the national security agenda, it seems justifiable to infer that they were a factor which installed a level of fear within the domestic electorate of a mass casualty terrorist attack using such weapons.

The specifics of this strategy meant that in cases where hostile states were viewed as *having the intention* or *actually* producing unconventional weapons, the United States would *prevent* their acquisition by resorting to anticipatory self-defence if a diplomatic/peaceful resolution in accordance with US zero-sum demands proved elusive. In other words, the United States would ultimately resort to the use of force if a state did not comply with US non-negotiable demands. This was based on the belief that such weapons could be used directly or asymmetrically against the United States, and therefore the scale of the threat justified the subjugation of state sovereignty. Bush unveiled this change in military strategy at the West Point Military Academy in June 2002 where he stated that "our security will require all Americans to be forward-looking and resolute, to be ready for preemptive action when necessary to defend our liberty and to defend our lives".[77]

In terms of the historical use of pre-emptive action, the National Security Strategy maintained that:

> The United States has long maintained the option of preemptive actions to counter a sufficient threat to our national security. The greater the threat, the greater is the risk of inaction – and the more compelling the case for taking anticipatory action to defend ourselves, even if uncertainty remains as to the time and place of the enemy's attack. To forestall or prevent such hostile acts by our adversaries, the United States will, if necessary, act preemptively.[78]

Bush's proposal, however, went beyond the traditional definition of *pre-emptive* war and encompassed the doctrine of *preventative* war.[79] It is important to recognise that *pre-emptive* warfare is a response in the face of an *imminent* attack whilst a *preventative* war is carried out long before a potential threat materialises.[80]

The use of pre-emptive force was not a new concept by any means in the history of US foreign policy. Indeed, the Kennedy administration had acted pre-emptively in its establishment of a naval quarantine around Cuba during the missile crisis. However, Robert Kennedy reminds us that the naval quarantine of Cuba was premised on the call to action from the Organization of American States, and the administration purposely refrained from referring to it as pre-emptive self-defence.[81] Nevertheless, a policy of pre-emptive action had never been a *formally declared policy* of the United States, *despite* its actual usage. The adoption of the *preventative* war doctrine was, therefore, very much a new concept in US foreign policy.

The Bush administration maintained that there was a clearly established legal basis for the pre-emptive use of force:

> For centuries, international law recognized that nations need not suffer an attack before they can lawfully take action to defend themselves against forces that present an imminent danger of attack. Legal scholars and international jurists often conditioned the legitimacy of preemption on the existence of an imminent threat – most often a visible mobilization of armies, navies, and air forces preparing to attack. We must adapt the concept of imminent threat to the capabilities and objectives of today's adversaries. [82]

This legal justification for the pre-emptive use of force, which should more accurately be referred to as *anticipatory self-defence,* stemmed from a narrow interpretation of Article 51 of the United Nations Charter. Article 2(4) provides for a clear prohibition of the use of force in the international system. The exception to this, carried in Article 51, allows for the "inherent right of individual or collective self-defence *if an armed attack occurs* . . . until the Security Council has taken measures to maintain international peace and security".[83] Apart from the Cuban missile crisis, there have been only two other relevant cases since the adoption of the UN Charter to *potentially* support its basis under customary international law: Israel's attack on the Egyptian army in 1967, and Israel's air strike on Iraq's nuclear reactor in Osirak in 1981. Even so, the legality of the preventative use of force rubric in the Bush Doctrine remains unproved at best under customary international law, but may well prove to be an evolving principle of customary international law.

In response to criticism, the Bush administration's position was clarified by William H. Taft IV, Legal Adviser to the State Department:

> The President's National Security Strategy relies upon the same legal framework applied to the British in Caroline and to Israel in 1981. The United States reserves the right to use force preemptively in self-defense when faced with an imminent threat. While the definition of imminent must recognize the threat posed by weapons of mass destruction and the intentions of those who possess them, the decision to undertake any action must meet the test of necessity. After the exhaustion of peaceful remedies and a careful, deliberate

consideration of the consequences, in the face of overwhelming evidence of an imminent threat, a nation may take preemptive action to defend its nationals from unimaginable harm.[84]

Whilst Taft's definition went some way to addressing the concerns of an *arbitrary* usage of this legal definition, the legality of invoking Article 51 as a justification for the use of force, *prior to an actual attack having occurred*, is not generally accepted by legal scholars.[85]

The case of the invasion of Iraq in March 2003 underscored this doctrine of the preventative use of force: Iraq was viewed as having such weapons in its possession, and also intent on further production whilst being unwilling to comply with the demands of the international community in a peaceful manner. The key issue to understand about this pillar was, however, that the preventative use of force was not seen as applicable in every circumstance. The Bush Doctrine only saw this as applicable in cases where hostile states remained committed to acquiring unconventional weapons once diplomacy to reverse this situation had been tried and failed. But the significance of this pillar is that it reduced US diplomacy to a *zero-sum game* where compromise is not possible on this issue. Therefore, under its rubric, the preventative use of force would occur once diplomacy, leading to a *full* compliance with US demands, was seen as tried and failed, which indicated that the notion of diplomacy in such circumstances was reduced to an anachronism.

Nonetheless, the Bush administration's adoption of the concept of the preventative use of force, premised on *unilateralism if necessary*, set a precedent for states defining their security interests and applying unilateral measures to achieve them. But the willingness of the Bush administration to resort to unilateralism has some vintage in US foreign policy, particularly in Republican circles.[86] Nevertheless, it is a course of action that held the risk of setting a precedent in the international system. Henry Kissinger succinctly commented that:

> As the most powerful nation in the world, the United States has a special unilateral capacity to implement its convictions. But it also has a special obligation to justify its actions by principals that transcend the assertions of preponderant power. It cannot be in either the American national interest or the world's interest to develop principals that grant every nation an unfettered right of preemption against its own definitions of threats to its security.[87]

Although the administration did caution other nations from using pre-emption as a pretext for aggressive military action, the ambiguity of what exactly warranted such state practice, if it is taken as a precedent for international action, underscores that the Westphalian order was truly in systemic crisis.[88]

The nature of the threat that became so apparent after the 9/11 attacks also ushered in other pillars which allow for the Bush Doctrine to be defined as a grand strategy. Indeed, it is the manner in which the threat was defined that prompted a departure from the Clintonian era. The nature of this difference lies firstly in the manner in which the Bush administration defined terrorism as being countered in the long term, and secondly in the recognition that the ultimate threat posed by terrorism was through the use of unconventional weapons, as has already been discussed. Therefore, this pillar saw the need to counter the threat posed by unconventional weapons and terrorists before they could possibly emerge, as the risks were deemed too great.

Democracy and Freedom Agenda
The second key pillar was the adoption of the neoconservative position on the promotion of democracy and freedom. Gaddis remarks that this was at the centre of the Bush Doctrine.[89] The desire to defend and spread such values drew from a historical vintage in US foreign policy which was most clearly articulated by Woodrow Wilson and Thomas Jefferson.[90] In contrast to previous administrations which saw its promotion as desirable, the Bush Doctrine saw the promotion of liberal democracy as a national security *requirement.*

The key reason why the Bush Doctrine equated democratic promotion with national security was on account of the interpretation that the absence of democracy and freedom actually spawned extremism under the guise of terrorism. Therefore, in the post-9/11 context, the root cause of the terrorist attacks was viewed as the lack of legitimate representative institutions within the Middle East and elsewhere as this resulted in the only outlet for dissent being religious fanaticism.[91] The Bush administration thus embraced the intellectual position on radical political Islam that it was the very lack of democracy and freedom in given countries that resulted in the rise of political extremism and terrorist action.[92]

In addition to democratisation actually combating the root causes of terrorism with global reach, the Bush administration also saw it as desirable on the grounds that representative democracies were more likely to engage in peaceful relations, and thus democratisation would provide stability and security for the international system. Indeed, this is a thoroughly Wilsonian ideal that believed like-minded democracies would opt to resolve differences through legal means and diplomacy. Therefore, when this was translated to the Middle East, a complete reordering of the political environment was desired in order to provide for regional stability in the long term. This was despite the transformation requiring a geopolitical overhaul which would create insecurity through socio-political changes. Indeed, this was in direct contrast to the Clinton administration's approach.

The nature of this pillar allowed the charge that it was exceptionally optimistic and ambitious. Indeed, it went well beyond the revolutionary vision Wilson articulated in the aftermath of the First World War. But for Bush, the 9/11 attacks marked an opportunity to restructure the world order. Bush remarked that "history has called us into action, and we are not going to miss that opportunity to make the world more peaceful and more free".[93]

With regard to the invasion of Iraq in March 2003, it was viewed by Bush as serving dual purposes commensurate with this pillar: firstly, it allowed the removal of Saddam Hussein's dictatorship and the installation of democratic polity; and secondly, a democratising Iraq was viewed as fostering pressures for democratic reform within neighbouring authoritarian states within the region.[94] In some respects this is akin to a reversal of the Cold War Domino Theory. Bush remarked in the aftermath of the Iraq invasion that "I believe that a free Iraq can be an example of reform and progress to all the Middle East".[95] Indeed, with Iraq serving as a beacon for democracy, the Bush administration believed that it would foster pressure within the civil society of neighbouring states for democratic reforms to be implemented.[96] As a consequence, this pillar fostered a wider geostrategic agenda for the Middle East which was in direct contrast to the Clinton era.

Therefore, the belief was that only through a complete reordering of the international system in the long term could the root causes of terrorism be countered. In addition to this, the Bush administration also saw democratic promotion as serving the goal of providing for international stability in the long term as it upheld the principle that democratic nations will resolve their differences through Wilsonian means.

American Hegemony

The final level of the Bush Doctrine called for the maintenance of US hegemony. It is noticeable that this was in keeping with the spirit of the Pentagon's Defense Policy Guidance of 1992.[97] As already highlighted, this called for the maintenance of US primacy through ensuring a qualitative superiority in military capability.[98] This can be translated as having an imperial connotation but will depend on the definition of hegemony and empire.[99] Either way, it was premised on the belief that the United States actually upholds universal values and thus maintenance of US primacy was required in order to promote and defend them in addition to the United States itself.[100] Indeed, Edward Rhodes highlights that the maintenance of the US hegemonic position "provides the aegis under which peace and freedom can be built".[101]

In an address to the West Point Military Academy in 2002, Bush remarked that "America has, and intends to keep, military strength beyond challenge – thereby making the destabilizing arms races of other eras pointless, and limiting rivalries to trade and other pursuits of peace".[102] But in the National Security Strategy of 2002, Bush announced that "[i]t is time to reaffirm the essential role of American military strength. We must build and maintain our defenses beyond challenge. Our military's highest priority is to defend the United States".[103] The strategy goes on to say that:

> The United States must and will maintain the capability to defeat any attempt by an enemy – whether a state or non-state actor – to impose its will on the United States, our allies, or our friends. We will maintain the forces sufficient to support our obligations, and to defend freedom. Our forces will be strong enough to dissuade potential adversaries from pursuing a military build-up in hopes of surpassing, or equalling, the power of the United States.[104]

This has been interpreted by Robert Jervis as seeking the dual objectives of ensuring that no nation could even contemplate matching US military supremacy through heightened levels of funding, in addition to actually preventing a rival from emerging.[105] Although Jervis believes that the United States would act militarily to ensure it maintains its primacy, it is difficult to envisage that military force would be used in the hypothetical situation of a liberal democratic rival emerging. Nevertheless, this aspect of the Bush Doctrine was aimed primarily at preventing a non-democratic state from gaining primacy over the United States.

Concluding Observations

The conclusions that can be drawn from these comparative observations are that the character, world view and vision for US foreign policy were markedly different in the Clinton and Bush administrations. The idiosyncratic differences of Bush and Clinton appeared to correlate with the character of key senior individuals in their given bureaucracies, and were ultimately commensurate with the nature their foreign policies have taken. On a bureaucratic level, Clinton's administration was staffed by individuals who shared his geoeconomic vision for foreign policy, but were not noted for holding particular views which would place them in conflict with this. In any case, the Clinton presidency could be characterised as risk averse in foreign policy concerns. Whilst its geoeconomic orientation and reluctance to take risks in the use of military power made it a more compatible policy for multilateral cooperation, its ad hoc approach to international affairs was weak and did result in contradictory positions being adopted. Bush's idiosyncrasies, however, lent themselves towards a clear and decisive foreign policy that was geared towards long-range and ambitious projections. It also resulted in a propensity for unilateralism which was in direct contrast to the Clinton presidency.

In direct comparison, the Bush presidency has been shown to have departed from Clinton's geoeconomic strategy in a radical fashion. After the 9/11 attacks, the Bush administration adopted a new strategic approach towards international affairs that resulted in a complete overhaul of US geostrategy towards the Middle East.

Taken as a whole, it is clear that a radical departure in US foreign policy has taken place. Whilst Bush's policy was more sophisticated in terms of complexity than Clinton's geoeconomic foreign policy strategy, the key issue was whether the radical transformation it required for the international system would actually provide the United States with the objectives it set out to achieve. Given the long-term nature of Bush's policy, an adequate evaluation at this stage is not viable, but the key observation that can be made is that it was inherently optimistic. This will lead to new challenges for the United States in terms of whether it can successfully accomplish its objectives in the face of the instability and insecurity that will likely follow as transitions to democracy occur.

When taking a long-term view on US foreign policy however, it is clear that the very principles, which are deemed to be universal, on which the republic was founded have gradually evolved to play a more assertive role in US diplomacy. Whilst such values were originally subordinated by a clear upholding of Westphalian notions of sovereignty, the evidence indicates that this principle began to break down for the United States during Wilson's presidency. Whilst America temporarily retreated back to isolationist zeal in the interwar period, what can be deduced is that there has been an inherent tension in US diplomatic history between a crusading universal moralism, and a *realpolitik* pursuit of the national interest – with both struggling to dominate the conduct of foreign policy. Nevertheless, in times of national threat a synergy develops between the two and serves a mutually reinforcing role with, however, different underlying reasons for their existence.

The War on Terror represented a new stage in this evolutionary process – one that did not allow for a clear historical parallel to be drawn. Unlike the Cold War era where Wilsonians and *realpolitik* strategists saw a common enemy – the latter military and the former moral – in the War on Terror, the nature of the threat, and how to counter it, differed in a key respect. The root causes of Islamic terrorism were seen as the very absence of free speech, democracy and equality, which are considered a product of colonialism and US interests in maintaining the status quo for a secure flow of hydrocarbon resources. Therefore, the intention of countering Islamic terrorism and thus securing US national security has a synergy with the crusading moralism ethic. So whilst Wilsonians may focus more on the moral obligation to promote such values, the key point is that even the more selfish Jacksonians, who seek to ensure US national security, see the lack of such values as being at the root of the problem. The final analysis is that US foreign policy has entered into a fundamentally new era where its main strands of thought are wholly mutually reinforcing.

The key challenge for US diplomacy towards the Islamic world is to recognise that there are two main streams of thought in the currently dominant neoconservative school, both moving towards the same endgame but for differential reasons: a global moralism and a *realpolitik* assessment of the national interest. Here it is necessary to recognise that this new strategic context is shaping two key debates on US foreign policy. The first point of debate is: should the United States uphold a crusading moralism as a determining force in its foreign policy? What relationship should moral values have in foreign policy to a *realpolitik* concept of the national interest? Indeed, the debate over the merits of the US-led invasion of Iraq in essence leads to the formulation of both sides of this debate: was the Iraq invasion a failure because of a misguided ideology that resulted in war or was it down to poor post-war planning?

In contributing to this debate, an initial observation is that US diplomacy has not learnt the historical lesson that an *unchecked* global moralism, as a determining factor in its foreign policy, is both an unwelcome and counterproductive force. Although US administrations do have genuine benevolent intentions premised on America's own experience with enlightened rationalism, an unhindered and crusading moralism leads to perceptions of imperialism and orientalism and makes the prospect of military force being used more likely as such action is justified morally. So whilst it may be morally justified, global moralism's use as a guiding force in foreign policy runs counter to not only its own theoretical objectives, but in the War on Terror its crusading nature also makes, on a practical level, such factors less likely to be adopted and thus serves to undermine US national interests in countering terrorism in the long term.

The second main debate for US foreign policy in the War on Terror is: how can political changes in Islamic countries be promoted most effectively in order to counter the root causes of Islamic terrorism? Whilst this proposition rests on the basis that the political structure is the key problem, the importance of this question for US foreign policy is that it will help foster a more sophisticated *realpolitik* approach in US diplomacy towards the Middle East in order for US national security interests to be satisfied. Therefore, it is of key importance to understand the nature of Middle Eastern politics, what impact US policy is having and how change can best be promoted in a productive manner, as this will be instrumental in countering the radicalism that has been inadvertently spawned from historic Western policies towards the Middle East.

As this chapter has provided an exposition and conceptualisation of US foreign policy in the post-Cold War and War on Terror periods, it is important to understand how this relates to the question of security in the Persian Gulf. Before analysing the nature of US foreign policy towards Iran and Iraq during this time frame, it is important to fully examine the intellectual context of political Islam and how this relates to the War on Terror rubric. Indeed, the question of political Islam and how it relates to extremism and democracy forms the essence of the debate on the character of the War on Terror and also the over-arching cause of the changed definition of Persian Gulf security. Therefore, the following chapter will provide a detailed examination of the issue of US foreign policy vis-à-vis political Islam as this will serve to provide a robust understanding of the fundamental change in grand strategy and geostrategy towards the Persian Gulf.

NOTES

1   Deborah J. Gerner, "Foreign Policy Analysis: Exhilarating Eclecticism, Intriguing Enigmas", *International Studies Notes* 16.3 (1991): 4–19; Deborah J. Gerner, "The Evolution of the Study of Foreign Policy", *Foreign Policy Analysis: Continuity and Change in Its Second Generation*, eds. Laura Neack, Jeanne A. K. Hey and Patrick Jude Haney (Englewood Cliffs: Prentice Hall, 1995) 17–32; and Yaacov Vertzberger, *The World in Their Minds: Information Processing, Cognition and Perception in Foreign Policy Decisionmaking* (Stanford: Stanford University Press, 1990) 342–64.

2   John Quincy Adams was the first President who was the son of a President, and was the sixth President of the United States.

3   Walter Russell Mead is the Henry A. Kissinger Senior Fellow for US Foreign Policy at the Council on Foreign Relations. See Walter Russell Mead, *Special Providence: American Foreign Policy and How It Changed the World* (New York: Knopf, 2001).

4   Philip E. Tetlock and Charles B. McGuire, "Cognitive Perspectives on Foreign Policy", *American Foreign Policy: Theoretical Essays*, ed. G. John Ikenberry, 5th ed. (New York: Georgetown University, 2005) 484–500.

5   Vertzberger, *The World in Their Minds: Information Processing, Cognition and Perception in Foreign Policy Decisionmaking* 111–91.

6   Robert Snyder, et al., 'Decision Making Approach to the Study of Foreign Policy'. *International Politics and Foreign Policy*, ed. James N. Rosenau (New York: The Free Press, 1969) 199–206; Robert Jervis, "Hypotheses on Misperception", *International Politics and Foreign Policy*, ed. James N. Rosenau (New York: The Free Press, 1969)

239–54; John Vogler, "Perspectives on the Foreign Policy System: Psychological Approaches", *Understanding Foreign Policy: The Foreign Policy Systems Approach*, eds. Michael Clarke and Brian White (Aldershot: Elgar, 1989) 135–58; and Graham T. Allison, *Essence of Decision; Explaining the Cuban Missile Crisis* (Boston: Little, Brown, 1971) 128–42.

7 Henry Kissinger, *Does America Need a Foreign Policy? Toward a Diplomacy for the 21st Century*, rev. ed. (London: Free Press, 2002) 29.

8 James Mann, *Rise of the Vulcans: The History of Bush's War Cabinet* (New York: Viking, 2004) 14–19.

9 Stephen Graubard, *The Presidents: The Transformation of the American Presidency from Theodore Roosevelt to George W. Bush* (London: Penguin, 2005) 669.

10 David Aikman and George W. Bush, *A Man of Faith: The Spiritual Journey of George W. Bush* (Nashville: W Publishing, 2004) 111–34.

11 William J. Clinton, "Remarks on Signing the Religious Freedom Restoration Act of 1993" (Washington, D.C.: GPO, 1993).

12 Kevin P. Phillips, *American Dynasty: Aristocracy, Fortune, and the Politics of Deceit in the House of Bush* (New York: Viking Penguin, 2004) 49–51.

13 Howard Fineman, "Bush and God", *Newsweek* 10 Mar. 2003: 3–5.

14 Fred Barnes, "God and Man in the Oval Office", *Weekly Standard* (2003), vol. 8, no. 26, 3pp.; Stephen Mansfield, *The Faith of George W. Bush* (Lake Mary, Fla.: Charisma House, 2003) 149–76; and Paul Kengor, *God and George W. Bush: A Spiritual Life* (New York: Regan Books, 2004) 89–290.

15 David Brady and D. Sunshine Hillygus, "Assessing the Clinton Presidency: The Political Constraints of Legislative Policy", *The Clinton Riddle: Perspectives on the Forty-Second President*, eds. Todd G. Shields, Jeannie M. Whayne and Donald R. Kelley (Arkansas: University of Arkansas Press, 2004) 47–78.

16 Betty Glad, "Bill Clinton: The Character Issue Revisited", *The Clinton Riddle: Perspectives on the Forty-Second President*, eds. Todd G. Shields, Jeannie M. Whayne and Donald R. Kelley (Arkansas: University of Arkansas Press, 2004) 1–22.

17 Graubard, *The Presidents: The Transformation of the American Presidency from Theodore Roosevelt to George W. Bush* 648.

18 Fred I. Greenstein, "The Leadership Style of George W. Bush", *The George W. Bush Presidency: An Early Assessment*, ed. Fred I. Greenstein (Maryland: Johns Hopkins Press, 2003) 1–16.

19 David Frum, *The Right Man: An Inside Account of the Surprise Presidency of George W. Bush* (New York: Random House, 2003) 12–74.

20 Ivo H. Daalder and James M. Lindsay, *America Unbound: The Bush Revolution in Foreign Policy* (Washington, D.C.: Brookings Institution, 2003) 36.

21 Anonymous, "The Odd Couple", *Economist Online* (2005); and Natan Sharansky and Ron Dermer, *The Case for Democracy: The Power of Freedom to Overcome Tyranny and Terror* (New York: Public Affairs, 2004) 18–38.

22 George W. Bush, "A Distinctly American Internationalism", *Remarks at the Ronald Reagan Presidential Library* (Simi Valley, California: FAS, 1999).

23 Ibid.

24 Robert Kagan, "Distinctly American Internationalism", *Weekly Standard* 29 Nov. 1999: 6–9.

25 Graubard, *The Presidents: The Transformation of the American Presidency from Theodore Roosevelt to George W. Bush* 547–87.

26 Hugh Heclo, "The Political Ethos of George W. Bush", *The George W. Bush Presidency: An Early Assessment*, ed. Fred I. Greenstein (Maryland: Johns Hopkins Press, 2003) 37–39.

27 William J. Clinton, "A New Covenant for American Security", *Speech at Georgetown University* (Washington, D.C.: GPO, 1991).

28 Ibid.

29 David Halberstam, *War in a Time of Peace: Bush, Clinton, and the Generals* (New York: Scribner, 2001) 174.

30 Ibid. 286.

31 Kissinger, *Does America Need a Foreign Policy?* 29.

32 John F. Harris, "New Security Adviser Berger Is Known as Consensus Builder", *Washington Post* 6 Dec. 1996: A27.

33 Halberstam, *War in a Time of Peace: Bush, Clinton, and the Generals* 244.

34 Graubard, *The Presidents: The Transformation of the American Presidency from Theodore Roosevelt to George W. Bush* 635.

35 Ibid. 629–30.

36 Halberstam, *War in a Time of Peace: Bush, Clinton, and the Generals* 386.

37 Harris, "New Security Adviser Berger Is Known as Consensus Builder" A27.

38 Kissinger, *Does America Need a Foreign Policy?* 19.

39 Daalder and Lindsay, *America Unbound: The Bush Revolution in Foreign Policy* 22.

40 Anne Norton, *Leo Strauss and the Politics of American Empire* (New Haven: Yale University Press, 2004) 141–43.

41 Mann, *Rise of the Vulcans* 1–9.

42 Norman Podhoretz, *Neoconservatism: A Eulogy*, 1996, AEI Press, Available: http://www.aei.org/publications/pubID.18103/pub_detail.asp, 10/08/05 2005.

43 Jeane Kirkpatrick, "Dictatorships and Double Standards", *Commentary* 68.Nov. (1979): 34–45.

44 Mann, *Rise of the Vulcans* 97–98.

45 Irving Kristol, *Neoconservatism: The Autobiography of an Idea* (New York: Free Press, 1995).

46 Mann, *Rise of the Vulcans* 164–78.

47 Joshua Muravchik, "The Bush Manifesto", *Commentary* 114.Dec. (2002): 28–29.

48 Elliott Abrams, et al., *Statement of Principles*, 3 Jun. 1997, Project for the New American Century, Available: http://newamericancentury.org/statementofprinciples.htm.

49 Mann, *Rise of the Vulcans* 148.

50 Ibid. 316.

51 Ibid. 29.

52 Patrick E. Tyler, "US Strategy Plan Calls for Insuring No Rivals Develop", *New York Times* 8 Mar. 1992: A12; and Patrick E. Tyler, "Lone Superpower Plan: Ammunition for Critics", *New York Times* 10 Mar. 1992: A10.

53 Tyler, "Lone Superpower Plan: Ammunition for Critics" A10.

54 Tyler, "US Strategy Plan Calls for Insuring No Rivals Develop" A12.

55 Norton, *Leo Strauss and the Politics of American Empire* 181–94.

56 Mann, *Rise of the Vulcans* 248–93.

57 Elliott Abrams, et al., *Letter to President Clinton*, 26 Jan. 1998, Project for a New

American Century, Available: http://www.newamericancentury.org/iraqclinton-letter.htm; and Elliott Abrams, et al., *Letter to Trent Lott and Newt Gingrich*, 29 May 1998, Available: http://www.newamericancentury.org/iraqletter1998.htm.

58 Mann, *Rise of the Vulcans* 29.

59 United States, "Quadrennial Defense Review Report", ed. Department of Defense (GPO, 2001).

60 United States, "Rumsfeld Commission Report", *Executive Summary of the Commission to Assess the Ballistic Missile Threat to the United States*, ed. Congress (Brookings Institution Press 1998).

61 Frum, *The Right Man: An Inside Account of the Surprise Presidency of George W. Bush* 100–01.

62 Martin E. Marty, "Bush and God", *Newsweek* Mar. 10 2003: 5–7.

63 George W. Bush, "President Delivers State of the Union Address", *The President's State of the Union Address* (Washington, D.C.: GPO, 2002).

64 Kissinger, *Does America Need a Foreign Policy?* 30.

65 Alexander Hamilton was the first US Secretary to the Treasury. He had a major impact on US economic policy and foreign policy. A Hamiltonian policy is one typically understood as being motivated by economic gain for the United States.

66 John Chipman, *Strategic Survey 2001/2002* (Oxford: OUP, 2002) 264–68.

67 John L. Gaddis, *We Now Know: Rethinking Cold War History* (Oxford: OUP, 1998) 281–95; and Henry Kissinger, *Diplomacy* (New York: Touchstone, 1995) 423–45.

68 Bob Woodward, *Bush at War* (New York: Simon & Schuster, 2002) 30.

69 United States, "The National Security Strategy of the United States of America," ed. President of the United States (GPO, 2002).

70 For an excellent study on Wilsonianism and foreign policy see: Robert S. McNamara and James G. Blight, *Wilson's Ghost: Reducing the Risk of Conflict, Killing, and Catastrophe in the 21st Century* (New York: Public Affairs, 2003) 17–58, 217–26.

71 Kenneth N. Waltz, *The Spread of Nuclear Weapons: More May Be Better*, Adelphi Papers, No. 171 (London: International Institute for Strategic Studies, 1981) 1–32; United States, "National Security Strategy to Combat Weapons of Mass Destruction", ed. President of the United States (GPO, 2002); and also see United States, "National Strategy for Combating Terrorism", ed. President of the United States (GPO, 2003).

72 Woodward, *Bush at War* 43.

73 Ibid. 137.

74 Paul R. Pillar, *Terrorism and US Foreign Policy* (Washington, D.C.: Brookings Institution Press, 2001) 164; David A. Kay, "Wmd Terrorism: Hype or Reality", *The Terrorism Treat and US Governmental Response: Operational and Organisational Factors*, eds. James M. Smith and William C. Thomas (Colorado: USAF Institute for National Security Studies, 2001) 69–78.

75 Bush, "President Delivers State of the Union Address."

76 United States, "The National Security Strategy of the United States of America".

77 George W. Bush, "West Point Commencement Speech", *America and the World: Debating the New Shape of International Politics*, ed. Gideon Rose (New York: Council on Foreign Relations, 2002) 367.

78 United States, "The National Security Strategy of the United States of America".

79 Walter B. Slocombe, "Force, Pre-Emption and Legitimacy", *Survival* 45.1 (2003): 123–28.
80 Jack Levy, "Declining Power and the Preventive Motivation for War", *World Politics* 40.Oct. (1987): 82–105.
81 Robert F. Kennedy, *Thirteen Days: A Memoir of the Cuban Missile Crisis* (Norwalk, Connecticut: Easton Press, 1991) 61–103; and John L. Gaddis, *Surprise, Security, and the American Experience* (Cambridge: Harvard University Press, 2004) 38–56.
82 United States, "The National Security Strategy of the United States of America".
83 Malcolm D. Evans, *Blackstone's International Law Documents*, Blackstone's Statutes, 4th ed. (London: Blackstone, 1999) 16. Emphasis added.
84 William H. Taft, "The Legal Basis for Preemption", *Roundtable on Old Rules, New Threats* (Washington, D.C.: Council on Foreign Relations, 2002), 3.
85 Miriam Sapiro, "Iraq: Shifting Sands of Preemptive Self-Defense", *The American Journal of International Law* 97.3 (2003): 602.
86 Jesse Helms, "American Sovereignty and the UN", *National Interest* 62.Winter (2000): 31–34.
87 Henry Kissinger, "Consult and Control: Bywords for Battling the New Enemy", *Washington Post* 16 Sept. 2002: A19.
88 Kissinger, *Does America Need a Foreign Policy?* 234-82.
89 John L. Gaddis, "Bush's Security Strategy", *Foreign Policy* 133 (2002): 50–57.
90 Robert Jervis, "Understanding the Bush Doctrine", *American Foreign Policy: Theoretical Essays*, ed. G. John Ikenberry, 5th ed. (New York: Georgetown University, 2005) 584–85.
91 Fouad Ajami, *The Dream Palace of the Arabs: A Generation's Odyssey*, 1st ed. (New York: Pantheon Books, 1998) 133–58; and Bernard Lewis, *What Went Wrong?* (London: Phoenix, 2002) 168–78; see also United Nations Development Programme, *The Arab Human Development Report 2004: Towards Freedom in the Arab World* (New York: United Nations Development Programme, Regional Bureau for Arab States, 2004).
92 Phillip H. Gordon, "Bush's Middle East Vision", *Survival* 45.1 (2003): 155–63.
93 George W. Bush, "President, Vice President Discuss the Middle East", *Remarks by the President and the Vice President Upon Conclusion of Breakfast* (Washington D.C.: GPO, 2002).
94 Gordon, "Bush's Middle East Vision" 155–63.
95 George W. Bush, "President Discusses the Economy with Small Business Owners", *Remarks by the President in the Rose Garden* (Washington D.C.: GPO, 2003); see also Colin Powell, "The US–Middle East Partnership Initiative: Building Hope for the Years Ahead", *Remarks at the Heritage Foundation* (Washington, D.C.: GPO, 2002).
96 Stephen Cook, "The Right Way to Promote Arab Reform", *Foreign Affairs* 84.2 (2005): 92–96; and Marina Ottaway, et al., "Democratic Mirage in the Middle East", *Critical Mission: Essays on Democracy Promotion*, ed. Thomas Carothers (Washington, D.C.: Brookings Institution Press, 2002) 229–36.
97 Tyler, "Lone Superpower Plan: Ammunition for Critics" A12.
98 Jervis, "Understanding the Bush Doctrine" 584–85.
99 G. John Ikenberry, "America's Imperial Ambition", *American Foreign Policy: Theoretical Essays*, ed. G. John Ikenberry, 5th ed. (New York: Georgetown

University, 2005) 564–75.; Zbigniew Brzezinski, *The Choice: Global Domination or Global Leadership* (New York: Basic Books, 2005) 131–49; Robert Jervis, *American Foreign Policy in a New Era* (New York: Routledge, 2005) 89–90; Niall Ferguson, *Colossus: The Rise and Fall of the American Empire* (London: Allen Lane, 2004) 169–99.

100 Ikenberry, "America's Imperial Ambition" 564–75; Andrew J. Bacevich, *American Empire: The Realities and Consequences of US Diplomacy* (Cambridge: Harvard University Press, 2002) 225–44; Bush, "West Point Commencement Speech" 369.

101 Edward Rhodes, "The Imperial Logic of Bush's Liberal Agenda", *Survival* 45.1 (2003): 134.

102 Bush, "West Point Commencement Speech" 369.

103 United States, "The National Security Strategy of the United States of America" 29.

104 Ibid. 29–30.

105 Jervis, *American Foreign Policy in a New Era* 89–90.

3

The Emergence of the War on Terror: Political Islam and Grand Strategy

"Which is more important in world history: the Taliban or the fall of the Soviet Empire? A few over-excited Islamists or the liberation of Central Europe and the end of the Cold War?"

Zbigniew Brzezinski
January 1998

The epigraph by Zbigniew Brzezinski is telling: prior to the attacks of 11 September 2001 it was difficult to equate the rise of radical political Islam with the ideological and military threat posed by the Soviet Union. But the scale and severity of the 9/11 attacks resulted in a radical foreign policy response. Whilst Brzezinski's assessment was correct prior to the 9/11 attacks, it is important to recognise that the overall product of the Soviet invasion of Afghanistan was the beginning of the development of a radical version of international political Islam that ultimately spawned al-Qa'ida. As the response of the United States to the 9/11 attacks marked the onset of a new grand strategic era, it is necessary to understand how political Islam fits in with the strategy underpinning the War on Terror.

The purpose of this chapter will be to analyse the position of the United States towards political Islam during the time period 1993–2003. Specifically, it will demonstrate how the linkage between neoconservatism and the advent of US grand strategy in the era of the War on Terror was premised, in the main, on countering the root causes of religious political extremism by promoting the values of political representation, freedom, human rights and equality on a global level. Indeed, their absence will be shown to be ultimately viewed as having created the conditions which bred international terrorism. So whilst promoting these values fulfilled the moral edge of neoconservatism and found a resonance with the values on which the American republic was founded, it also served a more realist function of safeguarding US national security.

[55]

In examining US foreign policy towards radical political Islam, it will be shown that the position of the United States towards political movements that are guided by Islam did not equate to a policy towards the Islamic religion. But in terms of these movements, a demarcation could generally be made between those that were moderate, and legitimately participated in the given political system, and extremists' movements which had a propensity towards violence in order to fulfil their political objectives. Extremist movements were viewed as illegitimate and fell under the United States' counterterrorism policy rubric: the focus of US foreign policy towards political Islam was therefore on moderate Islamic groups.

The issues facing US policy towards moderate Islamist groups revolved around whether their participation in a democratic process and the establishment of a government based on the Islamic *Shari'a* was legitimate. This chapter will show that the steadily evolving policy towards political Islam in the time period 1993–2003 was typically inconsistent: such groups' participation was seen as legitimate, but a majority electoral victory was deemed illegitimate.

Of more importance, however, was the manner in which the United States aimed to combat the root causes of extremism and terrorism in general. Although the academic literature quite rightly gives a diverse and rich account of the causes of extremism, the position of the United States in this time period can be characterised as viewing a democratic and free-dom deficit in Islamic countries as being at the root of Islamic-inspired extremism. Nevertheless, stated US policy towards reform as a means of countering the root causes of Islamic extremism was actually a secondary foreign policy concern to US policy strategy towards the Persian Gulf arena during the Clinton years. However, this chapter will show that the onset of the War on Terror resulted in a fundamental departure in this long-standing policy and redefined the strategic underpinnings of Persian Gulf security.

Overview of the Origins of Political Islam

In order to provide an appropriate analysis of US foreign policy towards political Islam, it is necessary to firstly provide a general overview of the intellectual framework of the subject.

Academic interpretations of political Islam have examined the origins, characteristics and perceived threats posed by political Islam.

However, the biggest question concerns whether or not political Islam is fundamentally compatible with democracy. The significance of these varying interpretations is that they advocate diverse and incompatible policy responses towards political Islam. In many respects, the debate over political Islam is one of the few remaining intellectual debates within US foreign policy: the legacy of the Iranian Revolution shows that differences of interpretation as to why the United States 'lost Iran' have a direct bearing on policy prescriptions towards Islamism.[1]

In terms of the classification and origin of Islamist movements, it has been argued that political Islam can be characterised as a complex socio-cultural response, which has evolved historically, rather than a simple product of the political structure.[2] Bernard Lewis approaches the issue by asking why the once vibrant and successful Islamic civilisation has declined and fallen in relation to the West. Lewis's lucid historical explanation argues that various inherent internal constrictions have resulted in the relative decline of the Islamic civilisation. But more importantly, he sees Islamic movements using politicised interpretations of history that explain this decline as a means of garnering support. Other scholars, such as François Burgat, echo Lewis's thesis by arguing that Islamism is a response to Westernisation and therefore should simply be considered a cultural response.[3] Burgat argues that "the process of re-Islamisation is a mere process of re-traditionalisation, developing in relative autonomy and exclusion to the dynamic of political liberalisation and social modernisation".[4] Bassam Tibi maintains this theme by highlighting that a Muslim identity has emerged as a cultural response to Muslim encounters with Western modernity.[5] These sociologically-grounded cultural responses draw from globalisation and regionalisation approaches which identify the reaffirming of a localised culture, or normative values, as being a product of an increased level of international interaction and interconnectedness.

Whilst increased interaction and awareness of foreign cultures, economies, political frameworks and religions results in a reaffirming of a cultural identity,[6] Hrair Dekmejian takes the position that this has occurred within the context of a failure of modernisation and development in the region.[7] The significance behind this is that it is the failure of competing ideologies in terms of delivering modernisation and development that has led to the adoption of Islamism as a new ideological paradigm. Again, this affirms Lewis's argument that an affirmation of

Islamic values in political life is viewed as the most apt way of restoring the Islamic world's position in relation to the West. Nazih Ayubi supports this approach but stresses that the lack of economic development in the Middle East can be attributed to it being 'artificial' development which was mainly geared towards catering for Western actors.[8] Moreover, this 'artificial' form of development is categorised as not only unsustainable, but also one which undermines socio-economic and political relations. In other words, Ayubi argues that modernisation in Muslim societies arose from the pressures of colonialism and its overall development has been inhibited.

Although the cultural response argument provides a credible reason for the existence of Islamist movements, Daniel Pipes considers Islamism as ultimately stemming from Western radicalism.[9] He highlights the fact that many Islamists are those who have been exposed to the West and are highly educated. They seek the modernisation of their own countries but blame the West for inhibiting their countries' indigenous development. Hence, not only does Pipes recognise that Islamism is fostered by a radical cultural response to modernity, but he also sees it as a product of the frustration at the lack of economic development within the Middle East. Therefore, in contrast to Dekmejian, Pipes highlights the Islamist view that the lack of modernisation and development in the Middle East is a result of Western capitalism.

Whilst both cultural and economic factors have been advanced as contributors towards the growth of Islamic movements, it should not be forgotten that Islamic political movements are first and foremost a political response. It has been widely argued that they are a natural successor to the ideological void left in the wake of Arab nationalism. John Esposito sees the emergence of political Islam as a result of the failure of alternative paradigms such as "Arab nationalism/socialism, Iranian (Pahlevi) nationalism, and Muslim nationalism in Pakistan".[10] With the apparent failures of these ideologies, political Islam became revitalised as a viable alternative in the Muslim world. Esposito and Voll both approach this so-called Islamic revivalism from a historical perspective that identifies political Islam as the only credible alternative to authoritarianism. They convincingly argue that:

> As the recent histories of Algeria, Tunisia and Egypt demonstrate, Islamist groups are more likely to emerge as the major opposition

party when they are 'the only game in town' that is, when they function in political environments in which they become the sole credible voice of opposition and thus attract the votes of those who simply wish to vote against the government or system, as well as the votes of their supporters.[11]

In many respects, Esposito and Voll's analysis correctly identifies that the key underlying cause of political Islam's success is the absence of any other credible political mobilising force. The key question is, therefore, why is there an absence of competing political mobilising agents? Esposito's analysis would have us believe that it is simply a product of the failure of competing political ideologies; but surely this overlooks why even limited democratic pluralism has failed to develop within Middle Eastern countries in general. Nevertheless, Maria do Céu Pinto reminds us that:

> [Political Islam is] mainly a protest movement against the current Arab regimes which suffer intrinsic weaknesses relative to the emerging Islamist challenge. The Muslim activists gain popular appeal by endeavouring to implement the very programme nationalist regimes devised but were unable to carry out.[12]

In other words, the growth in support for Islamism rather than other political movements is a result of the failure of indigenous Arab regimes to implement successful development programmes. Thus, Pinto implies that Islamism is a political response to the socio-economic context.

Whilst there are several origins of political Islam, for policy prescriptions the most important consideration is the political structure itself within countries where political Islam finds currency. Bernard Lewis rightly highlights that:

> Religious movements enjoy . . . practical advantage[s] in societies like those of the Middle East and north Africa that are under more or less autocratic rule: dictatorships can forbid parties, they can forbid meetings – they cannot forbid public worship, and, they can to only a limited extent control sermons. As a result the religious opposition groups are the only ones that have regular meeting places where they can assemble and have at their disposal a network outside the control of the state or at least not fully subject to it. The more oppressive the regime the more it helps the fundamentalists by giving them a virtual monopoly of opposition.[13]

Whilst this explains why political Islam has grown within the context of authoritarianism, it does not by itself explain why political Islam potentially leads to Islamic terrorism. The most likely explanation is that because of the failure to achieve reform within authoritarian countries, the use of violence is seen by some as a legitimate means of achieving their political objectives. Therefore, the very essence of the absence of freedom in authoritarian systems serves to foster the radicalisation of some Islamists into using terrorism as a political tool.

This line of argument is incorporated to a certain extent in Martin Indyk's analysis into why Islamist movements have seen a resurgence, coupled with the use of violence as a tool for achieving political object-ives.[14] Indyk argues that because of the frustration of the Islamists in dealing with their own government, opposition towards the United States and other Western powers has been fuelled, as they are seen as the reason why authoritarian regimes have been unwilling to reform. When viewed within the context of long-standing US policy towards Persian Gulf security, which specially sought the maintenance of the status quo, there is credibility in the argument which sees the US national interest as having been the barrier to political reform in the first instance. Islamic terrorism against the United States is thus a direct by-product of US policy efforts to promote its national interest in the Middle East.

Accommodation or Confrontation?

Islamic political movements use highly diverse methods in their attempts to gain political power. Islamists are generally classified in terms of their political behaviour as being either moderate or radical, based mainly on whether they use violence as a political tool. However, there are some commonalities which transcend political Islamic movements that should not be overlooked. Esposito highlights the following commonalities:

1. Islam is viewed as being a total way of life.
2. Westernisation is equated with secularism and other values contrary to Islam.
3. Islam is the divine route to success and therefore is superior to capitalism and socialism.
4. The introduction of the *Shari'a* will produce a more moral and just society.

5.   It is the duty of all Muslims to embrace the concept of Jihad – to make effort against the odds.[15]

Despite these commonalities, Esposito and Voll quite rightly emphasise the distinction between Islamic movements that pursue power in moderate fashion and those that are more radical:

> Radical groups which go beyond these principles such as Hezbollah, al-Jihad, Takfir wal Hijra and the Army of God believe in an over-throw of Muslim governments who they see as un-Islamic; that a historical battle exists against the West; Muslims and non-Muslims who do not accept this are infidels.[16]

They highlight that although such radical groups exist, they operate on the fringe of society and are not representative of the majority norms and values of mainstream Muslim societies.[17] The mainstream Islamic groups are highlighted as being non-violent:

> [They are] vibrant, multi-faceted movements that will embody the major impact of Islamic revivalism for the foreseeable future . . . its goal is the transformation of society through the formation of individuals at the grass roots level. Islamic societies work in education (schools, child care centres, youth camps), in religious publishing and broadcasting, in economic projects (Islamic banks, investment houses, insurance companies, local agrarian development) and in social services (hospitals, clinics, legal aid societies).[18]

Following the view that moderate Islamists exist, Esposito affirms the *accommodationist* view that Islam is *compatible* with democracy and should therefore be incorporated into the political spectrum as part of a wider drive towards political pluralism.[19] In any case, Esposito and James Piscatori remind us that Islam does indeed have an intrinsic representative element through the consultative mechanism of the *Shura*.[20] Moreover, the involvement in democratic polity is believed to be a moderating mechanism as participation within it forces the moderation of policy for simple political expediency. This is seen as further marginalising radical Islamists.[21]

Graham Fuller takes a comparable position by highlighting that Islamists' involvement in democratic political processes would have to be suitably moderated for them to effectively cooperate with other movements and to enable them to fulfil their objective of gaining political support for election to power.[22] Mumtaj Ahmad and I. William Zartman comment that:

> Even if we consider the profession of democracy by the present leadership of Islamist countries as tactical or opportunistic, there is reason to believe that the very process of working within a democratic framework will transform this opportunistic commitment to a more substantive and effective commitment among the next generation of leaders and supporters.[23]

Piscatori goes even further by arguing that it is far from certain that even if political Islamic parties gained power, we would see it "degenerate into the obscurantist beliefs, priestly tyrannies, and sacred violence that secular ideologues anticipate".[24] Therefore, this highlights the prospect that political Islam is indeed compatible with democratic polity.

Overall, the *accommodationist school* not only stresses the distinction between radical and moderate Islamists, but also highlights the advantages of incorporating moderates into the democratic political process in order to moderate political behaviour. Political Islam is viewed as compatible with democracy and the inclusion of Islamists in a free and pluralistic system is seen as desirable. The *confrontationalist school* on the other hand sees an inherent tension existing between democracy and Islam. Bernard Lewis argues that Islamist participation in the democratic process is tactical as elections would effectively result in "one man, one vote, once".[25] He argues it is basically illegitimate for a democracy to effectively vote itself away and, with the democratic election of an Islamic theocracy, that is precisely what would happen. But the reason why Islam is seen as unable to function within a democratic system is taken up by Samuel Huntington as being a direct result of its incompatible culture.[26] Huntington argues that an Islamic theocracy is incompatible with the very notion of fundamental freedoms that underpin liberal democracy.[27] He suggests that this inherent tension may well result in some form of civilisation confrontation rather than the traditional state-based conflict.

Lewis picks up on the theme of the desirability of an Islamic theocracy by arguing that Islamic governance not only results in the abrogation of fundamental human rights, it also serves to stifle economic and social development.[28] Lewis writes "[i]n the course of the twentieth century it became abundantly clear in the Middle East and indeed all over the lands of Islam that things had indeed gone badly wrong. Compared with its millennial rival, Christendom, the world of Islam had become poor, weak, and ignorant".[29] But Lewis does not limit his analysis to nation-specific Islamist groups, he sees international ones, epitomised by al-Qa'ida, as equally undesirable: "For Usama bin Laden, his declaration of war against the United States marks the resumption of the struggle for religious dominance of the world that began in the seventh century."[30] Lewis goes on to conclude that "[i]f the fundamentalists are correct in their calculations and succeed in their war, then a dark future awaits the world, especially the part of it that embraces Islam".[31] Overall, Lewis suggests that the equation of Islam with peaceful rule is a fallacy, and thus political Islam cannot be allowed to reach its logical conclusion of the establishment of an Islamic theocracy governed by the *Shari'a*.

Given this incompatibility and potential threat, Daniel Pipes argues that despite the degree of diversity of all Islamic political movements, they are inherently hostile and pose a threat to Western civilisation.[32] He identifies Islamism as analogous to other ideological movements such as communism and fascism which are widely considered inimical to Western norms and values.[33] Amos Perlmutter echoes his theme by arguing that Islamism is an "aggressive revolutionary movement as militant and violent as the Bolshevik, Fascist, and Nazi movements of the past".[34] This view is grounded in the argument that underlying commonalities exist amongst all political Islamic movements, though there are also insurmountable differences between movements which usually amount to differences of ideology.

Martin Kramer continues by drawing our attention to inherent common characteristics, which allows us to question if any real distinction exists between radical and moderate Islamic movements.[35] He goes as far as to argue that this commonality indicates a unified political ideology, comparable with communism, which threatens the West.[36] He specifically highlights Iran as being at the centre of this monolithic Islamist civilisation.

The accommodationist approach, which sees the *Shari'a* as compatible with democratic polity and Islamists' involvement in the democratic process resulting in a moderation of behaviour, is firmly rejected by Daniel Brumberg. He echoes Lewis's premise that moderate Islamists are essentially only engaging in the democratic political process for tactical reasons in that they believe it to be the most legitimate and likely way they will achieve power. Such behaviour is seen as tactical, since democracy could be subverted once power is gained; then the adoption of the *Shari'a* will usher in an authoritarian theocracy.[37] Kramer continues with this theme by highlighting that although democracy was promised by Islamists in Iran, candidates are vetted by the Guardian Council in order to see if they meet the requirements set out in the Iranian constitution: "the regime in Tehran thus fails the key test of democracy, for it cannot be voted out of power".[38] He argues that by their very essence Islamic theocracies are expansionist, aggressive and inherently anti-Western. The reason for this stems from the belief that Western culture is perceived as the antithesis of Islamic values.[39] Indeed, Kramer argues that by positioning themselves as the bastion against Western culture, fundamentalist regimes indirectly serve to self-legitimise their presence.

Oliver Roy approaches this issue from a unique perspective by arguing that Islamic polity cannot be an effective and lasting form of governance. He comments that:

> Even if Islamist regimes are authoritarian and coercive, why is there no Islamic totalitarianism? My answer is that there is a contradiction in Islamist ideology. If it does respect the basic idea of the Shari'a, it cannot control the family and has to admit the existence of a private sphere beyond the reach of the state. If it does not respect the Shari'a, then this ideology might be opposed in the very name of Islam . . . true Shari'a would mean devolution of law from the state to a religious court.[40]

Therefore, Roy argues the position that governance under *Shari'a* law not only has inherent contradictions, which make it unworkable along its own ideals, but also that it is incompatible with Western models of liberal democratic polity.

Overall, the characteristics of political Islam are a clear matter of contention. It is accepted by scholars and commentators that Islamic political movements do share common characteristics in terms of their goals and values, as well as having diversity in the methods by which they attempt to gain political power. Notable academics such as Esposito, Piscatori and Voll take the position that radical and violent movements are unrepresentative, as the majority of Islamic movements are moderate and engage in peaceful participation in the political process. They highlight that such moderate movements should be accommodated in the democratic process as they would necessarily moderate their objectives further for expediency, and would consequently not pose a threat to the democratic framework. Although this view has a great deal of credibility, other commentators such as Kramer and Pipes affirm that no real distinction can be drawn between moderate and radical Islamist movements. They highlight that the difference between moderate/peaceful and violent/radical Islamists is inconsequential as both seek the establishment of a regime based on the principles of the *Shari'a*. They highlight that the *Shari'a* is incompatible with liberal democratic rule, human rights and Western culture. Although an Islamic theocracy would not necessarily equate with extremism, the belief that it would not, on religious principles, allow itself to be voted out of power makes it inherently incompatible with democratic rule. The net effect of such incompatibility is an overriding tension with the West. The final analysis that can be made is that the compatibility of Islam and democracy is a fundamental moot point in examining how political Islam should be viewed.

The Historical Context

The position of the US government towards political Islam began to germinate during the Carter presidency. The Carter administration saw the Islamic *Mujaheddin* in Afghanistan as a geostrategic means of drawing the Soviet Union into a 'Vietnam-style' conflict in order to counter the Soviet threat to the Persian Gulf. Indeed, Brzezinski regarded the Soviet invasion of Afghanistan as being a direct result of a successful covert US operation to draw them into an invasion. Brzezinski stated:

> According to the official version of history, CIA aid to the Mujaheddin began during 1980, that is to say, after the Soviet army invaded Afghanistan, 24 Dec 1979. But the reality, secretly guarded until now, is completely otherwise. Indeed, it was July 3 1979 that President Carter signed the first directive for secret aid to the opponents of the pro-Soviet regime in Kabul. And that very day, I wrote a note to the president in which I explained to him that in my opinion this aid was going to induce a Soviet military intervention.[41]

Brzezinski's analysis of the situation was correct. The US-induced invasion marked the onset of a strategic relationship which involved the supply of armaments to Islamists. The significance of this covert US policy was that Afghanistan became the locus of an Islamic guerrilla-style insurgency against the Soviet Union, which attracted numerous recruits from across the world. In many respects, it can be described as the beginning of an international *jihad,* which was in contrast to the nation-specific Islamists who merely opposed their own government. But significantly, the use of the Afghan *Mujaheddin* was a tactical means by which the United States secured wider interests in accordance with the Cold War strategic environment. Although this episode marked the beginnings of US involvement with political Islamic movements, it was a covert strategy and thus not representative of an over-arching US policy framework.

The Iranian Revolution of 1979 was, however, the key issue that brought political Islam into the spotlight. Unlike the *Mujaheddin* in Afghanistan which was seen as a tactical asset, the Iranian Revolution was seen as a clear strategic threat to US interests in the Gulf. The revolution was highly significant in that it not only marked a fundamental change in US policy towards Persian Gulf security, it also marked the emergence of political Islam as a credible political force. On a wider level, the Shi'a uprisings in the eastern province of Saudi Arabia in 1979, in addition to the seizure of the Grand Mosque in Mecca by Islamists, underscored that the ramifications of Iran's Islamic Revolution had a much wider significance.

Although the United States did have several other encounters with radical Islamists during the 1980s, a comprehensive policy framework does not appear to have been established. It would be more accurate to describe a *perception* of political Islam as having developed at this time: political Islam was almost consistently seen as posing varying degrees of risk.[42] The terrorist bombing of the US marine barracks in Lebanon in 1983 underscored the recognition that radical Islamists posed a threat, but the focus of the Reagan administration generally remained centred on the Cold War strategic environment. Political Islam remained a secondary concern.

It was not until the Algerian Revolution in 1991 that political Islam was seen as posing a potential threat through the democratic process. Unlike the manner in which Khomeini came to power in Iran, Algeria showed that Islamists could gain power through democratic means and thus underscored Bernard Lewis's point that democracy could be used illegitimately: many believed an Islamic theocracy would result in the abolition of future elections. The victory by the Islamic Salvation Front in Algeria's parliamentary elections resulted in a bloody civil war when the military intervened to nullify the elections. In many respects, a parallel can be drawn with the 1970 democratic election of the socialist Salvador Allende in Chile: both were legitimate electoral victories but were deemed by the United States as a usurpation of democracy. In essence it was an illegitimate, yet democratic, outcome. Nevertheless, the Islamists' democratic victory demonstrated that an Islamic theocracy could occur through democratic means.

But the realisation of the threat posed by political Islam through the ballot box coincided neatly with the end of the Cold War era. To many writers, Islamism became the ideological successor to communism. In terms of US foreign policy, the Algerian scenario represented a clear threat to US interests within the Middle East. George H. W. Bush's Assistant Secretary of State for Near Eastern Affairs, Edward Djerejian, stated that "a coherent policy framework towards Islam has become a compelling need as foreign policy challenges erupt involving an 'arc of crisis' extending from the Balkans, the Caucasus, North Africa, the Middle East, and Central and South Africa".[43] Given the end of the Cold War and the realisation, from the causes of Algerian civil war, that US interests on a wider level were potentially at risk from political Islam, a coherent policy position was thus seen as warranted.

The formation of a policy framework was unveiled by Djerejian in June 1992. In his 'Meridian House Declaration', Djerejian made clear that despite the end of the Cold War, Islam was not seen as a monolithic threat to the United States. Djerejian remarked that "the US Government does not view Islam as the next 'ism' confronting the West or threatening world peace. That is an overly simplistic response to a complex reality".[44] But whilst the diversity amongst political Islamic movements was recognised and accepted as part of the political process, Djerejian outlined that certain Islamist groups were not supported by the United States: "we are suspect of those who would use the democratic process to come to power, only to destroy that very process in order to retain power and political dominance. While we believe in the principle of 'one person, one vote', we do not support 'one person, one vote, one time'."[45]

Therefore, the policy formulation saw a clear distinction between moderate and radical Islamist groups. Radical Islamist groups were demarcated as having the following characteristics:

1. They practise terrorism, oppress minorities, preach intolerance, or violate internationally accepted standards of conduct regarding human rights;
2. They are insensitive to the need for political pluralism;
3. They cloak their message in another brand of authoritarianism;
4. They substitute religious and political confrontation for constructive engagement with the rest of the world;
5. They do not share our commitment to peaceful resolution of conflict, especially the Arab–Israeli conflict; and
6. They align themselves with those who would pursue their goals through repression or violence.[46]

In contrast, moderate Islamist groups were seen as seeking a gradual reform and affirmation of Islamic ideals for their given country. Importantly, these Islamic ideals were viewed as *compatible with democratic rule*. Djerejian commented that:

> In countries throughout the Middle East and North Africa, we thus see [moderate] groups or movements seeking to reform their societies in keeping with Islamic ideals. There is considerable diversity in how these ideals are expressed. We detect no monolithic or coordinated international effort behind these movements. What we do see are believers living in different countries placing renewed emphasis on Islamic principles and governments accommodating Islamist political activity to varying degrees and in different ways.[47]

The key point about this policy formulation was that it demonstrated a synthesis of both the accommodationist and confrontationalist schools of thought: both were applied respectively to whether the Islamist group was defined by the United States as moderate or radical. Nevertheless, this definition was fluid and applied on a case-by-case approach. Therefore, whilst it was clear that the United States opposed extremism which manifested itself through violence, ambiguity remained as to whether the United States "was genuinely committed to the principle of free elections in a case in which political Islamists could win power".[48] Although the

Meridian House address had its limitations, it was also politically helpful. Maria do Céu Pinto comments that:

> On the one hand [Djerejian's formulation] enabled Washington to oppose any Islamic group that espoused violence and challenged moderate pro-Western regimes such as Egypt and Saudi Arabia. On the other it made it possible to resist groups opposed to the peace process and anti-American Islamic regimes in power – such as Sudan and Iran – which met his criteria of being violent, intolerant and coercive. [49]

In essence, Djerejian's formulation rested on three distinct tiers: moderate Islamists who were compatible with US foreign policy interests and were a non-issue; extremist Islamists who were *compatible* with US foreign policy interests; and extremist Islamists, who were *incompatible* with US foreign policy interests. That is to say, analytically speaking, US policy towards extremist Islamists was dependent not on whether violence was used, but whom it was being used against. On the other hand, a rejection of violence as a political means was clearly present, thus ruling out a condoning of extremism. From this, it appears that there was a degree of ambiguity and lack of coherence in US policy statements which encompassed political Islamic movements.

Instructively, Fawaz Gerges is correct to argue that the real importance of the Meridian House Declaration was that it left a contextual framework for the Clinton administration.[50] It interpreted political Islam very broadly and thus was far from a comprehensive policy framework. But it did stress two important themes: firstly, that a clear dichotomy existed, separating moderate from extremist Islamism; and secondly, that extremist Islamism could be identified not only by its willingness to use violence as a political tool, but also by its wider political agenda which was seen as incompatible with democracy. Thus the point of contention for this framework was whether moderate Islamists could be viewed as compatible with democratic rule despite the differentiation from extremist groups.

Although it was an important framework, Gerges argues that the George H. W. Bush administration did not translate this position into policy as it conflicted with Persian Gulf security: *the strategic objective of maintaining security through supporting the status quo did not correspond with the competing objective of political reform and accommodation.* Therefore, when US policy towards political Islam under the first Bush administration is put into context, it amounted to very little operationally. Indeed, its flexibility and lack of clarity underscored it as a *secondary foreign policy issue* to wider US policy interests in the Middle East.

The United States and Political Islam 1993–2001

With the onset of the Clinton administration in 1993, a key issue which appeared to be facing US foreign policy towards political Islam was how to maintain the fine balance between accommodation and confrontation, whilst not allowing US policy to be charged with being anti-Islam per se. The Bush administration had been vocal in the Meridian House Declaration in stating that it neither saw Islam as a threat nor extremist Islamists as representative of the Islamic faith. By maintaining the Bush administration's position of stressing that the United States did not equate extremist political Islam with the Islamic faith, it underscored the dichotomy and legitimised a confrontationalist approach against extremism. In other words, by stressing that radical Islamism was nothing to do with the Islamic religion, the United States could reject accusations that it was adopting a confrontationalist strategy towards political Islam. While moderate political Islam was essentially a non-issue, extremist Islamism was seen as demanding a policy response, as it was equated with terrorism.

Throughout Clinton's two terms of office, it is striking that the presidency was consistent in the manner in which extremist Islamism was portrayed: policy pronouncements carefully and consistently dispelled any linkage between the Islamic faith and terrorism, in addition to rejecting the notion that political Islam was a successor to communism. Clinton personally affirmed these points during his visit to Indonesia in November 1994. He commented "[I] say to the American people and the West generally that even though we have had problems with terrorism coming out of the Middle East, it is not inherently related to Islam – not to the religion, not to the culture".[51] On a similar note, Clinton remarked in an address to the Jordanian parliament in October 1994 "[that] America refuses to accept that our civilizations must collide . . . [w]e respect Islam".[52]

Robert Pelletreau succeeded Djerejian as Assistant Secretary of

State and maintained what appeared *analytically* to be the three-tier approach towards political Islam:

> In the foreign affairs community, we often use the term 'political Islam' to refer to the movements and groups within the broader fundamentalist revival with a specific political agenda. 'Islamists' are Muslims with political goals. We view these terms as analytical, not normative. They do not refer to phenomena that are necessarily sinister: there are many legitimate, socially responsible Muslim groups with political goals. However, there are also Islamists who operate outside the law. Groups or individuals who operate outside the law – who espouse violence to achieve their aims – are properly called extremists.[53]

Martin Kramer sees this as a three-tiered approach as it demonstrates a clear analytical inconsistency in US foreign policy: it arguably allowed the United States to condone extremism, which can manifest itself in the form of terrorism, as legitimate, providing the United States agrees with its objectives.[54] Nevertheless, this is an academic point of contention and is in direct contrast to the long-standing official position of the US government that it does not condone or support terrorism. In September 1995, Pelletreau underscored this point by stating that "I have trouble defining exactly where one category starts and another stops . . . [we] ought not color every party or group or government the same way, nor should we simplistically condemn them all as anti-Western".[55] He also stated that "[w]e must deal with fundamentalist Islam in a variety of contexts – how it impacts on issues of importance to the United States, such as the peace process, or combating terrorism, or encouraging open markets or political pluralism or respect for human rights. The starting point is our own objectives, not political Islam as such."[56] As a result of a lack of clarity and coherence in distinguishing moderate from extremist groups, even amongst those that used violence, US policy pronouncements regarding political Islam could be interpreted as being both contradictory and ambiguous.

Therefore, the United States' position on extremist political Islam was clearly confrontational providing it was commensurate with US policy objectives. Indeed, although we know the Clinton administration's *position* towards both moderate and extremist political Islam, it was not part of a specific stated policy towards Islam, or indeed politicised Islam.

Therefore, political Islam mainly became an issue for the United States when it used terrorism as a means of achieving its political objectives, and thus fell under the rubric of US counterterrorism policy. Strictly speaking, it is inaccurate to view the Clinton administration as having had a policy towards Islam. This point was underlined by the Deputy Assistant Secretary of State, Robert Neumann: "[l]et me be clear and emphatic: the United States of America does not and should not have a political policy towards Islam".[57]

This point underscored the argument that if the United States did not have a specific policy towards political Islam, and extremist Islamism was not seen as representative of the Islamic faith, the central issues were: firstly, the position of the United States towards moderate political Islam vis-à-vis democracy; and secondly, the nature of US counterterrorism policy towards extremist political Islam. The importance of the compatibility of moderate political Islam with democracy was that it demonstrated whether the United States supported moderate political Islamic movements in a democratic polity. With regard to counterterrorism, this highlighted the more operational sphere of US policy towards extremist political Islamic movements.

Islam and Democracy

The position of the United States towards political Islam's compatibility with democracy was changed by the events in Algeria. As has already been stated, the George H. W. Bush administration did not view the election of the Algerian Salvation Front as legitimate as it believed democracy could not vote itself out of existence. This was a view which was upheld throughout the Clinton presidency.

Pelletreau's ambiguous distinction of moderate from extremist Islamists was not helpful. The case-by-case approach, which recognised overlapping criteria for the two definitions, did not allow for a clear analytical interpretation of whether US foreign policy saw Islam as inherently compatible with democratic rule. Clinton's National Security Advisor, Anthony Lake, saw Islamic extremism as separate from the Islamic faith, but also as posing a threat to freedom itself. Lake commented in May 1994 that "[w]hat distinguishes Islamic extremism from other forms of extremism is not terrorism, but the naked pursuit of political power".[58] Lake's statement was important in that it expanded on the Meridian

House Declaration by showing that extremism had a dual dimension with its propensity for the use of violence, in addition to its underlying political objectives. Previous declarations had basically confined extremism to the sole definition of whether it resorted to violence.

Lake's formulation raises more questions than it answers. It is questionable to what extent moderate or extremist Islamists could be separated if they both desired the establishment of an Islamic theocracy as their strategic objective. Trying to decide whether there were different forms of an Islamic theocracy, which might be more or less acceptable to the US, was simply not a viable means of analytically assessing US policy towards political Islam.

In contrast, Pelletreau confined the definition of extremist Islamists as being centred on acts rather than objectives.[59] Pelletreau stated in May 1994 that Islamists "who operate outside the law"[60] could be classified as extremists. This legalistic formulation, made within days of Lake's *objective-based* definition, indicated a lack of clarity in US policy towards defining extremism. For instance, the US designation of Hezbollah in 1997 as an extremist group demonstrated that this was a flawed approach as they are a democratically elected party in Lebanon.[61] Nonetheless, it does underscore the point that analytically, there was inconsistency in whether the United States interpreted political Islam as a threat based on its *actions* or its *strategic objectives*.

By 1996, Pelletreau's definition of Islamism had incorporated the issue of extremists' objectives in addition to their actions. Pelletreau commented that:

> Extremists around the world use whatever resources they have to achieve their goals. In the Middle East, religious rhetoric can be made into one of those resources. A fatwa or incitement to violence can be just as dangerous as bombs and bullets. The impulse that motivates the Izz al-Din al-Qassam brigades of Hamas, the Algerian Armed Islamic Group (or GIA) and the Iranian Revolutionary Guards is not Islamic piety, but a mixture of revenge, fanaticism and pursuit of political power.[62]

The classification of extremists as using whatever means available to them in order to achieve their objectives, suggests that the goal of an Islamic theocracy was viewed as synonymous with extremism and contrary to US interests. Indeed, this indicates that the distinction between moderate and extremist Islamists was not as clear as Pelletreau's previous comments would have us believe. From this, one could argue that, at the very least, the United States viewed even moderate political Islam with a degree of scepticism because of its potential to usurp democracy in the event of the establishment of an Islamic theocracy. However, when viewed within the context of previous policy statements, there was a clear lack of clarity as to whether the United States viewed moderate Islamists' objectives as being in favour of US interests.

In June 1998, Robert Neumann compounded this uncertainty by seemingly reverting to the classification of an Islamist group as being based on their actions. But Neumann went further than previous administration statements as he rejected the school of thought which advocated that the United States should have a policy towards Islamist groups that used democracy as a tactical means of achieving their incompatible strategic objective of an Islamic theocracy. He rejected the confrontation of moderate Islamist groups as it was seen as incompatible with the underlying Jeffersonian tenets of US foreign policy.[63] He indicated that even though the Islamist groups' strategic objective was flawed, the United States would not view their activities as illegitimate.

When US policy statements towards the objectives of Islamists and their compatibility with democratic rule are examined from the onset of the Clinton presidency, there appears to be a lack of consistency or clarity, and at times the statements are contradictory. There were, however, some consistencies that can be highlighted during the time period 1993–2001. The most noteworthy consistency has been US opposition to the use of violence as a political tool. Although the flexible nature of US policy has allowed for an analytical criticism of whether this is true, at an operational level there is good reason to believe that this has been applied in practice. The key issue is, however, whether the United States views an Islamic theocracy as commensurate with democracy, and therefore to what extent moderate and extremist Islamists can be equated given that they seemingly seek the shared goal of an Islamic theocracy. At a base level, Clinton's policy in this regard was inherently contradictory as it saw moderate Islamists' participation in the democratic process as legitimate, but their endgame objective as illegitimate. The indication is that Islamists' political participation is fine, providing they only remain on the fringes of democratic polity and thus do not usurp democracy in favour of an Islamic theocracy.

As the general indication is that the United States favoured a widening of the political system in Middle Eastern authoritarian countries and the inclusion of moderate Islamists, the key issue is how this equated within the wider context of US policy. Within the Persian Gulf, the key to maintaining the security of the region and the status quo therefore safeguarding US interests, was the containment of Iran and Iraq. The key interest was that the security of the oil-producing GCC countries was ensured in order to safeguard US economic interests. Political reform and the inclusion of Islamists in the political process posed risks for the stability and security of these countries. Therefore, US interests within the Persian Gulf were widely viewed as being potentially jeopardised by the US position towards moderate Islamist groups.

On an international level, the key pillar of the Clinton administration was the expansion of free markets and democracy. Although this was in keeping with US policy towards political Islam, it contrasted sharply with US policy towards the Persian Gulf. Whilst there was clearly a policy quagmire, the Clinton administration cannot be regarded as having pressed Middle Eastern countries to implement substantive reform. Although there were clear rhetorical statements which called for this, attempts at reform amounted to very little. This indicates that Clinton's policy was contradictory in that while it called for a widening of political participation, US interests towards Persian Gulf security remained its primary concern. Political Islam and the furthering of its inclusion in democratic polity can thus be interpreted as a secondary concern at that time.

International Terrorism

With the onset of the Clinton administration in 1993, terrorism was, according to Richard Clarke, "far down on the new team's priority list".[64] The Clinton administration had come to power with its global foreign policy objectives premised on the expansion of democracy and free markets: counterterrorism was undoubtedly a key issue but, as with the previous Bush White House, it was not viewed as an imminent threat. The significance of terrorism with regard to political Islam was simply that extremist Islamism could manifest itself in what the United States defined as terrorism: "premeditated, politically motivated violence perpetrated against non-combatant targets by sub-national groups or clandestine agents, usually intended to influence an audience".[65] International Islamic terrorism is therefore an important contextual issue in allowing for an understanding of US foreign policy towards extremist political Islamic movements and is of direct relevance to the grand strategic era of the War on Terror.

The January 1993 bombing of the World Trade Centre in New York was the first high profile Islamic terrorist attack within the United States. The arrest of Omar Abdel Rahman, a blind Egyptian cleric, uncovered what was to turn out to be an al-Qa'ida terrorist cell with direct links to Khalid Sheikh Mohamad and Ramzi Yousef. Investigations at the cleric's apartment in New York uncovered references to the Afghan Services Bureau (*Mahktab al Kiddimah*). The Afghan Services Bureau, better known as al-Qa'ida, was a form of international political Islam that had developed in the wake of the Soviet defeat in Afghanistan, and was headed by Osama bin Laden and Ayman al-Zawahiri.

Unlike indigenous extremist political Islamic movements operating within Middle Eastern countries, al-Qa'ida's modus operandi stems directly from the circumstances surrounding the Cold War guerrilla-style insurgency within Afghanistan. The decision by the United States to instigate a Soviet invasion, coupled with its support for the Afghan *Mujaheddin*, served both the strategic purpose of embroiling the Soviet Union in a Vietnam-style conflict, and as a locus point for attracting numerous recruits from across the Muslim world. The CIA purchased armaments from China and Egypt using Saudi and US funds in order to back the insurgency.[66] It was in essence the Vietnam conflict but with role reversal.

Unlike other indigenous nation-specific political Islamic groups, the Afghan *Mujaheddin* was directed against a foreign power. Significantly, the total number of *Mujaheddin* fighters has been estimated at between 175,000 and 250,000 from over 40 countries.[67] The eventual withdrawal of the Soviet Union from Afghanistan was seen as a religious victory for the *Mujaheddin*. That is to say, the withdrawal of the Soviet Union reinforced the conviction that their insurgency had defeated a super-power: but crucially, it created a strategic vacuum. Peter Bergen quite rightly comments that:

> The victory against communism in Afghanistan was an intoxicating moral victory: a superpower had been defeated in the name of

Allah. It was an important lesson for the Afghan Arabs and for bin Laden himself, who applied it to the next holy war – against the United States.[68]

The Iraqi invasion of Kuwait in 1990 prompted the deployment of US forces onto the Arabian Peninsula to defend Saudi Arabia from potential Iraqi invasion, and ultimately a counter-invasion of Kuwait to liberate it from Iraq and place it under a UN mandate. This was the key event which seemingly resulted in the United States being viewed by bin Laden and his affiliates as the immediate successor to the Soviet Union. Within the context of their extremist Wahhabi interpretation of Islam, the presence of a non-Islamic force on the Arabian Peninsula was a key trigger given the location of the two holy shrines in Mecca and Medina. Bernard Lewis reminds us, however, that bin Laden's reasoning was highly complex: "[t]he catalog of American offences they cite is long and detailed, beginning with the conquest, colonization, and settlement – emotive words – of the New World and continuing to the present day".[69] Indeed, bin Laden saw the 'New World Order', first outlined by George H. W. Bush to a joint session of Congress on 11 September 1990, as symbolic of the onset of a new phase in the United States' relations with the world, and the Islamic world in particular.[70] The specific date of the 9/11 attacks, some eleven years later, may even have been symbolic of this. In an interview with Peter Arnett in 1997, Bin Laden stated:

> After the collapse of the Soviet Union in which the US has no mentionable role, but rather the credit goes to God, Praise and Glory be to Him, and the Mujahidin in Afghanistan, this collapse made the US more haughty and arrogant and it has started to look at itself as a Master of this world and established what it calls the *new world order*.[71]

With bin Laden locating himself in Sudan and later in Afghanistan, the establishment of a loose network of former *Mujaheddin* fighters known as al-Qa'ida had emerged. Al-Qa'ida is by no means a monolithic organisation: it is a loosely organised *international* political Islamic organisation which is represented across the world. The informal nature of al-Qa'ida is what provided it with its operational effectiveness, as infiltration by governmental intelligence agencies was highly difficult.

For US foreign policy at the onset of the Clinton administration, the sphere of political Islam was very much seen under the guise of indigenous Islamist groups, but al-Qa'ida was a different threat altogether as its objectives encompassed *and also* localised nation-specific issues into wider goals which saw a need for the United States to be directly attacked.

Although al-Qa'ida was implicated in the 1993 World Trade Centre bombing and the subsequent debacle in Somalia, it was not initially clear to the Clinton administration what they were facing.[72] The focus of the Clinton administration towards international terrorism was arguably *state-centric*. Iran, Sudan and Syria were the focus of the initial efforts by the Clinton administration towards international terrorism.[73] Indeed, Iranian-backed Saudi Hezbollah was reported by the US government as being behind the attack at al-Khobar in Saudi Arabia, which killed nineteen US military personnel in 1996. During the first Clinton administration, the threat from international terrorism was seen as squarely coming from state-sponsored terrorism. Non-state international terrorist groups were still recognised as a real threat, but were viewed as less operationally effective than state-sponsored terrorist groups. Although the trial of the World Trade Centre bomber, Omar Abdel Rahman, showed the first signs that the United States faced a threat from international non-state political Islam, and that bin Laden was *potentially* involved in financing transnational terrorist operations,[74] the focus of US counterterrorism strategy was generally on state actors. Indeed, it appears that much of the intelligence the United States was receiving about al-Qa'ida was unsubstantiated at this point.

By the summer of 1995, the CIA recognised that the United States was facing a loosely organised international terrorist network headed by bin Laden.[75] The steady flow of intelligence underlined this fact. But by 1998, al-Qa'ida had become a more comprehensive organisation as it reportedly 'merged' with Egyptian Islamic Jihad, headed by Ayman Zawahiri. Whilst bin Laden remained the public figurehead of al-Qa'ida, it has been widely speculated that Zawahiri acted in a more operational capacity than bin Laden. Around the same time, bin Laden issued a fatwa which called upon Muslims to target the United States. Although al-Qa'ida had attacked the United States before, this was the rhetorical declaration of war. The true scale of the threat facing the United States from al-Qa'ida surfaced shortly afterwards. In August 1998, the US embassies in Tanzania and Kenya were simultaneously attacked causing over two hundred and fifty fatalities and injuries to over five thousand. The Clinton administration responded with targeted air strikes in Afghanistan after receiving actionable intelligence about an al-Qa'ida leadership meeting. This, however, amounted to very little and did not succeed in its objective of killing al-Qa'ida's leadership.

The bombings of the US embassies galvanised the administration's view that al-Qa'ida posed a clear and present danger to the United States. Al-Qa'ida had steadily evolved and the embassy bombing underscored its operational ability. Crucially, this was the juncture at which the Clinton administration actually sanctioned the use of lethal force against bin Laden and thus was the point when bin Laden was viewed as an imminent threat rather than a fugitive from the law requiring trial and imprisonment. Politically speaking, an unequivocal response from the Clinton White House was a necessity given the scale of the attack. The response of the Clinton administration was to implement several new counterterrorist policies and increase funding to homeland security programmes. Nevertheless, despite the fact that the Clinton administration took the al-Qa'ida threat very seriously and implemented several counterterrorist measures, its policy response was *reactive* and thus not geared towards combating the perceived *root causes* of al-Qa'ida's support base.[76] As has already been discussed, the root causes of support for political Islamic movements are varied but most important among them are the structural barriers to political reform in authoritarian countries which make political Islam an attractive and viable means of expressing discontent and striving for political objectives. The priority of the Clinton presidency towards the Persian Gulf throughout remained geared towards ensuring the security of the region through upholding the status quo.

This allows us to conclude that Clinton's policy towards international Islamic-inspired terrorism was, although an issue of great importance, a secondary issue to Persian Gulf security. Of course, there is the argument that the Clinton administration may not have seen the removal of the structural barriers to political reform as the most effective means of combating the base support level of al-Qa'ida; but when US policy pronouncements toward political Islam are taken into account, it seems that the administration did indeed see the political structure of authoritarian countries as being the main cause of political Islam's support base. Therefore, Clinton's policy towards international Islamic extremism was geared towards a military response and, as with his policy towards indigenous nation-specific political Islam, pressing for substantive political reforms in authoritarian countries was not viewed as compatible with the key interest of preserving Persian Gulf security.

With the onset of the George W. Bush administration, it appears that this policy trajectory was continued. In the initial months of the new administration, a comprehensive policy review was conducted. As a result, there was no substantive change in operational US foreign policy relating to political Islam. According to Richard Clarke, the former National Coordinator for Security and Counterterrorism, this policy review was slow and continued up until the attacks of 11 September 2001. Nevertheless, it is interesting to note that the findings of the Deputies' level policy review showed that a *more comprehensive non-state-centric solution* was agreed for the National Security Presidential Directive on Terrorism. Indeed, it seems that this stemmed not only from the realisation that the Clinton administration had been overly state-centric and the nature of al-Qa'ida warranted a change of tactics, but also because President Bush wanted to eliminate al-Qa'ida rather than continue "swatting flies".[77] Although the indication is that prior to the 9/11 attacks the Bush administration was planning a more vigorous counterterrorism policy, the available evidence does not indicate that this was anything more than an escalation of Clinton's reactive-based policy. There is no indication that the Bush administration was going to alter its policy towards Persian Gulf security in order to usher in a reformist agenda in an attempt to combat the *root causes* of extremist political Islam and international terrorism.

Equally, there were some bureaucratic changes, which are also worthy of note. Most importantly, according to Clarke, the newly incumbent Bush administration did not grasp the complexity of the terrorist threat.[78] Clarke argues that Condoleezza Rice saw the National Security Council as a "foreign policy coordination mechanism and not some place where issues such as terrorism in the US"[79] should be addressed, and thus was arguably viewing terrorism as a secondary national security concern. Moreover, Clarke implies that Rice's decision to downgrade his position of National Coordinator for Security and Counterterrorism from Cabinet level was further evidence of the priority to which the Bush administration gave the threat from terrorism. Nevertheless, although Clarke is right to highlight this bureaucratic restructuring, it does not analytically demonstrate that the Bush administration had adopted, or was indeed planning, a different foreign policy *strategy* towards terrorism, or saw terrorism in general as any less of a threat.

United States and Political Islam post-9/11

Following the devastating attacks of 9/11 on the World Trade Centre and the Pentagon, the foreign policy priorities of the Bush administration underwent a comprehensive revision. The shock and horror of the attacks on US society was overwhelming, and was akin to the reaction of the surprise Japanese attack on Pearl Harbour. But 9/11 was arguably more telling: it was an attack against the symbols of American military and economic power and resulted in a significant loss of civilian life, rather than military personnel as occurred in Pearl Harbour. A foreign policy response of one form or another was inevitable given the domestic political outcry.

The basis of the Bush administration's neoconservative foreign policy response was that a new grand strategic era in US foreign policy had begun. As with the Cold War era, the White House defined an over-arching external threat to the national security of the United States and its allies. Unlike the communist threat, which was seen in purely state-centric terms, international Islamic terrorism was seen as a by-product of the socio-political conditions present within particular countries, most notably the Islamic countries of the Middle East, which could be described as undemocratic in character. As with the Clinton administration, Bush's interpretation accepted the formulation, advocated most notably by Bernard Lewis, that the root causes of political Islam and radical international Islamic terrorism were the structural conditions present within authoritarian countries. As has already been discussed, it is the perpetuation of authoritarian rule in Middle Eastern countries that ultimately results in a furthering of the support base of radical Islamists: both nation-specific and international.

US policy towards combating the radical manifestation of political Islam in the time period 1993–2001 was subservient to US strategy towards the Persian Gulf arena. Although the Clinton administration recognised that democratisation and the spread of freedom were necessary remedies against radical political Islam, the US strategy of promoting a balance of power through maintaining the status quo was its primary foreign policy concern. The significance of the Bush administration's policy response to the attacks of 9/11 was that these priorities became reversed: combating the *root causes* of radical Islamism became a priority over *immediate* US interests in the Persian Gulf arena. Indeed, through combating the root causes of radical political Islam, US national security was seen to be enhanced. Instructively, the Bush administration saw the widespread adoption of democracy and freedom throughout the Middle East as actually catering for Persian Gulf security concerns, but it was recognised that this transition would result in a period of insecurity.

The Bush administration's invasion of Afghanistan in October 2001 reflected this grand strategic vision in addition to immediate operational concerns: the ousting of the Taliban was to serve the purpose of denying sanctuary and a formal base of operations for al-Qa'ida. But within Bush's strategic framework, the implementation of democracy and freedom in Afghanistan served the over-arching goal of safeguarding US national security through combating what it defined as the root causes of radical Islamism. The invasion of Iraq in March 2003 will be shown to have been based on the same strategic objective. But with Iraq, it was a much more important policy as it was seen as the means by which democracy and freedom could be promoted throughout the Middle East and the Persian Gulf countries in particular. Indeed, the Iraq invasion underscored the point that US policy towards political Islam had risen to become a foreign policy priority, and the altered definition of Persian Gulf security was in keeping with this. Therefore, unlike the Clinton administration where there was a clear inconsistency in the two policy agendas, Bush's post-9/11 policies were strategically compatible.

With the overall grand strategy dictating the supremacy of both Jeffersonian and Wilsonian guides to foreign policy, the key analytical question about Bush's policy was whether moderate political Islam was viewed as compatible with democracy. Anoush Ehteshami is correct to ask whether the Bush administration "would fathom the emergence of Islamist-leaning governments across the Arab world?"[80] According to Bush, however, Islam and democracy are indeed compatible:

> It should be clear to all that Islam – the faith of one-fifth of humanity – is consistent with democratic rule. Democratic progress is found in many predominantly Muslim countries – in Turkey and Indonesia,

and Senegal and Albania, Niger and Sierra Leone. Muslim men and women are good citizens of India and South Africa, of the nations of Western Europe, and of the United States of America. More than half of all the Muslims in the world live in freedom under democratically constituted governments. They succeed in democratic societies, not in spite of their faith, but because of it. A religion that demands individual moral accountability, and encourages the encounter of the individual with God, is fully compatible with the rights and responsibilities of self-government.[81]

Bush's comments were echoed by Condoleezza Rice who stated that "the Islamic faith and striving for democracy and human rights are not only fully compatible, they are mutually reinforcing".[82] Richard Armitage, the Deputy US Secretary of State, reinforced this view by stating that "I think a democratic election held in the Muslim world will be a further sign that there's nothing antithetical about democracy and the great religion of Islam".[83]

Although from the above statements one can conclude that the Bush administration shared the Clintonian position that moderate Islamic parties' participation in a democratic process was legitimate, it is not altogether clear if an *Islamic theocracy* would be viewed within the same light. Indeed, given the possibility that such a government could, as Bernard Lewis highlights, result in the subjugation of democratic rule, it is reasonable to take the position that although Bush held Jeffersonian democratic values as universal, an Islamic theocracy would have been seen as an illegitimate outcome. More to the point, this indicates a policy continuation from the Clinton era: legitimate participation but with the recognition of it *potentially* leading to an illegitimate outcome.

The key issue, therefore, is how would the outcome of the Iraq invasion be seen as legitimate? Michael Hirsh writes that the combination of democracy and Islam does pose a potential contradiction, but there is also the possibility of a true compatibility. According to Bernard Lewis, who acted as one of a select group of academic consultants to the Bush White House, the solution is viewed as coming from the adoption of the Kemalist democratic model exhibited by Turkey.[84] Michael Hirsh comments that:

The administration's vision of post-war Iraq was also fundamentally Lewisian, which is to say Kemalist. Paul Wolfowitz repeatedly invoked secular, democratic Turkey as a 'useful model for others in the Muslim world', as the deputy secretary of defense termed it in December 2002 on the eve of a trip to lay the groundwork for what he thought would be a friendly Turkey's role as a staging ground for the Iraq war. Another key Pentagon neocon and old friend of Lewis's, Harold Rhode, told associates a year ago that 'we need an accelerated Turkish model' for Iraq.[85]

In support of Hirsh's argument, Bush remarked in July 2004 on a visit to Turkey that "I appreciate so very much the example [Turkey] has set on how to be a Muslim country and at the same time a country which embraces democracy and rule of law and freedom".[86] Here the significance is that the *ideal* end product of what Bush viewed as a desirable and legitimate outcome from democratic polity within an Islamic society was a separation of religion from government. From this conception, moderate political Islamic parties can legitimately participate in a pluralistic democratic polity, but the adoption of an Islamic theocracy resulting in the potential scenario of one person, one vote, one time would continue to be viewed by the United States as an illegitimate outcome.

In many respects, the Bush administration's position towards political Islam clarified and expanded on what was an ambiguous and at times contradictory position of US foreign policy prior to the attacks of 9/11. Although the Bush presidency saw the compatibility of democratic rule in an Islamic society as more clearly achievable and, most importantly, desirable, than any preceding administration, it still appears to have held the same position that an Islamic theocracy would have been an illegitimate political outcome.

Concluding Observations

What can be deduced from US foreign policy with respect to political Islam and terrorism in the time period 1993–2003 is that there was consistency in some respects and a reversal of policy in others. In terms of continuity, the United States maintained a consistent opposition towards violent political expression during this time period. Nevertheless, the lack of clarity and consistency in the Clinton era brought this supposition into question as one could analytically conclude from the Clinton administration's position that it condoned political extremism, providing its objective was commensurate with US policy interests. But, as has already been discussed, at an operational level, it is reasonable to conclude that the United States remained firmly opposed towards extremism as a means of achieving political objectives.

With regard to the scope of US policy towards political Islam, it is important to recognise that there is no evidence to support the conjecture that the United States had a policy toward Islam per se. Indeed, it is noticeable that the United States had gone to great pains to underscore the point that it did not have a policy towards one of the world's great religions. But it would be accurate to describe a steadily evolving understanding of Islamic political movements and how this fitted in with US policy. The key issues for US policy towards political Islam in this time period were essentially twofold: firstly, whether the establishment of an Islamic state premised on the *Shari'a* would be compatible with democratic principles; and secondly, how Islamic-inspired terrorism should be countered.

United States foreign policy during the Clinton era towards whether an Islamic state premised on the *Shari'a* was compatible with democracy was slow in developing. The statements on the issue which gradually flowed from administration officials were often unclear and inconsistent. The Clinton administration saw the participation of Islamic political parties, which desired the adoption of the *Shari'a*, as legitimate in a democratic process. However, it saw a potential majority election as an illegitimate outcome due to the belief that the adoption of the *Shari'a* would ultimately result in a subjugation of democracy. In many respects, a historical parallel can be drawn with US Cold War policy towards communist political parties' involvement in democratic politics.

The onset of the War on Terror strategic environment for US foreign policy greatly clarified and expanded upon the importance of political Islam in policy calculations. With the external threat being defined as terrorism with global reach, the issue of how to combat its *root causes* became a defining feature of US grand strategy for the Bush administration. Whilst there was recognition in the Clinton era that the authoritarian nature of Islamic states was the prime cause of terrorism, Clinton's policy remained firmly *reactive-based* and, crucially, *a secondary foreign policy concern* to US interests in the Persian Gulf strategic arena. Indeed, it is widely accepted that the Clinton administration accepted the balance of power in the Persian Gulf by failing to substantively press for reform. Although Clinton articulated that the spread of democracy and global capitalism was a priority, Clintonian foreign policy appears to have been overly cautious and lacking in a clear strategic vision. Nevertheless, the combating of the root causes of political Islam as part of a comprehensive counterterrorism strategy had been a secondary foreign policy concern to Persian Gulf security since the Cold War era.

The advent of the War on Terror changed these priorities: the need to combat the root causes of terrorism with global reach became a primary foreign policy concern and thus supplanted the post-Cold War policy towards Persian Gulf security. Although the definition of Persian Gulf security will be shown to have also changed, counterterrorism, directed at combating its root causes, had taken on a status of grand strategy. The key point here is that Bush's policy priority was *offensive-based* and had resulted in a new definition of Persian Gulf security.

The central issue, with regard to the Bush administration's new-found priority of countering the root causes of terrorism was, however, whether Islamic governance based on the *Shari'a* was compatible with the democracy and freedom agenda. The Bush administration's statements greatly expanded upon those of the previous presidency, as any notion that democracy could not work in an Islamic society were comprehensively dispelled by them. However, the new-found commitment towards democracy and freedom did not clarify whether all democratic outcomes would be viewed as acceptable. Indeed, there is good reason to conclude that the Bush administration saw democracy as compatible within an *Islamic society*, providing the *Shari'a* was not adopted.

NOTES

1 Robert Satloff, *US Policy Towards Islamism: A Theoretical and Operational Overview* (New York: Council on Foreign Relations, 2000) 3–5.
2 Dale F. Eickelman and James P. Piscatori, *Muslim Politics* (Princeton, NJ: Princeton University Press, 2004) 22–166.
3 François Burgat, "Ballot Boxes, Militaries and Islamic Movements", *The Islamism Debate*, ed. Martin Kramer (The Moshe Dayan Center for Middle Eastern and African Studies, Tel Aviv University, 1997) 41.
4 François Burgat, "Ballot Boxes, Militaries and Islamic Movements" 41.
5 Bassam Tibi, *The Challenge of Fundamentalism: Political Islam and the New World Order* (Berkeley: University of California Press, 2002) 64–113.
6 John O. Voll, *Islam: Continuity and Change in the Modern World*, 2nd ed. (Syracuse: Syracuse University Press, 1994) 289–392.

7   R. Hrair Dekmejian, *Islam in Revolution: Fundamentalism in the Arab World*, 2nd ed. (Syracuse: Syracuse University Press, 1995) 3–72; R. Hrair Dekmejian, "Islamic Revival: Catalysts, Categories, and Consequences", *The Politics of Islamic Revivalism: Diversity and Unity*, ed. Shireen Hunter (Bloomington: Indiana University Press, 1988) 103-15.

8   Nazih N. M. Ayubi, *Political Islam: Religion and Politics in the Arab World* (London: Routledge, 1991) 120–77.

9   Daniel Pipes, "The Western Mind of Radical Islam", *The Islamism Debate*, ed. Martin Kramer (The Moshe Dayan Center for Middle Eastern and African Studies, Tel Aviv University, 1997) 51–67.

10 John L. Esposito, "The Persian Gulf War, Islamic Movements and the New World Order", *The Iranian Journal of International Affairs* Spring (1991): 346.

11 John L. Esposito and John O. Voll, *Islam and Democracy* (Oxford: OUP, 1996) 196.

12 Maria do Céu Pinto, *Political Islam and the United States: A Study of U.S. Policy Towards Islamist Movements in the Middle East* (New York: Ithaca Press, 1999).

13 Bernard Lewis, *The Crisis of Islam* (London: Phoenix, 2003) 114.

14 Martin Indyk, "Back to the Bazaar", *Foreign Affairs* 82.1 (2002).

15 Esposito, "The Persian Gulf War, Islamic Movements and the New World Order" 342–43.

16 Ibid. 344.

17 John L. Esposito and John O. Voll, "Islam's Democratic Essence", *Middle East Quarterly* 1.4 (1994): 5–10; John L. Esposito and John O. Voll, "Islam and Democracy: Rejoinder", *Middle East Quarterly* 1.4 (1994): 74.

18 Esposito, "The Persian Gulf War, Islamic Movements and the New World Order" 344.

19 Esposito and Voll, "Islam and Democracy: Rejoinder" 73–75.

20 John L. Esposito and James P. Piscatori, "Democratization and Islam", *Middle East Journal* 45.3 (1991): 427–40.

21 Ibid.

22 Graham Fuller, "Islamism(S) in the Next Century", *The Islamism Debate*, ed. Martin Kramer (The Moshe Dayan Center for Middle Eastern and African Studies, Tel Aviv University, 1997) 141–60.

23 Mumtaz Ahmed and I. William Zartman, "Political Islam: Can It Become a Loyal Opposition", *Middle East Policy* 5.1 (1997): 72.

24 James P. Piscatori, "The Turmoil Within: The Struggle for the Future of the Islamic World", *Foreign Affairs Editors' Choice: The Middle East Crisis*, ed. Gideon Rose (New York: Council on Foreign Relations, 2002) 178.

25 Bernard Lewis, "Islam and Liberal Democracy", *Atlantic Monthly* 271.2 (1993): 91.

26 Samuel Huntington, "The Clash of Civilizations?" *Foreign Affairs* 72.3 (1993): 22–32.

27 Samuel Huntington, "Religion and the Third Wave", *National Interest* 24. Summer (1991): 40–41.

28 Bernard Lewis, *What Went Wrong?* (London: Phoenix, 2002) 168–78.

29 Ibid. 168.

30 Lewis, *The Crisis of Islam* 139.

31 Ibid. 140.

32 Robert H. Pelletreau, et al., "Symposium: Resurgent Islam in the Middle East", *Middle East Policy* 2.2 (1994).

33 Daniel Pipes, "There Are No Moderates: Dealing with Fundamentalist Islam", *National Interest* 41. Fall (1995): 48.

34 Amos Perlmutter, "Wishful Thinking About Islamic Fundamentalism", *Washington Post* 19 Jan. 1992, A5.

35 Martin Kramer, "The Mismeasure of Political Islam", *The Islamism Debate*, ed. Martin Kramer (The Moshe Dayan Center for Middle Eastern and African Studies, Tel Aviv University, 1997) 167–72.

36 Martin Kramer, "Islam vs. Democracy", *Commentary* 95.Jan. (1993): 38–39.

37 Daniel Brumberg, "Rhetoric and Strategy: Islamic Movements and Democracy in the Middle East", *The Islamism Debate*, ed. Martin Kramer (The Moshe Dayan Center for Middle Eastern and African Studies, Tel Aviv University, 1997) 11–18.

38 Kramer, "The Mismeasure of Political Islam" 49.

39 Ibid.

40 Oliver Roy, "Islamists in Power", *The Islamism Debate*, ed. Martin Kramer (The Moshe Dayan Center for Middle Eastern and African Studies, Tel Aviv University, 1997) 82.

41 Bill Blum, "The CIA's Intervention in Afghanistan: Interview with Zbigniew Brzezinski", *Le Nouvel Observateur* 15–21 Jan. 1998, 12/06/03 <http://www.globalresearch.ca/articles/BRZ110A.html>.

42 Paul R. Pillar, *Terrorism and US Foreign Policy* (Washington, D.C.: Brookings Institution Press, 2001) 41–72; Richard A. Clarke, *Against All Enemies: Inside America's War on Terror* (New York: Free Press, 2004) 35–72.

43 Pinto, *Political Islam and the United States* 206.

44 Edward Djerejian, "The US and the Middle East in a Changing World", Address at Meridian House International, Washington, D.C.: GPO, 2 Jun. 1992. 8pp. 04/05/02 <http://dosfan.lib.uic.edu/ERC/briefing/dispatch/1992/html/Dispatchv3no23.html>.

45 Ibid.

46 Edward Djerejian, "The US and the Middle East in a Changing World".

47 Ibid.

48 Fawaz A. Gerges, *America and Political Islam: Clash of Cultures or Clash of Interests?* (Cambridge: Cambridge University Press, 1999) 83.

49 Pinto, *Political Islam and the United States* 207.

50 Gerges, *America and Political Islam* 85.

51 Thomas W. Lippman, "To Islam, an Olive Branch", *Washington Post* 28 Dec. 1994: A3.

52 William J. Clinton, "Speech by President to the Jordanian Parliament", Remarks by the President to the Jordanian Parliament, Amman: GPO, 26 Aug. 1993. 2pp. 11/10/04 <http://www.clintonfoundation.org/legacy/102694-speech-by-president-to-jordanian-parliament.htm>.

53 Robert H. Pelletreau, "Symposium: Resurgent Islam in the Middle East", *Middle East Policy* Fall (1994): 2.

54 Martin Kramer, "Coming to Terms: Fundamentalists or Islamists?", *Middle East Quarterly* 10.2 (2003): 7.

55 Daniel Pipes and Patrick Clawson, "Robert H. Pelletreau Jr.: Not Every Fundamentalist Is a Terrorist", *Middle East Quarterly* 2.3 (1995): 7.

56 Ibid. 7.

57 Satloff, *US Policy Towards Islamism: A Theoretical and Operational Overview*, 8.

58 Anthony Lake, "Conceptualizing US Strategy in the Middle East", Address to the Soref Symposium, Washington, D.C.: Washington Institute for Near East Policy, 17 May 1994. 4pp. 19/04/02 <http://www.washingtoninstitute.org/pubs/soref/lake.htm>.

59 Satloff, *US Policy Towards Islamism*, 10.

60 Ibid.

61 Ibid.

62 Robert H. Pelletreau, "Dealing with the Muslim Politics of the Middle East", Address to the Council on Foreign Relations, New York: GPO, 8 May 1996. 7pp. 15/09/02 <http://dosfan.lib.uic.edu/ERC/bureaus/nea/ 960508PelletreauMuslim. html>.

63 Walter Russell Mead, *Special Providence: American Foreign Policy and How It Changed the World* (New York: Knopf, 2001) 100–73.

64 Clarke, *Against All Enemies* 73.

65 United States, CIA, *The War on Terrorism: Frequently Asked Questions* (Washington, D.C.: GPO, 2005) 2pp. 20/11/02 <http://www.cia.gov/terrorism/faqs.html>.

66 Steve Coll, "CIA in Afghanistan: In CIA's Covert War, Where to Draw the Line Was Key", *Washington Post* 20 Jul. 1992: A3.

67 Mark Urban, *War in Afghanistan* (London: Macmillan, 1988) 244–45.

68 Peter Bergen, *Holy War Inc.: Inside the Secret World of Osama Bin Laden* (London: Phoenix, 2002) 78.

69 Lewis, *The Crisis of Islam* 134.

70 George H. W. Bush, "Toward a New World Order", Address before a joint session of Congress, Washington, D.C.: GPO, 11 Sept. 1990. 27pp. 15/06/04 <http://dosfan.lib.uic.edu/erc/briefing/dispatch/1990/html/Dispatchv1no03.html>.

71 Peter Arnett, "March 1997 Interview with Osama Bin Laden", *CNN Online* March 2001, 12/07/04 <http://news.findlaw.com/hdocs/docs/binladen/binladenintvw-cnn. pdf>. Emphasis added.

72 Clarke, *Against All Enemies* 79.

73 Ibid. 101–32.

74 Ibid. 147.

75 Ibid. 148.

76 For further details on US counterterrorism policy see: David Tucker, "Combating International Terrorism", *The Terrorism Threat and US Governmental Response: Operational and Organisational Factors*, eds. James M. Smith and William C. Thomas (Colorado: USAF Institute for National Security Studies, 2001) 129–54.

77 Clarke, *Against All Enemies* 235.

78 Ibid. 229–32.

79 Ibid. 230.

80 Anoushiravan Ehteshami, "The Delicate State of Muslim Democracy", *Global Agenda* 2004: 216.

81 George W. Bush, "President Bush Discusses Freedom in Iraq and Middle East", Remarks by the President at the 20th Anniversary of the National Endowment for Democracy, Washington, D.C.: GPO, 6 Nov. 2003. 6pp. 15/09/04 <http://www.whitehouse.gov/news/releases/2003/11/20031106-2.html>.

82 Condoleezza Rice, *Rice Says Values of Islam, Democracy, Human Rights Mutually Reinforcing*, (Washington D.C.: GPO, 4 Dec. 2002) 3pp. 15/09/04 <http://tokyo.usembassy.gov/e/p/tp-soc20021206a2.html>.

83 Richard Armitage, "Armitage: Afghan Vote to Show Democracy, Islam Compatible", Deputy Secretary of State interviewed by Italian newspaper, Washington, D.C.: GPO, 6 Oct. 2004. 4pp. 17/12/04 <http://tokyo.usembassy.gov/e/p/tp-20041012-26.html>.

84 Michael Hirsh, "Bernard Lewis Revisited: What If Islam Isn't an Obstacle to Democracy in the Middle East but the Secret to Achieving It?" *Washington Monthly* 45. Nov. (2004) 6pp. 13/12/04 <http://www.collectiveinterest.net/homepage/bernard_lewis%20revisited.pdf>.

85 Ibid.

86 George W. Bush, "Remarks Prior to Discussions with Prime Minister", Remarks prior to discussions with Prime Minister Recep Tayyip Erdogan of Turkey, Ankara: GPO, 27 Jun. 2004. 1pp. 17/02/05 <http://www.findarticles.com/p/articles/mi_m2889/is_27_40/ai_n6148652>.

PART 2

THE UNITED STATES AND THE PERSIAN GULF IN THE POST-COLD WAR ERA

4

The Clinton Years and Iran:
Containment and Engagement

---

*"The purpose of foreign policy is not to provide an outlet for our own
sentiments of hope or indignation; it is to shape real events in a real world."*

John Fitzgerald Kennedy
September 1963

By 1993, bilateral relations with Iran had been affected by both historical
and contemporary differences. For the United States, one of the main
issues hampering a rapprochement concerned Iran's continual opposition
to the Arab–Israeli peace process both rhetorically and substantively. In
addition, its conventional military capability and alleged efforts to acquire
a nuclear arsenal served as active barriers to the goal of reconciliation.
Regionally, Iran was seen by the United States as posing a potential threat
to US allies in the Persian Gulf and also to the freedom of the seas
through its potential ability to disrupt shipping access through the Strait
of Hormuz.

The overlapping interests of the US and Iran do not lead to any
conclusion that there should have been mutual hostility.[1] On a geostrategic level, politically and strategically important areas flank Iran's
borders. Its large oil reserves coupled with its large deposits of natural gas
clearly indicate that Iran has great importance for the global economy.
Moreover, its role as the most populous Shi'a country gives it a special
role in Islamic jurisprudence. For Iran, trade relations with the United
States have the potential for rapid economic development and regional
ascendancy. Although cooperative relations could fulfil mutual interests
and be beneficial, relations since 1979 had been void of such cooperation.

The foreign relations of the United States and Iran in the time
period 1993–2001 were remarkable in that one state's foreign policies
appeared to mutually reinforce the other's and thus lessened the prospects
of substantive diplomacy. Indeed, from the United States' point of view,
Iran's unwillingness to moderate its sponsorship of terrorist organisations,

in addition to its vocal opposition to the peace process, fuelled Congressional legislation against Iran. This was important because it created a domestic political environment within the United States which made any 'softening' of US policy a politically charged option for the executive.

Overall, the Clinton administration will be shown to have sought a moderation of Iran's policies in order to achieve a degree of reconciliation. Without this, Iran was seen as posing a direct threat to Persian Gulf security. However, Iran did not moderate its policies to a level which could have made reciprocal measures by the executive a credible political option. Indeed, Iran's policies served as a means by which US interest groups were able to mobilise support for a punitive containment of Iran through unilateral sanctions. This will be shown to have restricted the options available to the executive and, in essence, to have usurped the foreign policy prerogative of the President. Nevertheless, Iran's failure or inability to moderate its provocative foreign policies resulted in a deepening of the bilateral hostility despite some aspects of Iranian foreign policy being, to a certain extent, a reaction to the unilateral measures enacted by Congress.

Domestic Political Contexts

The CIA's involvement in overthrowing Iranian Prime Minister Mossadegh in 1953, coupled with support for Shah Mohamed Reza Pahlavi, were very significant historical grievances for Iran. However, the revolution itself did not immediately mark the onset of bilateral hostility; rather it was the decision to allow the Shah into the United States for medical treatment which triggered a domestic backlash against America. The resulting seizure of the United States Embassy and the popular support it received allowed for what Said Amir Arjomand has classified as a "clerical *coup d'état*".[2] This saw the radical clerics ultimately extend their power over the moderates and any remaining areas of the Iranian government and military. The resulting effect was that the Islamic Revolution became self-legitimising through being defined as diametrically opposed to the United States and the West. Even with the accession of Ali Akbar Hashemi Rafsanjani to the presidency following the death of Ayatollah Khomeini, these constraints arguably thwarted his efforts at détente. Therefore, there were significant domestic and institutional contextual factors within Iran which made a rapprochement with the United States an arduous policy quagmire from the start.[3]

Similarly, in the United States, historical relations have had an institutional bearing on its foreign policy towards Iran. As has already been discussed, the embassy hostage crisis and Iran's implication in terrorist attacks against the United States and Israel have been highly significant issues that have had a bearing on US foreign policy.

Domestically, Iran was generally portrayed in the Western media as a pariah nation inherently linked with terrorism. With images of Iranians chanting 'Death to America!' after a religious sermon and occasional burnings of the US and Israeli flags, generally speaking, little distinction was usually made in the media between the ruling theocracy's supporters as compared with the wider diversity in Iranian civil society and even within the government itself. Nevertheless, the Mullahs' attempts to gain legitimacy amongst their supporters both rhetorically and substantively through their opposition towards the United States, placed clear pressures on the US foreign policy agenda. Nevertheless, although the American domestic perception of Iranian policies was important, in the case of the construction of US foreign policy towards Iran, the actions of Congress were even more instrumental.

A central issue to understanding the driving force of Congressional impingement on US relations with Iran has been the role of special interest groups. Given Iran's hostile position towards Israel, Jewish groups have played a key role in lobbying for the adoption of a pro-Israeli policy. With Iran's hostile rhetoric and its alleged support for terrorist attacks against Israel, the pro-Israeli interest groups generally categorised Iran as a clear and present danger.

The umbrella organisation for the Jewish lobbies is the American Israel Public Affairs Committee (AIPAC). Although US legislation prevents Israel from directly providing funding or acting as a client of AIPAC, "Israel is the *de facto* client of several Jewish lobbies: it is with its interests alone that they are concerned".[4] Although there are several diverse pro-Jewish lobbies, they act in a fairly coordinated manner:

> Many AIPAC groups (among them the American Jewish Congress and the Anti-Defamation League of B'nai B'rith) have their own representatives in Washington. AIPAC has close working relations with other Jewish organisations, some of which are represented on

its board. It also advises numerous Jewish PAC's across the United States.[5]

The Jewish lobby is, along with the National Rifle Association, one of the most influential and successful special interest groups in the United States. It wields a great deal of influence within Congress and its ability to have some bearing on Congressional voting is an important consideration in any evaluation of US policy that either directly or indirectly concerns Israel.

In addition to lobbyist groups, domestic voting blocks are also an important consideration. The so called 'Jewish vote' is significant in some areas such as New York and some North Eastern areas of the United States, but with there being in the region of six million Jewish individuals in the United States, they are a clear voting minority.[6] However, it is worthwhile distinguishing the 'Jewish vote' from the 'pro-Jewish vote', which stems mainly from diverse conservative Christian communities. Indeed, Clinton's election campaign pronouncements on the Middle East were noted for being very supportive of the Israeli state. Whilst this could likely be accounted for by his genuine affinity towards the Israeli state and the Jewish people,[7] it also indirectly served the political purpose of catering to the interests of the significant American Christian and Jewish voting blocks.

Although these factors are significant to varying degrees, it is important to recognise that contextual issues external to the United States were also fundamental in shaping US relations with Iran in the time period of this study. Raymond Tanter has argued that Israeli national politics were linked with the direction of AIPAC's lobbying on the US Congress following the liberation of Kuwait in 1991. Tanter maintains that AIPAC shifted its focus towards Iran following the defeat of the Likud party in Israeli national elections in 1992.[8] He suggests that as a result of AIPAC being, in effect, linked with the Likud, its defeat at the Israeli elections lessened AIPAC's influence within the Congressional halls of power. He goes on to say that by AIPAC immediately shifting its focus onto Iran, it was able to use this as a means of maintaining its influence within Washington following the defeat of the Likud.[9]

Additionally, many critics saw the Clinton administration as having an inherent pro-Israeli character of its own on account of the sizeable number of Jewish individuals that were present within it. Hossein

Alikhani argues that within Clinton's National Security Council, seven out of eleven of its most senior Directors were Jewish, along with a large number of senior individuals within the White House and State Department. For some, this indicates that there was an inherent pro-Israeli bias from the offset in Clinton's administration. Whilst Alikhani's argument has some merit, it should be viewed with caution as it is not methodologically feasible to measure its effect on US policy. However, it is reasonable to conclude that it was a factor that potentially fostered a degree of bias within the administration towards Israel.

Iran–Iraq Arms Non-Proliferation Act of 1992
During the course of the Iran–Iraq War, the military presence of the United States had progressively increased in the region as a means of securing its allies and ensuring the unrestricted supply of oil. Given the state of relations since the Islamic Revolution, the increased US military presence in the Persian Gulf was understandably seen by Tehran as a real threat to its national security. Coupled with this was its aggressive neighbour, Iraq, and its historical suspicion of Russia with its borders stretching from Afghanistan to the states on the Caspian basin. Given the threats Iran perceived, and the fact that its conventional military forces had been significantly degraded following its war with Iraq, it understandably saw a strategic need to rebuild its armed forces.

As Iran was not self-sufficient in domestic weaponry production, it made a concerted effort to rebuild its armed forces from sources overseas. Iran's decision to increase the size of its armed forces in the aftermath of the Iran–Iraq War was strategically provocative to Washington on account of the risk this potentially posed to US interests in the Persian Gulf and towards Israel. However, the availability of armaments had been curtailed as a result of the actions of successive US administrations since 1979. The view held by the majority in Congress and in US policy circles in general was that post-revolutionary Iran posed a threat to US interests in the Middle East, and thus its armaments and military procurement should be restricted. As a result of the conditions on the supply of conventional weapons, Tehran had little choice about whom it could actually enter into supply relationships with. The most notable military arms and technological suppliers in the aftermath of the Iran–Iraq War proved to be Russia, China and North Korea.[10]

Iran's relations with Russia had historically been characterised by hostility and suspicion.[11] However, a thaw in relations occurred in February 1989 following a meeting between Ayatollah Khomeini and the Soviet Foreign Minister Edouard Shevardnadze. This ultimately developed into a military and nuclear technology trade agreement following the visit to Moscow by the Speaker of the Iranian Parliament, Ali Akbar Hashemi Rafsanjani, in June 1989.

The US-led liberation of Kuwait in 1991 had important ramifications for Russia's influence in the Persian Gulf. The United States forged close political and military relations with the GCC countries,[12] which effectively closed off the market to Russian arms manufacturers. It seems clear that, despite their poor historical relations, Russia's need for capital and Iran's need for armaments thus allowed both countries to develop their bilateral relations based on mutual interests. Geopolitics also accounts for the Russian–Iranian arms cooperation following the break-up of the Soviet Union in 1991. It has also been speculated that the supply of armaments to Iran allowed Russia to control the spread of revolutionary Islam on its borders. [13]

During the Clinton presidency, Russia's arms trade with Iran did have ramifications for Moscow's bilateral relations with the United States. The degree of concern about Iran's procurement of Russian armaments and technology was so high within the Clinton administration that Clinton raised it as a serious concern with President Yeltsin at their summit meetings.[14] Clinton made Russia's acceptance of the multilateral export trading control relationship, the Waasenaar Agreement,[15] dependent upon Russia not concluding any new arms agreements with Tehran. Following the 1995 Clinton–Yeltsin summit meeting, Russia bowed to American pressure and agreed not to conclude any *new* arms agreements with Iran.[16]

China was also willing to provide armaments and technology to Iran in spite of US pressures to the contrary.[17] Following a visit to Beijing in 1985 by Ali Akbar Hashemi Rafsanjani, Iran entered into an armament trading relationship with the People's Republic.[18] A range of advanced conventional weapons and technology was purchased by Iran, including alleged assistance for Iran's *Shihab* missile programme. However, the main focus of Sino-Iranian conventional arms trade concentrated on advanced antiship missiles. Iran entered into an agreement to purchase the sophisticated Chinese-manufactured Silkworm surface-to-surface antiship missiles. This represented a strategic escalation in Iran's military capability. This was ultimately realised in the final stages of the Iran–Iraq War when Iran used Silkworm missiles against US-escorted oil tankers in the Persian Gulf and also against Kuwaiti oil installations.

The trade in armaments between China and Iran does seem to have been motivated by commercial interests on the part of China: specifically revenue from the arms trade and also the regular supply of oil from Iran. China's willingness to supply Iran with arms and technology did prove to be a point of contention in US–Sino bilateral relations. It has been suggested that this was a 'tit for tat' strategy by Beijing in response to US military support for Taiwan.[19]

Similarly, Iran engaged in a range of military and technological procurements from North Korea.[20] The focus of the relationship was, however, concentrated on ballistic missile technology. North Korea allegedly sold Iran Scud and North Korean-manufactured *Nodong* and *Tapeo-Dong* surface-to-surface missiles, in addition to technology for Iran's own *Shihab* surface-to-surface missile project.[21] North Korea's sale of military technology did have an impact on its own bilateral relationship with the United States, but in terms of US–Iranian relations, its proliferating ballistic missile stockpile, together with the development of longer-range *Shihab* rockets,[22] served to further aggravate bilateral relations. Indeed, Iran's missile proliferation compounded fears within Israel for its own national security,[23] which in turn had an impact on the US foreign policy agenda.

In the aftermath of the liberation of Kuwait in 1991, the level of Congressional dissatisfaction towards Iran was aggravated by Iran's procurement of such weaponry and also by the fact that the United States was one of Iran's major trading partners. Dissatisfaction had been mounting at the inconsistency of Washington's policy towards the Islamic Republic: it categorised Iran as a 'rogue state' whilst burgeoning bilateral trade was allowed to go unchecked. Indeed, the level of trade was significant as "US exports to Iran in 1987 amounted to US$54 million, growing to US$60 million by 1989. In 1990, exports shot up to US$168 million, reaching US$750 million by 1992, making the United States Iran's sixth-largest trading partner."[24]

By early 1992, with the dissatisfaction of the Department of Commerce's export licensing towards a proliferating Iran, Congress was prompted into adopting the Iran–Iraq Non-Proliferation Act of 1992.[25] Proposed by Republican Senators John McCain and Alfonse D'Amato, the Iran–Iraq Non-Proliferation Act of 1992 suspended the ability of the United States government to engage in trade with Iran, issue trading licences and provide economic and technical assistance. It specifically placed restrictions on entities trading in advanced conventional weapons of a type or size that would have a destabilising impact on the region. Moreover, it prohibited the trade in technology that could assist Iran's unconventional weapons programmes. It was justified by its sponsor, Senator John McCain, and its co-sponsor, Senator Alfonse D'Amato who claimed that "tighter curbs on shipments to Iran were necessary if a repetition of US export control errors with Iraq prior to the Gulf War was to be avoided".[26]

This legislation was also extra-territorial in that it extended these provisions to foreign states and companies. An important factor of this Act, which subsequently had a bearing on the Clinton administration, was that it did not quantify what constituted "destabilizing numbers and types of advanced conventional weapons".[27] This later provided the Clinton administration with some degree of latitude in implementing the Act. However, the legislation had no bearing on Russian transfers of armaments to Iran as it was not enacted retrospectively over previously signed arms agreements.

It is important at this point to recognise that the Iran–Iraq Arms Non-Proliferation Act of 1992 was very much a Congressional response towards the problems posed by Iran and was the "most restrictive legislation passed against Iran since 1980".[28] This legislation was not welcomed by the Bush administration as it was seen as subjugating the Constitutional authority of the President to construct US foreign policy. President Bush notably commented that:

> I am particularly concerned about provisions that purport to derogate the President's authority under the Constitution to conduct US foreign policy, including negotiation with other countries . . . Consistent with my responsibilities under the Constitution for the conduct of diplomatic negotiations, and with established practice, I will construe these provisions to be precatory rather than mandatory.[29]

Nevertheless, the signing into law of this Act did have a direct bearing on US policy as Washington began to further its efforts to enlist the cooperation of allied nations to restrict their exports to Iran,[30] and marked the onset of a clear unilateral containment strategy towards Iran.

Geostrategic Policy for Gulf Security: Dual Containment

In the immediate post-war scenario 1991–1993, Iraq obstructed the UNSCOM inspections by restricting access to various sites, and prevented the seizure of official Iraqi documents by the inspectors. The UN responded to Iraqi non-compliance by adopting UNSCR 707 and 715, which effectively reaffirmed the legitimacy of inspections and the necessity for full and complete Iraqi compliance. It was, however, in the period immediately prior to Bill Clinton being inaugurated into office that Iraq prohibited the use of UNSCOM flights,[31] and also made incursions into the demilitarised zone with Kuwait.[32] This violation by Iraq resulted in it being found in material breach of prior resolutions on 8 January 1993.[33] In this instance, it seems likely that Iraq was testing the willingness of Washington to enforce compliance in the run-up to the US administration handover. These factors resulted in the coalition responding with a series of air strikes against Iraq.[34] Therefore, with the onset of the Clinton presidency, the new administration inherited the policy position of being committed to upholding UN resolutions designed to contain the threat Iraq posed to US interests in the Persian Gulf region.

Although President-elect Clinton supported this policy position, he made it clear that when he entered office he was "ready for a fresh start with Saddam Hussein".[35] After receiving political criticism for a seemingly 'softer' approach towards Iraq, Clinton refined his position on Iraq as being the maintenance of the Bush administration's policy but with a *new policy initiative*.[36] Crucially, Clinton made it clear that he could not conceive "[the] United States ever having any kind of normal relationship with Iraq as long as Saddam Hussein [was] there".[37] It was, therefore, clear that George H. W. Bush's position on Iraq was widely favoured within Congress and any radical departure by Clinton would have been politically costly to the new Democrat administration. Indeed, given this accepted political wisdom in Washington, it would have been a difficult departure for the incoming Clinton presidency.

Martin Indyk, the Special Assistant to the President for Near East and South Asian affairs, outlined the Clinton administration's 'new' initiative towards regional security in an address to the pro-Israeli Washington Institute for Near East Policy in May 1993. The strategy outlined by Indyk was that of dual containment towards both Iran and Iraq.[38] Dual containment rested on the premise that both states had a history of aggressive action in a variety of spheres, and posed a threat to the Persian Gulf states and Israel. The emphasis was thus on a moderation of their policies.

Clinton's Persian Gulf strategy rested on the recognition that a singular containment of Iraq was insufficient to guarantee regional security on account of the geopolitical situation which was defined as follows:

1. The threat posed by potential Iranian hegemony in the context of Iraqi containment;
2. The threat posed by Iranian attempts to procure unconventional weapons;
3. The inability of the GCC countries to mobilise a credible defence cooperation arrangement.[39]

The clearest exposé of the dual containment strategy occurred, however, in an academic article in 1994, by Anthony Lake, the Assistant to the President for National Security Affairs:

> The Clinton administration's policy of 'dual containment' of Iraq and Iran derives in the first instance from an assessment that the current Iraqi and Iranian regimes are both hostile to American interests in the region. Accordingly, we do not accept the argument that we should continue the old balance of power game, building up one to balance the other. We reject that approach not only because its bankruptcy was demonstrated in Iraq's invasion of Kuwait. We reject it because of a clear-headed assessment of the antagonism that both regimes harbor towards the United States and its allies in the region. And we reject it because we don't need to rely on one to balance the other.[40]

Lake outlined Clinton's dual containment policy as not entailing a duplication of policy towards both Iran and Iraq, as the administration saw both states posing differential threats and thus warranting unique responses. Whilst the policy towards Iraq was multilateral in scope and based on UN resolutions, the US containment policy towards Iran was clearly a unilateral policy undertaking. The Iranian policies that warranted these responses were highlighted by Lake as:

1. Clandestine efforts to procure unconventional weapons with long-range missile technology;
2. Provision of direct and asymmetric support for radical political Islamic movements who use violent terrorist style methods of political expression;
3. Efforts to undermine the Arab–Israeli peace process;
4. Efforts to destabilise Gulf countries such as Bahrain, and also Islamic countries in Africa;
5. High levels of conventional weapons production and procurement, which posed a potential threat to the security of GCC states.[41]

For the Clinton administration, these factors ultimately posed a significant threat to US interests in the Persian Gulf, and were seen to warrant the *continuation* of a unilateral containment policy.[42] The objective of the Clinton administration towards Iran was thus: the United States would unilaterally attempt to economically, politically and militarily contain the threat posed by Iran to the region and would seek a change in Tehran's behaviour through *meaningful dialogue*, leading ultimately to reconciliation rather than a regime change strategy. This was very much a continuation of the unilateral policy of the previous Bush administration towards Iran.

Lake was careful to distinguish the administration's policy towards Iraq as being separate from that towards Iran, though it was still encompassed under the same strategic policy of dual containment:

> In post-Khomeini Iran, a revolutionary regime remains engaged in outlaw behavior. Nevertheless, the Clinton administration does not oppose Islamic government, nor does it seek the regime's overthrow. Indeed we remain ready for an authoritative dialog in which we will raise aspects of Iranian behavior that cause us so much concern.[43]

Clinton's dual containment strategy towards regional security was therefore, in essence, a policy continuation towards both Iran and Iraq from the previous Bush administration. However, it was original because no previous *declared* US policy rested on the premise of simultaneously containing both Iran and Iraq as a means of ensuring Persian Gulf and wider regional security.

The accepted historical diplomatic wisdom of the application of containment theory is one possible explanation as to why the Clinton administration was willing to pursue this strategy towards Iran and Iraq. Throughout the Cold War, the United States pursued a strategy of containment towards the Soviet Union as its primary means of strategically combating the ideological and military threat it posed. It is also a strategy that the United States employed against other states such as Cuba and North Korea. The origins of strategic containment are found in George Kennan's long telegram in 1946 on how to combat the Soviet threat. Expanded upon and clarified in Kennan's famous article in *Foreign Affairs*, containment emerged as the cornerstone of US grand strategic policy throughout the Cold War period.[44]

The credibility of containment as a strategy for dealing with nations that pursue policies contrary to US interests was greatly enhanced with the fall of the Soviet Union. Containment has credibility in US political discourse as it is seen to control the short and medium threats posed by 'rogue states' and arguably forces change to occur at a socio-political level. It is important, however, to recognise that the containment strategy also emerged as a result of its perceived suitability for the geopolitical environment and the recognition within Congress that the United States should apply its power given its hegemonic position.

Henry Kissinger eloquently captures the essence of the US application of containment theory:

> Containment was an extraordinary theory . . . [t]horoughly American in its utopianism, it assumed that the collapse of a totalitarian adversary could be achieved in an essentially benign way. Although this doctrine was formulated at the height of America's absolute power, it preached America's relative weakness. Postulating a grand diplomatic encounter at the moment of its culmination, containment allowed no role for diplomacy until the climactic final scene in which the men in white hats accepted the conversion of the men in black hats.[45]

Even during containment, Kissinger argued that the prospect of a meaningful dialogue taking place between the United States and a perceived rogue country will very much hinge on whether Washington views the regime as having *diplomatic credibility*.[46] Kissinger highlights that US 'exceptionalism'[47] in its foreign policy requires the negotiating partner to act in a legalistic, honest and moral manner in its diplomacy. The prospect of meaningful dialogue thus ceases when Washington views the given regime as lacking in this. This is important when we examine US diplomacy towards both Iraq and Iran.

Clinton's Foreign Policy Objectives Towards Iran

With the onset of the Clinton Presidency, Robert Pelletreau, the Assistant Secretary of State for Near East Affairs, outlined the objective of the administration towards Iran as being geared towards altering Iran's behaviour with respect to five key areas:

1. Its quest for nuclear and other weapons of mass destruction, and the means for their delivery;
2. The continued involvement of the Iranian government in terrorism and assassination worldwide;
3. Its support for violent opposition to the Arab–Israeli peace process;
4. Iran's threats and subversive activities against its neighbours;
5. Its dismal human rights record at home.[48]

Importantly however, Pelletreau made it clear that a resumption of relations was an objective, but would very much depend on such activities being curtailed. Pelletreau commented:

> Our policy is not aimed at changing the Iranian government, but at inducing Iran to change its behavior in these areas. We are prepared to enter into dialog with authorised representatives of the Iranian government to discuss the differences between us. We seek to persuade Iran that it cannot expect to enjoy normal state-to-state relations so long as it violates basic standards of international behavior. This means working with other countries to deny Iran access to technology, new credits, and other means by which it can facilitate the pursuit of policies of destabilization, terrorism and acquiring weapons of mass destruction.[49]

Congressional Usurpation of Foreign Policy

Although the Clinton administration was fortunate to come to power with a Democrat-controlled Congress, the Republican Party gained control of both Houses of Congress following the 1994 midterm elections. The loss of Democrat control over Congress was highly significant for two distinct reasons:

1. The end of the Cold War signalled the end of the over-arching global grand strategy geared towards the containment of the Soviet Union. With the loss of a clear strategy, Congress inevitably lost its general bipartisan approach towards foreign policy. When this is considered along with the administration's loss of partisan control over Congress, Clinton was facing a clear obstacle in the conduct of his foreign policy.
2. As a result of the end of a general bipartisan approach towards foreign policy and the context of a Democrat Presidency, the Republicans within Congress inevitably adopted the strategy of being reactive to domestic political concerns on foreign issues as a means of garnering wider political support. This translated into interest groups receiving a much wider political voice within Congress.

The interplay of the political forces from interest groups and Congressional politics was a constant source of pressure on the Clinton administration from the conception of the dual containment strategy. By March 1994, AIPAC released its highly influential policy document: *Comprehensive US Sanctions against Iran: A Plan for Action*.[50] The 76-page document outlined a strategy to combat Iran through a variety of means. AIPAC also lobbied "strenuously for a total trade embargo and for a secondary boycott of foreign companies trading with Iran".[51] But it was Senator Alfonse D'Amato's adopting this strategy that ultimately saw Congress force it onto the US foreign policy agenda.

D'Amato, a fiercely pro-Israeli Republican Senator from New York, had a large Jewish constituency and was seen by many as a champion of AIPAC. Indeed, Senator D'Amato and AIPAC had a long-standing relationship as the organisation allegedly deterred potential Democrat candidates from running against him in his 1986 re-election bid.[52] At the end of January 1995, D'Amato tabled the Comprehensive Iran Sanctions Act of 1995 in the Senate.[53] Indeed, D'Amato's proposed bill was inherently linked with AIPAC as, according to Keith Weissman, AIPAC's Chief Middle East Analyst, it was AIPAC who actually wrote the proposed legislation. Drawing from AIPAC's 1994 strategy paper on comprehensive sanctions against Iran,[54] D'Amato's proposed legislation called for a prohibition on:

1. Any transfer in the currency exchange of Iran;
2. The transfer of credit or payments between, by, through, or to any banking institution, to the extent that such transfers or payments involve interest of Iran or thereof;
3. The importing from, or exporting to, Iran of currencies or securities;
4. Any acquisition, holding, withholding, use, transfer, withdrawal, transportation, importation or exportation of, or dealing in, or exercising any right, power or privilege with respect to, or any transaction involving, any property in which Iran or any national thereof has any interest; by any person, or with respect to any property, subject to the jurisdiction of the United States;
5. The licensing for export to Iran, or for export to any other country for re-export to Iran, by any person subject to the jurisdiction of the United States of any item or technology controlled in the Export Administration Act of 1954;
6. The importation into the United States of any good or service which is, in whole or in part, grown, produced, manufactured, extracted, or processed in Iran.[55]

Clearly, D'Amato's proposed legislation was comprehensive and a large escalation in US unilateral sanctions towards Iran. Although it was very much based on the framework of the Cuban Democracy Act of 1992, it added additional provisions that made it potentially the most restrictive legislation against a foreign country by the United States.

In the interim period before D'Amato's bill received a hearing in the Senate, pressure on the Clinton administration mounted as Republican Representative Peter King tabled a bill in the House that was identical to D'Amato's. With it being clear that sanctions would be implemented, the Iranian National Oil Company (INOC) concluded a US$1 billion contract with US oil giant Conoco, to develop the Sirri-A and Sirri-E oil fields. The conclusion of the agreement did indicate a clear attempt from Iran to open up political relations,[56] but as a result of the political situation within Congress, it was doubtful that it would have been politically feasible for the administration to pursue such an avenue at that time.

The conclusion of the INOC–Conoco oil agreement served to

highlight the inconsistency of the dual containment strategy: on the one hand, the US$1 billion agreement was lawful, but on the other, it ran contrary to the stated objectives and spirit of the containment strategy. Given this inconsistency, conflicting remarks emerged from the administration on the agreement.[57] Whilst the White House appeared to condone the agreement by stating that it was legal, Secretary of State Christopher unequivocally condemned the agreement as inconsistent with the interests and policies of the United States.[58]

The response of the Clinton administration to this politically damaging situation was, in effect, to implement many of the provisions of D'Amato's bill in order to regain lost political ground and to be seen as responsive to the INOC–Conoco Agreement. On 15 March 1995, Clinton issued Executive Order 12957, which basically precluded:

1. [T]he entry into or performance by a United States person or the entry into or performance by an entity owned or controlled by a United States person, of (i) a contract that includes overall supervision and management responsibility for the development of petroleum resources located in Iran, or (ii) a guaranty of another person's performance under such a contract.

2. [T]he entry into or performance by a United States person or the entry into or performance by an entity owned or controlled by a United States person, of (i) a contract for financing of the development of petroleum resources located in Iran, or (ii) a guaranty of another person's performance under such a contract.

3. [A]ny transaction by any United States person or within the United States that evades or avoids, or has the purpose of evading or avoiding, or attempts to violate, any of the prohibitions set forth in the Order.[59]

The Clinton administration, however, opposed the D'Amato bill, which was heard at the Senate on 16 March 1994, as it felt that milder sanctions were more appropriate, especially given the difficulties in applying unilateral sanctions.[60] Given this opposition, D'Amato introduced the Iran Foreign Sanctions Act of 1995, dubbed D'Amato II by AIPAC; it went even further than his previous bill. The bill was designed to be extra-territorial in jurisdiction, whereby any foreign firm that trades with Iran would be subject to sanctions. Compounding this, identical legislation was introduced in the House by Republican King, with the caveat that a sanctioned foreign entity that had traded with Iran would not be able to trade at all within the United States. In effect, the combined nature of the bills potentially called for a foreign entity to choose to trade either with the United States or with Iran.

The bills were subject to a great deal of criticism as a result of the impact they would have on US multilateral relations. Gary Sick highlighted that the result of the legislation, if enacted, would be that:

> [A] blizzard of Presidential waivers will be required . . . making a travesty of the legislative process and clogging the courts with frivolous litigation . . . corporate lawyers and entrepreneurs with a taste for complex legal dodges will have a field day, creating a swamp of evasive corruption and thriving business for eager prosecutors.[61]

Both bills received public backing from AIPAC, as well as from the influential Jewish Institute for National Security Affairs (JINSA). It should have been clear to Clinton that the wise words of Senator William Fulbright in 1973, on how the Israelis exercise a great deal of influence in the Senate, had merit.[62]

Clinton was therefore faced with a clear dilemma for if he opposed the bills it would have been very politically damaging to his administration and thus to the Democrats in Congress. Clinton was thus left with little political choice. The administration's response was to steal the initiative yet again and propose the policy as its own, before the Senate and House voted on the D'Amato–King bills. With Clinton aiming to regain his domestic position with the pro-Jewish electoral factions, he duly announced his new policy undertaking at none other than a World Jewish Congress dinner, whilst wearing a *yarmulke*. Clinton stated:

> I am formally announcing my intention to cut off all trade and investment with Iran and to suspend nearly all other economic activity between our nations. This is not a step I take lightly, but I am convinced that instituting a trade embargo with Iran is the most effective way our Nation can help to curb that nation's drive to acquire devastating weapons and its continued support for terrorism . . . In my discussions with President Yeltsin and with the G–7 leaders in Halifax in June, I will urge other countries to take

similar or parallel actions. I do want you to know that I do oppose the suggestion some have made that we impose a secondary boycott and prohibit foreign firms doing business with Iran from doing business with the United States. I don't agree with that. I think that decision would cause unnecessary strain with our allies at a time when we need our friends' co-operations.[63]

Clinton therefore proposed implementing tighter sanctions on trade with Iran, but fell short of the D'Amato–King bills which called for sanctioning foreign entities that traded with Iran. D'Amato stated that the policy would mean "a foreign corporation or person will have to choose between trade with the United States and trade with Iran".[64] His proposals were, however, commensurate with the dual containment strategy doctrine, but Clinton made it clear that he did not support a secondary application of sanctions against foreign entities because of the detrimental impact this would have had on US multilateral relations. Given that Clinton's official policy towards Iraq relied on multilateral support, it was commensurate with US interests to refrain from provocative foreign policies.

Adding to Executive Order 12957 of 15 March 1995, Clinton issued Executive Order 12959 of 6 May 1995 which prohibited virtually all trade and investment with Iran. The Executive Order towards Iran:

1. Prohibits exportation from the United States to Iran or to the Government of Iran of goods, technology or services, including trade financing by US banks;
2. Prohibits the re-exportation of certain US goods and technology to Iran from third countries;
3. Prohibits transactions such as brokering and other dealing by United States persons in Iranian goods and services;
4. Prohibits new investments by United States persons in Iran or in property owned or controlled by the Government of Iran;
5. Prohibits US companies from approving or facilitating their subsidiaries' performance of transactions that they themselves are prohibited from performing;
6. Continues the 1987 prohibition on the importation into the United States of goods and services of Iranian origin; and
7. Allows US companies a 30-day period in which to perform trade transactions pursuant to contracts pre-dating this order that are now prohibited.[65]

With the issuing of this Executive Order, Clinton had in effect been forced to implement policy that was designed by pro-Israeli lobbyist groups and tabled by Republican Congressmen. Although this was policy that was commensurate with Clinton's dual containment strategy, the domestic political conditions limited his options and prevented him from exploring further the political opening made by Iran under the guise of the INOC–Conoco oil agreement. Indeed, this serves to highlight the trend of an intrusion by Congress into the foreign policy agenda of the United States towards Iran. This usurpation could ultimately be traced back to the factors leading to the adoption of the Iran–Iraq Non-Proliferation Act of 1992.

The Iran–Libya Sanctions Act of 1996

Following Clinton's Executive Order 12959 of 6 May 1995, an understanding was reached with Senator D'Amato whereby he and his counterparts in the House would postpone having their respective bills considered by Congress. As a condition of this postponement, Clinton ambitiously agreed to actively gain support from US allies to reduce, or even cease, their bilateral trading with Iran.

Clinton had made it clear, in his speech at the World Jewish Congress on 20 April 1995, that he would pursue this objective at the G-7 summit in Halifax, Nova Scotia, in June 1995.[66] Predictably, the G-7 countries were unwilling to adopt this policy proposal towards Iran. The failure of the Clinton administration to gain international backing for its policy towards Iran prompted D'Amato to submit legislation to the Senate on 8 September 1995. D'Amato's introduction of the Iran Foreign Oil Sanctions Act of 1995, co-sponsored by Senators Inouye, Pressler, Faircloth and Kohl, drew from, but ultimately differed from, the legislation he introduced on the 27 March 1995. D'Amato had amended his previous bill so that it would specifically target *foreign entities* trading in petroleum or natural gas products with Iran.[67] This, however, was still directly opposed to the stated position of the Clinton administration that it would not impose any secondary sanctions on foreign entities trading with Iran.[68]

Although the Clinton administration opposed the legislation,[69] the Chairman of the House International Relations Committee, Benjamin Gilman, introduced a similar bill in the House of Representatives. Gilman's legislation, co-sponsored by Representatives Berman, Forbes,

King and Shaw, was equally as comprehensive as D'Amato's Senate bill. Although the White House maintained its adamant opposition to the bills, within Congress the bills received bipartisan support. Compounding this, Representatives Gejdenson and Burton introduced a bill which supported Gilman's position.[70] As a result of the high level of support the bills were receiving within both Houses of Congress, the Clinton administration changed its policy from direct opposition to a stated willingness to compromise.[71]

Senator D'Amato duly altered his legislation as a compromise measure towards the administration so that sanctions on entities trading on Iran's oil and gas fields would only qualify on investments of more than US$40 million. With the White House lending its support to this modified bill, it had clearly undertaken a policy reversal towards secondary sanctions on foreign entities engaged in trade in Iran's oil and gas sectors as a direct result of domestic political factors.

Whilst the Senate bill was being approved, Democrat Senator Edward Kennedy added an amendment requiring the same sanctions be applied to Libya. Kennedy was representing the families of the victims of the notorious bombing of Pan Am Flight 103 over Lockerbie. With Libya providing sanctuary to Abdel Basset Ali Mohammed al-Megrahi and Lamen Khalifa Fhimah, the two suspects in the bombing, Kennedy argued that it would serve as a means to both deter future terrorist attacks by Libya and hopefully compel Gaddafi to hand over the suspects.

Although the legislation was a 'watered down' version of its original incarnation, it was subject to a barrage of heavy criticism by US allies, as well as oil and gas companies, for having no basis under international law on account of the extra-territorial application of the jurisdiction of the United States.[72] The Senate bill was technically illegal under international law, and it had not come into force within the United States. The requirement was for it to be reconciled with Gilman's bill in the House. However, Gilman's bill was diplomatically uncomfortable for the White House as it was more comprehensive than the modified D'Amato bill. Specifically speaking, Gilman's legislation called for sanctions on any entity that engaged in trade with Iran, which would understandably have had diplomatic repercussions for the United States internationally.

The administration strongly opposed Gilman's bill in Congressional hearings, but ultimately reached a compromise that allowed the bill to proceed with the support of the White House. The main compromises entailed Libya being essentially treated differently to Iran, as sanctions were to be *mandatory* for contraventions of UN resolutions and were only *optional* for investment in the oil and gas sectors.

With the passage to the Senate of the bill on 26 June 1996 for final approval, Senator Kennedy reintroduced an amendment that required the lifting of the distinction within the bill in applying differential sanctions on the two countries. Whilst this was opposed by AIPAC, it was the pressure of the Pan Am Flight 103 victims' families on the Senate that allowed the bill, now jointly proposed by D'Amato and Kennedy, to be passed on 16 July 1996.

With the Kennedy amendment, there was a requirement to reconcile the two bills. This unexpectedly occurred as a direct consequence of the crash of TWA Flight 800 over Long Island on 17 July 1996. The initial view that it may have been a result of a terrorist attack resulted in a loss of opposition to the bill within the House.[73] The unanimous adoption of the House bill paved the way for it to be signed into law by Clinton.

Therefore, with a Republican-controlled Congress, Congressional pressure and domestic political forces on the executive and the wider Democrat party, Clinton was forced to alter his policy position towards Iran. Although the application of prohibitive unilateral sanctions was entirely commensurate with the rubric of the dual containment strategy, the extra-territorial sanctioning of entities trading with Iran was not. Moreover, Congressional legislation, which strengthened sanctions against Iran, was arguably not commensurate under the rubric of the dual containment strategy. Specifically speaking, with Congress legislating foreign policy, Clinton's flexibility in conducting diplomacy with Iran to achieve the strategic objective of reconciliation was very much thwarted. Moreover, given the priority of the Clinton administration to maintain the multilateral sanctions-based policy towards Iraq, the Congressional legislation very much usurped the foreign policy prerogative of the executive and ultimately served to hamper the implementation of the overall dual containment policy strategy.

Dual Track Diplomacy: Beyond Containment

US policy towards Iran during the first Clinton administration had been clearly dominated by Congressional legislation as previously discussed.

This had restricted the scope of options available to the White House and had effectively set the foreign policy agenda. Moreover, structural impediments within Iran were further active barriers towards any efforts at a rapprochement.[74] However, in May 1997, the political context in Iran changed as Mohammad Khatami, a self-declared reformer whose record was not tainted with hostile rhetoric towards the United States, was elected President. Khatami's election came as a surprise to many international observers and was dubbed the Second Khordad Movement after the date of his election.

In an interview with CNN in January 1998 Khatami presented a more conciliatory tone towards the United States. He drew parallels between the United States and Iran's revolutionary movement towards independence and, most notably, he called for a "dialogue of civilizations".[75] He expressed his "respect for the great American people"[76] and his desire for relations to be built on a cultural exchange involving scholars, tourists, journalists and artisans, etc. Although it was a notable change in rhetoric, the substance of Khatami's remarks received a cautious response as some of these exchanges had already been occurring:

> American tourists go to Iran, although the State Department warns
> them that it is unwise, and many Iranians visit the U.S. and even
> attend American universities. Academics from both sides fly back
> and forth to give lectures and take part in conferences. There is no
> sign such exchanges have warmed the icy political climate much.[77]

Nevertheless, Khatami highlighted that "[o]ne of the major flaws in the U.S. foreign policy . . . is that they continue to live with cold war mentality and try to create a perceived enemy". He saw the D'Amato legislation as epitomising this framework of thinking. Although Khatami's remarks were effectively a departure in official Iranian rhetoric towards the United States, in terms of US foreign policy Iran's continued opposition towards the Arab–Israeli peace process, along with other contextual issues, prevented any substantive alteration in US foreign policy.

According to former Secretary of State Madeleine Albright, the opportunity for a shift in US foreign policy towards Iran did indeed occur in January 1998. However this was not as a result of Khatami's conciliatory remarks in the CNN interview but rather as a result of a substantive change in Iran's policy towards the Arab–Israeli peace process. Yasser Arafat had received a letter from Khatami which "backed Palestinian participation in the Middle East peace process, acknowledged Israel's legitimacy, and discussed the possibility of a region-wide peace if the Palestinians were allowed to establish a state on the West Bank and Gaza".[78] Also, Khatami publicly denounced terrorism and the killing of Israeli citizens, which was a significant move towards accommodating the demands of the United States. The overall situational context leading to a change in US foreign policy was not, however, just limited to Iran's conciliatory overtures towards the United States and policy change towards the peace process. Albright commented:

> Iran's record in the war against drugs has greatly improved – at least within its own borders – and it has received high marks from the UN for its treatment of more than two million Iraqi and Afghan refugees. Iran is also participating in diplomatic efforts to bring peace and stability to Afghanistan and is making a welcome effort to improve relations with Saudi Arabia and other neighbors in the Gulf.[79]

Albright concluded that given this alteration in policy, "Iran no longer belonged in the same category as Iraq",[80] and consequently "[t]he time was ripe to move beyond dual containment".[81]

The US response to Iran's policy changes under Khatami was a cautious welcome, but significant obstacles towards reconciliation remained. Albright commented that:

> We view these developments with interest, both with regard to the possibility of Iran assuming its rightful place in the world community, and the chance for better bilateral ties. However, these hopes must be balanced against the reality that Iran's support for terrorism has not yet ceased; serious violations of human rights persist; and its efforts to develop long-range missiles and to acquire nuclear weapons continue. The United States opposes, and will continue to oppose, any country selling or transferring to Iran materials and technologies that could be used to develop long-range missiles or weapons of mass destruction. Similarly, we oppose Iranian efforts to sponsor terror. Accordingly, our economic policies, including with respect to the export pipelines for Caspian oil and gas, remain unchanged.[82]

Whilst a positive move towards resolving substantive differences had occurred, the contextual divide was, nevertheless, unlikely to lead to a period of détente in any real sense. Indeed, a shift in US policy could not have realistically occurred without Iran ending its policies – most notably its alleged support for terrorist groups – which placed pressure on the foreign policy agenda from special interest groups and from within Congress. Also it appears that there were structural obstacles within Iran which prevented a more substantive alteration of its own foreign policies,[83] in addition to the perceived need for a moderation of US policies, the lack of which provided legitimacy for Iran's provocative stance. Indeed, in late 1998, Khatami's reformist Second Khordad Movement suffered a government clampdown which further weakened their influence against the conservative clerics.[84]

The options available for US diplomacy were few: given the challenges Khatami was facing from his conservative opponents, any public backing for him from Washington would have probably caused the reformist movement more harm than good. Although a significant relaxation of US sanctions policy would potentially have bolstered Khatami's position, wider contextual issues relating to Iran's foreign policies made this an unrealistic foreign policy choice for the United States, in spite of the Clinton administration being in its final years of its second term of office. These issues included:

1. The unresolved issue of whether Iran was covertly pursuing a nuclear weapons programme in contravention of its international obligations;
2. Iran's implication in an attack on US forces stationed in Khobar Towers, Saudi Arabia, in June 1996;
3. Iran had arrested thirteen Jewish individuals and several Muslims on the charge of espionage. Despite EU and UN pressure on Tehran, twelve were imprisoned. This resulted in domestic political pressures within Congress which rejected the engagement approach;
4. Without a substantive change in Iran's policies that were provocative to the United States and Israel, a significant relaxation in US sanctions policies would have been politically unworkable for the White House given the likely response within Congress.

Despite these contextual obstacles on the options available to it, the Clinton administration made a second attempt at improving relations following the Iranian February 2000 elections, in which Khatami's supporters gained control of the parliament. Again, it was the political situation in Iran which prompted the administration to make political overtures at providing concessions towards the Islamic Republic to indirectly bolster the reformist movement. The United States lifted its import restrictions on "Iran's principal non-oil exports – carpets, pistachios, dried fruit, and caviar. Whilst these are considered luxury items in the United States, their production and marketing in Iran are associated with the middle class, much of which had voted for Khatami."[85]

According to Albright, the Iranian reaction to the relaxation of US sanctions was mixed despite the positive response from the EU and domestically within the United States.[86] However, the US concessions did not go far enough to overcome the structural impediments facing the reformers within Iran. The context which created the policy quagmire is usefully summarised by Albright:

> The Clinton administration's policy towards Iran was calibrated appropriately. We could have achieved a breakthrough only by abandoning our principals and interests in non-proliferation, terrorism, and the Middle East, far too high a price. We could have avoided the charge that we were too soft on Iran by ignoring the reform movement entirely, but that would have left us isolated internationally and provided no incentive for Iran to change further.[87]

Therefore, at the end of the Clinton administration, the prospects for achieving a normalisation of relations with Iran were remote. US policies in the Middle East, such as its support for Israel, military presence and restrictive sanctions policy, presented clear political obstacles for any change in Iranian foreign policy towards meeting the benchmark required for meaningful dialogue to take place.

Assessing Clinton's Foreign Policy towards Iran
What can be discerned from the above analysis is that US policy towards Iran during the time period 1993–2001 can be divided into two distinct phases determined by the change in foreign policy. These two distinct phases are separated by the election of President Mohammad Khatami in 1997.

The above analysis indicates that US foreign policy towards

Iran 1993–1997 was primarily the product of domestic structures outside the traditional government bureaucracy. Although the executive and the government bureaucracy had a clear foreign policy agenda, the international context, as determined on a domestic level by Iran's foreign policy,[88] resulted in a sustained effort on behalf of special interest groups on Congress to direct the foreign policy agenda. Interestingly, traditional foreign policy analysis concentrates on the role of the government bureaucracy, or executive, as the principal determining force in foreign policy. Indeed, the construction of the foreign policy of the United States is constitutionally enshrined as being the prerogative of the executive. However, the special nature of the international context, coupled with the highly mobilised and privileged position the Jewish and pro-Israeli lobbies occupied, resulted in an exceptional application of influence onto the legislative branch of the American government.

The significance of this situation was twofold: firstly, the prerogative of the President to conduct foreign policy was subjugated; secondly, special interest groups, which traditional foreign policy analysis fails to fully account for, actually determined the course of US foreign policy. Although a strict application of sanctions on Iran was commensurate with the containment policy, the extra-territorial application of sanctions was not.

The second phase of US policy towards Iran during the Clinton Presidency occurred after a change in the domestic political situation in Iran which, in turn, resulted in a change in Iran's foreign policy. Despite the election of Mohamed Khatami and the subsequent alteration in Iran's foreign policy, it did not alter to a level sufficient for meaningful dialogue and a détente to occur. Whilst the reason for the lack of substantive changes to Iran's own foreign policy in order to enable reconciliation is a moot point, the available evidence underlines the fact that for the United States, a policy of engagement faced a number of obstacles. Instructively, the evidence indicates that a policy shift towards engagement would overlook the structural impediments within the United States as highlighted in this chapter. Crucially, this prevented a policy of engagement occurring *before* a satisfactory change in Iran's foreign policy had occurred. Finally, the above analysis indicates that a complex range of structural factors and special interests prevented any scope for meaningful diplomacy in the absence of a substantive change in Iran's foreign policy.

NOTES

1 Zbigniew Brzezinski, et al., *Iran: Time for a New Approach* (Washington D.C.: Council on Foreign Relations, 2004), 9.
2 Qtd in Robert Snyder, *The United States and Iran: Analysing the Structural Impediments to a Rapprochement* (Abu Dhabi: Emirates Center for Strategic Studies and Research, 2001) 11.
3 Ibid. 10–25.
4 Nigel Bowles, "The Government and Politics of the United States", *Comparative Government and Politics.* (Basingstoke: Macmillan, 1993) 227.
5 Ibid.
6 Ibid. 227.
7 William J. Clinton, *My Life* (New York: Knopf, 2004) 294.
8 Raymond Tanter, *Rogue Regimes: Terrorism and Proliferation* (Basingstoke: Macmillan, 1999) 55–57.
9 Ibid. 56.
10 The Czech Republic and Poland were also countries that traded arms with Iran.
11 Kenneth Katzman, "Iran: Arms and Technology Acquisitions", *CRS Report for Congress*, (97–474F), Washington, D.C.: CRS, Congress, 22 Jun. 1998, 6pp. 01/04/03 <http://www.globalsecurity.org/wmd/library/report/crs/97-474.htm>.
12 The Gulf Cooperation Council comprises: Oman, Saudi Arabia, UAE, Bahrain, Qatar and Kuwait.
13 Katzman, "Iran: Arms and Technology Acquisitions".
14 The Clinton–Yeltsin summits were held in: Vancouver, 1993; Washington D.C. 1994; and Moscow 1995.
15 The Waasenaar Agreement is the successor to the Coordinating Committee for Multilateral Export Controls.
16 Clinton, *My Life* 654–56.
17 John Calabrese, "China and the Persian Gulf: Energy and Security", *Middle East Journal* 52.2 (1998): 265.
18 For further details on Iran's procurement of conventional weapons from China see Kenneth Katzman, "Iran: Military Relations with China," *CRS Report for Congress*, (96–572), Washington, D.C.: CRS, Congress, 26 Jun. 1996, 13pp.
19 Katzman, "Iran: Arms and Technology Acquisitions".
20 For further details on Iran's procurement of conventional weapons from North Korea see Kenneth Katzman and Rinn-Sup Shinn, "North Korea: Military Relations with the Middle", *CRS Report for Congress*, (95-754F), Washington, D.C.: CRS, Congress, 23 Jun. 1994, 19pp.
21 For a detailed study on Iran's ballistic missile programme see Andrew Feickert, "Iran's Ballistic Missile Program", *CRS Report for Congress*, (RS21548), Washington, D.C.: CRS, Congress, 23 Aug. 2004, 6pp. 12/02/05 <http://fpc.state.gov/documents/organization/39332.pdf>.
22 John Chipman, *The Military Balance*, ed. Christopher Langton, vol. 2003–2004 (Oxford: Oxford University Press, 2003) 102–03.
23 Thomas W. Lippman, "Israel Presses U.S. To Sanction Russian Missile Firms Aiding Iran", *Washington Post* 25 Sept. 1997: A31.

24 Hossein Alikhani, *Sanctioning Iran: Anatomy of a Failed Policy* (London: I.B. Tauris, 2000) 163.
25 Ibid. 63.
26 Ibid. 164.
27 The Iran–Iraq Non-Proliferation Act of 1992.
28 Alikhani, *Sanctioning Iran* 164.
29 Ibid. 164.
30 Ibid. 165.
31 Iraq informed the UN that it would no longer permit UNSCOM fixed-wing aircraft to operate within Iraq on 7 Jan. 1993.
32 Iraq began positioning anti-aircraft missiles in the demilitarised zone on 27 Dec. 1992.
33 Yoshio Hatano, "Situation between Iraq and Kuwait", Statement by UN Security Council President Hatano, New York: 8 Jan. 1993. 12/08/02 <http://dosfan.lib.uic.edu/ERC/briefing/dispatch/1993/html/Dispatchv4no03.html >.
34 Coalition air strikes commenced on 13 Jan. 1993.
35 Thomas Friedman, "Clinton's Warning to Saddam: I'm Going to Judge You by Your Behaviour", *International Herald Tribune* 15 Jan. 1993: 2.
36 George Stephanopoulos, *All Too Human: A Political Education* (London: Hutchinson, 1999) 157–59; also see Leslie Gelb, "A Reformed Iraq to Offset Iran? Forget It", *International Herald Tribune* 18 Jan. 1993: 2.
37 William J. Clinton, *Public Papers of the Presidents of the United States 1993: William J. Clinton (Bk. 1)*, Washington, D.C.: GPO, 1993. 05/11/04 <http://frwebgate.access.gpo.gov/cgi-bin/getdoc.cgi?dbname=1993_public_papers_vol1_misc&docid=f:pap_pre.htm#1993v1contents>.
38 Martin Indyk, "The Clinton Administration's Approach to the Middle East", Address to the Soref Symposium, Washington, D.C.: Washington Institute for Near East Policy, 18 May 1993. 4pp. 12/07/03 <http://www.washingtoninstitute.org/pubs/soref/indyk.htm >.
39 David W. Lesch, *The Middle East and the United States: A Historical and Political Reassessment* (Oxford: Westview, 1996) 356–58.
40 Anthony Lake, "Confronting Backlash States", *Foreign Affairs* 73.2 (1994): 48.
41 Ibid.
42 Ellen Laipson, et al., "Symposium: US Policy Towards Iran: From Containment to Relentless Persuit", *Middle East Policy* 4.Sep (1995): 2.
43 Lake, "Confronting Backlash States" 50.
44 Anonymous [George Kennan], "The Sources of Soviet Conduct", *Foreign Affairs* 25.4 (1947): 852–68.
45 Henry Kissinger, *Diplomacy*, (New York: Touchstone, 1995) 471.
46 Ibid. 471–75.
47 Exceptionalism in US foreign policy refers to the widely held belief that the values which underpin American society are *universal* values. This interpretation has a direct bearing on US diplomacy in that in the pursuit of US national interests, other nations will benefit from such values being imparted to them.
48 United States, House. Foreign Affairs Committee. Subcommittee on Europe and the Middle East, *Developments in the Middle East*, 105th Cong., 2nd Sess. (Washington, D.C.: GPO, 01 Mar. 1994).
49 Ibid.

50 American Israeli Public Affairs Committee, *Comprehensive US Sanctions against Iran: A Plan for Action* (Washington D.C.: AIPAC, 1994) 1–72.
51 Alikhani, *Sanctioning Iran* 178
52 Bowles, "The Government and Politics of the United States" 228.
53 United States, Senate, *Comprehensive Iran Sanctions Act*, 104th Cong., 2nd Sess. (Washington D.C.: GPO, 25 Jan. 1995) 5pp. 12/04/04 <http://thomas.loc. gov/cgi-bin/query/z?c104:S.277.IS:>.
54 American Israeli Public Affairs Committee, *Comprehensive US Sanctions against Iran* 1–72.
55 United States, *Comprehensive Iran Sanctions Act*.
56 Elaine Sciolino, "Iranian Leader Says US Move on Oil Deal Wrecked Chances to Improve Ties", *New York Times* 16 May 1995: A5.
57 Alikhani, *Sanctioning Iran* 182.
58 United States, Department of State, "Daily Press Briefing", Conoco Oil Agreement, Washington, D.C.: GPO, 7 Mar. 1995. 12pp. 12/09/03 <http:// dosfan.lib.uic.edu/ERC/briefing/daily_briefings/1995/9503/950307db.html>.
59 Department of Defence, *United States Security Strategy for the Middle East* (Washington, D.C.: GPO, 3 May 1995) 48.
60 Alikhani, *Sanctioning Iran* 186.
61 Gary Sick, "How Not to Make Iran Policy", *MEES* 38.31 (1995): D5.
62 Alikhani, *Sanctioning Iran* 189.
63 Clinton, *Public Papers of the Presidents of the United States 1994: William J. Clinton (Bk. 1)*, 1054.
64 Thomas W. Lippman, "Hill Races White House to Get Tough with Iran", *Washington Post* 2 Apr 1995: A5.
65 Clinton, *Public Papers of the Presidents of the United States 1994: William J. Clinton (Bk. 1)*, 654.
66 Ibid.
67 United States, Senate, *Iran Oil Sanctions Act Report*, 104th Cong., 1st Sess. (Washington, D.C.: GPO, 15 Dec. 1995) 9pp. 12/03/03 <http://thomas.loc. gov/cgi-bin/cpquery/T?&report=sr187&dbname=cp104&>.
68 Ibid.
69 United States, Senate, *Iran Oil Sanctions Act Report*.
70 Alikhani, *Sanctioning Iran* 295.
71 Ibid.
72 Anonymous, "A Review of US Unilateral Sanctions against Iran", *Middle East Economic Survey* 45.34 (2002).
73 Alikhani, *Sanctioning Iran* 310.
74 Robert Snyder, *The United States and Iran: Analysing the Structural Impediments to a Rapprochement*, The Emirates Occasional Paper, vol. 32 (Abu Dhabi: Emirates Center for Strategic Studies and Research, 2001) 10–19.
75 Christiane Amanpour, "Transcript of Interview with Iranian President Mohammad Khatami", *CNN Online* 7 Jan. 1998, 12/07/04 <http://www.cnn. com/WORLD/9801/07/iran/interview.html>.
76 Ibid.
77 Bruce W. Nelan, "New Day Coming?" *Time* Jan. 19 1998: 4–5.
78 Madeleine Albright and William Woodward, *Madam Secretary: A Memoir* (London: Macmillan, 2003).

79 Madeleine Albright, "Albright Speech 6/17/98", Remarks at 1998 Asia Society Dinner Waldorf-Astoria Hotel New York, New York: GPO, 18 Jun. 1998. 4pp. 13/06/04 <http://www.aghayan.com/alb061798.htm>.
80 Albright and Woodward, *Madam Secretary* 320–22.
81 Ibid.
82 Albright, "Albright Speech 6/17/98".
83 Richard A. Roth, et al., "U.S. Policy Towards Iran: Time for a Change?" *Middle East Policy* 3.1 (2001): 4–8.
84 Albright and Woodward, *Madam Secretary* 323.
85 Ibid. 324.
86 Ibid.
87 Ibid.
88 Roth, et al., "U.S. Policy Towards Iran: Time for a Change?" 11–13.

5

The Clinton Years and Iraq:
Strategic Regime Change

"We recognize this area as vital to US interests and we will behave, with others, multilaterally when we can and unilaterally when we must."

Madeleine Albright
October 1994

Following the liberation of Kuwait in 1991, President George H. W. Bush used the unprecedented agreement within the international community towards Iraq to formulate a post-war sanctions and inspections mandate through the United Nations. Washington's post-liberation agenda was positioned on a multilateral effort towards ensuring Iraq did not possess unconventional weapons. But crucially, the key by-product of this for the US was that it was seen to provide Persian Gulf security. The Bush administration's policy had been formulated in the context of widespread uprisings within Iraq that followed the liberation of Kuwait.[1] Indeed, it is widely known that there was high confidence in the administration and in many policy circles that Saddam would be overthrown by a national revolutionary civil uprising or through an internal military *coup d'état*. Therefore, a direct military invasion of Iraq was not seen as necessary given the widely held belief that Saddam's regime was in its dying days. For the Bush administration, resorting to the United Nations allowed Iraq to be multilaterally contained *until* regime change actually occurred. Therefore, whilst the strategic objective was to achieve regime change, the tactics employed were geared towards nullifying the threat posed by Iraq during this period.[2]

The adoption of UNSCR 687 in April 1991, which was ultimately enforceable under Chapter VII of the UN Charter, placed obligations on Iraq to *verifiably* dismantle its chemical, biological and nuclear programmes, in addition to any ballistic missiles and related components with a range greater than one hundred and fifty kilometres. Also, in accordance with the US regional security agenda, UNSCR 687 established an embargo on military procurement and laid the basis for sanctions on imports and exports in order to pay for damages incurred following the invasion and occupation of Kuwait. With the Iraqi threat to Persian Gulf security being curtailed through a multilateral containment strategy by the Bush administration, the key issue was how to prevent Iranian hegemony within this context.

The response in Congress to these pressures, coupled with both the newly emerging post-Cold War strategic arena and the geopolitical context in the Persian Gulf, resulted in the Iran–Iraq Arms Non-Proliferation Act of 1992. That is to say that Congress considered the pressures, and additional domestic political considerations, then applied pressure on the Bush administration. The presidency was forced by Congress to implement a restrictive unilateral sanctions policy towards Iran. Therefore, the over-arching nature of the Bush administration's policy towards Persian Gulf security, which Clinton inherited in 1993, was the dual characteristic of a multilateral containment of Iraq through the United Nations, and a unilateral sanctions-based policy towards Iran.·

Clinton's Iraq Policy 1993–2001

For the US, the imposition of sanctions brought about the by-product of a contained and controlled Iraq. A multilaterally contained Iraq thus catered for the US objective of ensuring the security and a balance of power within the vital area of the Persian Gulf. Nevertheless, it is important to recognise that the reason why sanctions were supported by the international community was to compel Iraq to comply with its obligations: this is in contrast with the underlying US objective of ensuring Persian Gulf security through a contained and controlled Iraq.

The *official policy* of the Clinton administration towards Iraq was, up until 1998, for a continuation of sanctions until a complete compliance with UN resolutions had been achieved. Following Iraq's full compliance with UN resolutions, a normalisation of relations would be possible. Comparatively, in the previous Bush administration, the US position towards Iraq differed slightly in that the emphasis was on the continuation of sanctions until Saddam was displaced from power, rather than a simple compliance with UN resolutions.[3] For the Clinton administration, Lake commented that "we will want to be satisfied that any successor [Iraqi] government complies fully with all UN resolutions".[4] This placed the official objective clearly on Iraqi compliance with UN resolutions, rather than regime change per se. However, from the outset of his term of office in 1993, Clinton made it clear that he could not "conceive of the United States ever having any kind of normal relationship with Iraq as long as Saddam Hussein is there".[5] This makes the strategic priority in his foreign policy very much open to question: was Clinton's overall strategic object-ive regime change or reconciliation following Iraq's full compliance with UN resolutions? The two strategic objectives are not compatible. With this in mind, the following section will provide analysis of US foreign policy towards Iraq and aims to separate the tactical from the strategic in order to provide a comprehensive understanding of US foreign policy towards Iraq. It will begin with a discussion of the tactical multilateral containment before moving on to the strategic element of regime change. The tactical policy will necessarily focus on the international context and the UN inspections mandate upon which US policy rested.

Tactical Policy: Multilateral Containment

Following the liberation of Kuwait by coalition forces,[6] Iraq was subject to stringent post-war obligations under UNSCR 687.[7] Specifically speak-ing, UNSCR 687 called on Iraq to *verifiably* render harmless all of its "chemical and biological weapons and all stocks of agents and all related subsystems and components and all research, development, support and manufacturing facilities".[8] Iraq was viewed as having a well-established offensive surface-to-surface missile programme: the test flight of the upgraded 'Scud B' missile, with a range of more than six hundred kilo-metres, posed a clear threat to the security of the states in the Persian Gulf.[9] UNSCR 687 stated that Iraq's "ballistic missiles with a range greater than one hundred and fifty kilometres and related major parts, and repair and production facilities" were to be rendered harmless.[10]

UNSCR 687 laid the basis for on-site inspections within Iraq by a United Nations Special Commission to verify compliance with these issues. Also, UNSCR 687 placed obligations on Iraq to comply with its commitments under the Treaty on the Non-Proliferation of Nuclear Weapons and laid the basis for Iraq to verifiably render harmless its nuclear weapons programme under the supervision of the IAEA (International Atomic Energy Agency) in conjunction with UNSCOM.[11]

Following the Iraqi invasion of Kuwait, President George H. W.

Bush declared a national emergency with respect to Iraq, through Executive Order No. 12722 on 2 August 1990: this blocked all Iraqi assets within the United States and placed restrictions on the importation and exportation of goods and services between the two countries. Subsequent Executive Orders Nos. 12724 and 12817 were implemented by the Bush administration to align US policy with UN Security Council Resolutions 661 and 778 respectively. With the Bush administration having based its policies on the prediction that Saddam would be internally ousted from power following the *intifadah* in 1991, Washington was left with little choice but to adopt a containment policy through supporting UN resolutions until it had been achieved.[12] As already highlighted, this was adopted on the premise that it would ensure both Persian Gulf security, and weaken Saddam Hussein's regime, with the ultimate objective of bringing about the conditions for an internal regime change.[13] In essence, the Bush administration saw its support of sanctions as a tactical means of ensuring Persian Gulf security until this strategic objective had been achieved.

UNSCR 699 and 715 provided the mandate for UNSCOM and the IAEA to conduct continual on-site inspections within Iraq in order to search and render harmless any prohibited materials.[14] Despite this being mandated by the United Nations, Iraq demonstrated little intention of allowing its unconventional weapons to be destroyed by the IAEA and the UN Special Commission. Saddam created a covert Concealment Operations Committee, which was headed by his son Qusayy, in order to hide his WMD programmes and stockpiles from the inspectors. Despite Iraqi attempts to inhibit the inspections process and conceal its prohibited nuclear programmes, in 1991 the IAEA inspection team successfully uncovered three uranium enrichment programmes: one using electromagnetic isotope separation technology; a second programme using centrifuge technology; and a third programme using chemical methods.[15] In addition to this, Iraq was found to be experimenting with a laboratory-scale plutonium separation technique. Following these discoveries, in July 1991 the sixth IAEA inspection uncovered further proof of a nuclear programme that included several kilograms of highly enriched uranium and approximately 400 tons of natural uranium.[16]

The findings of the IAEA inspectors alarmed the international community as Iraq's nuclear programme was more advanced than commonly thought. The discoveries made by the inspectors on Iraq's biological and chemical weapons programmes compounded this concern.[17] Following the uncovering by UNSCOM and the IAEA of details of Iraq's nuclear and biological weapons programme in 1992, Iraq began to cooperate and disclosed to the inspectors details on its chemical and nuclear stockpiles, as well as admitting that it had a *defensive* biological programme. Although Iraq did make these declarations on its weapons stockpiles, its cooperation was consistently brought into question on numerous levels, especially given that the inspectors would make discoveries that were not listed in Iraq's declaration to the Security Council.

With the onset of the Clinton administration and the confirmation of the containment policy in May 1993, US policy towards Iraq continued to rest clearly on the effectiveness of the implementation of UN Security Council resolutions. The weapons inspections process continued to be highly problematic with specific regard to Iraq's obligation to give a full, final and complete declaration on its weapons programmes, as prohibited by UNSCR 687 and required by UNSCR 707.[18] Iraq's declarations were consistently found to be insufficiently detailed and incomplete by UNSCOM.[19] In addition to failing to provide a full, final and complete declaration of its prohibited weapons, UNSCOM and the IAEA found Iraq to be carrying out "a continuing pattern of obstruction and intimidation" towards its mandate.[20] According to UN reports, up until 1995, there were numerous instances of Iraqi obstruction towards inspectors and it has been suggested that the obstruction was "directed by the highest levels of the Iraqi government and by the Office of the Presidential Palace (OPP) and personnel in Saddam's private Diwan (office)".[21]

Saddam's defiance also extended to provoking a potential military engagement with the United States in October 1994 after his deployment of ground forces near the Kuwaiti border. Saddam apparently wanted to provoke a crisis with the United States to have the UN sanctions lifted. Clinton's response, however, was to deploy 170 aircraft and 6,500 personnel to Riyadh under the rubric of Operation Vigilant Warrior. It is worthy of note that Clinton retained 120 aircraft and 5,000 personnel as a permanent military deployment in order to deter future transgressions by Iraq, thus placing a greater degree of pressure on Baghdad to comply.

However, despite Iraq's persistent obstruction and provocations, by 1995 the UN inspection process had yielded positive results. UNSCOM and the IAEA had severely degraded Iraq's WMD programmes, which involved the destruction of "over 480,000 litres of chemical warfare agents, over 28,000 chemical munitions and nearly 1,800,000 litres, over

1,040,000 kilograms and 648 barrels, of some 45 different precursor chemicals for the production of chemical warfare agents".[22]

The official view of the United States was that the IAEA had "effectively disbanded the Iraqi nuclear weapons programme at least for the near term".[23] However, questions remained as Iraq was unable to account for its stockpiles of *precursor* ingredients for the production of chemical weapons. Most notably, Iraq was unable to account for precursor chemicals required for the production of 200–250 tons of the advanced nerve agent VX.[24] Therefore, although Iraq was failing to fully comply with the inspectors, the UN and the IAEA had achieved a great deal by destroying sizeable amounts of Iraq's chemical arsenal, dismantling its nuclear programme and destroying its declared defensive biological weapons programme.

Post-1995 Inspection Process

Although by 1995 UNSCOM and the IAEA were reasonably satisfied that they had rendered harmless the majority of Iraq's prohibited weapons and were ready to implement the long-term monitoring phase,[25] it was with the defection to Jordan of Lt. General Hussain Kamal Hassan al-Majeed and Lt. Colonel Saddam Kamal Hassan al-Majeed that a new phase in the weapons inspections process was ushered in.[26] Hussain Kamal al-Majeed was the former Minister of Industry and Military Industrialisation in Iraq and was one of Saddam Hussein's inner circle. The defection was prompted by Saddam's son Udayy issuing threats against Hussain Kamal and his family.[27] As Hussain Kamal was intimately involved in a deception of UNSCOM and the IAEA by way of a covert illicit weapons programme, it was clear to the Iraqi regime that information on this would be provided to UNSCOM and the IAEA. The Iraqi government thus opted to pre-empt any possible information Hussain Kamal would give the Special Commission by providing documentation pertaining to its covert illicit weapons programme to the IAEA. Baghdad provided "documentary material, which included technical records, drawings, suppliers catalogues and extracts from scientific and technical publications [that] amounted to some 680,000 pages, of which some 80% related to Iraq's past nuclear programme".[28]

These new declarations showed that Baghdad's prohibited weapons programmes were more advanced than previously thought, especially with regard to the development of the advanced VX nerve agent.[29] Also, by October 1995, the Special Commission had concluded that Iraq had significantly misled UNSCOM and the IAEA over the issue of prohibited missile technology:

> Iraq has been misleading the Commission by withholding information that, before the Gulf war, it had secretly produced Scud-type missile engines and carried out research and development on a variety of projects on missiles of prohibited ranges. Furthermore, Iraq's efforts to conceal its biological weapons programme, its chemical missile warhead flight tests and work on the development of a missile for the delivery of a nuclear device led it to provide incorrect information concerning certain of its missile activities. [30]

In terms of Iraq's weapons programme, the most alarming aspect of the new revelations was that Iraq had a secret, *offensive* biological warfare programme and a covert chemical weapons programme that included the production of the advanced VX nerve agent on an industrial scale.[31] According to UNSCOM, Iraq declared it had produced sizeable quantities of the chemical precursors exclusive to the development of VX and that it possessed sufficient amounts to produce 90 tons of VX.[32] It was noted at the United Nations that:

> In the chemical weapons area, the Special Commission's investigations have led to disclosure of activities [aimed] at the acquisition of a considerable capability for the production of the advanced nerve agent VX. Whether Iraq still keeps precursors in storage for immediate VX use has not been fully clarified.[33]

These damning revelations about Iraq's undisclosed illicit weapons programmes, in addition to a continuation of the policy of non-cooperation with the UN inspectors, demonstrated that Iraq was failing to comply with its obligations which gave it little diplomatic credibility in the face of its previous false declarations.

The response at the UN was predictable and Iraq's failure to comply with its obligations was greeted with condemnation. This mood in the UN was further exacerbated by the seizure of advanced missile components destined for Iraq via Jordan in 1995.[34] This showed that the provisions of UNSCR 687, paragraph 20, which placed control on Iraqi imports, was insufficient in the face of a defiant Iraq. The response at the United Nations was the unanimous adoption of UNSCR 1051,[35] which strengthened the import and export controls on Iraq by requiring all imports to Iraq to be declared and ultimately accounted for by Iraq. Despite the efforts at the United Nations to further strengthen the sanctions mandate, Iraq was found by UNSCOM to be continuing in a persistent and deliberate obstruction of the inspections process.[36] This pattern of obstructing the mandate of UNSCOM and the IAEA continued throughout 1996–1998 and ultimately saw Iraq being found in breach of its obligations by a series of UN Security Council resolutions.[37]

The Dilemma of Verifiability

The defection of Lt. General Hussain Kamal Hassan al-Majeed was a turning point in Iraq's situation vis-à-vis the UN, and also demonstrated to the United States that Iraq had little intention of complying with UN resolutions. UNSCOM recognised in a report to the Security Council in January 1999 that "the overall period of the Commission's disarmament work must be divided into two parts, separated by the events following the departure from Iraq, in August 1995, of Lt. General Hussain Kamal".[38]

In Hussain Kamal's testimony to the IAEA, he was categorical that Iraq did indeed have nuclear, chemical and biological weapons programmes that dated back to the Iran–Iraq War. Moreover, he stated that previous declarations given by Iraq were flawed as its biological and chemical weapons programmes, particularly with regard to the VX nerve agent, were more advanced than previously known by the UN. His statement, however, was enlightening in that by August 1995 he said he personally ordered the unilateral destruction of all of the prohibited weapons, precursor chemicals and missile components, in order to have the sanctions on Iraq lifted. In his testimony to the IAEA, Hussain Kamal stated "I ordered the destruction of all weapons. All weapons – biological, chemical, missile, nuclear were destroyed".[39] He commented: "I made the decision to disclose everything so that Iraq could return to normal".[40] He went on to confirm that the destruction of the prohibited weapons took place "after visits of inspection teams", who were "very effective in Iraq".[41]

The significance of Hussain Kamal's testimony cannot be underestimated as any assessment of its truthfulness would impinge on the maintenance of the US containment policy through multilateral sanctions: without the possession of unconventional weapons, the official justification for multilateral sanctions would have been nullified. Given the scope of the new information he provided to the IAEA, the detrimental impact it had on Iraq's diplomatic credibility, and the fact that Hussain Kamal was executed upon his return to Iraq after falsely being promised a pardon by Saddam, it seems reasonable to conclude that he was being truthful. However, if Iraq had indeed destroyed all of its weapons and any trace of them, why was it continuing to persist in an obstruction of the UN Special Commission if it had nothing to hide? Even if the international community accepted Hussain Kamal's testimony that Iraq had unilaterally destroyed all its prohibited weapons, there remained the key problem of *verifiability* for a complete compliance with UN resolutions. The paradox was thus how could Iraq prove to the UN Special Commission and the international community that it had destroyed its stockpiles, listed in official Iraqi documents, when it had concealed the destruction process and any evidence of it having taken place?

Consequently, there was a possibility that Iraq possessed fewer, or indeed none, of the prohibited weapons and technologies post-1995 that it had failed to account for. In addition to this issue, there was the matter of whether Iraq's unaccounted-for weapons actually still posed a threat. The majority of chemical and biological weapons were a relic of the Iran–Iraq War: many of those that had been weaponised would have been defunct anyway as the chemical weapons Iraq was known to possess, such as the nerve agents sarin and tabun, have a limited shelf life of five years if stored in *ideal conditions*. The advanced nerve agent VX has only a slightly longer shelf life. Biological weapons also suffer from the same problem: even if stored in ideal conditions, botulinum and liquid anthrax have a shelf life of three to four years.

A further factor, which warranted consideration, was that during the 1991 conflict a number of the weapons would have conceivably been destroyed in the bombing campaign. Indeed, Iraq's chemical weapon site at al-Muthanna was completely destroyed, along with weapons stored there. It was also likely that other weapon stores were destroyed in the intensive bombing campaign across Iraq in 1991.

Overall, it seems reasonable to conclude that even if the prohibited weapons had not been unilaterally destroyed as indicated by Hussain Kamal, it was unrealistic to take the position that Iraq would have been able to verify the destruction of *all* its weapons and related components following the 1991 bombing campaign. Moreover, by 1995, virtually all remaining weapons would likely have been past their shelf life thus rendering them defunct anyway. The threat Iraq potentially posed was therefore more to do with its capacity to produce new weapons from *unaccounted-for precursor ingredients*. But even when considering potential production from precursor ingredients, it is open to question how effectively an estimate could take into account wastage during production. Therefore, it was reasonable to take the position that the majority of Iraq's illicit weapons had indeed been destroyed by 1995, and that Iraq was not in the position of being able to *fully* verify their destruction to the United Nations.

Air Exclusion Zones

As highlighted earlier, following the liberation of Kuwait in 1991, President Bush called upon the Iraqi people to "take matters into their own hands", and oust Saddam's regime from power.[42] Various civilian areas in Iraq, and in particular the Kurdish areas, openly rebelled against the Iraqi regime. It was following the Iraqi military repression of these rebellions that the international community condemned these actions and adopted UNSCR 688 of 5 April 1991. UNSCR 688 condemned the oppression of the Iraqi civilians and demanded that Iraq immediately halt the repression. Of significance however, was the appeal by the Security Council that "all Member States and all humanitarian organizations . . . contribute to these humanitarian relief efforts".[43] Following the adoption of UNSCR 688, the United States, the United Kingdom and France adopted a northern air exclusion zone in April 1991. This had the express objective of creating a safe haven for the Kurdish civilians by making the area north of the 36th parallel in Iraq a fixed-wing and rotary-wing aircraft free zone.[44] This northern no-fly zone was justified by the United States as being consistent with UNSCR 688 in terms of it providing the adequate security needed for the humanitarian relief effort. The United States, the United Kingdom and France established a second air exclusion zone in southern Iraq in the area below the 32nd parallel on 26 August 1991 in order to provide protection for the Shi'ite population. This southern air exclusion zone was subsequently expanded to the 33rd parallel in September 1996.

At issue, however, was whether UNSCR 688 actually provided the legal justification for the US, UK and French enforcement of the no-fly zones. UNSCR 688 was *not* enacted under Chapter VII, and thus did not provide any *explicit provisions* for the use of force.[45] Although Congress called upon Bush to press the Security Council to agree on the enforcement of UNSCR 688 in accordance with Chapter VII, no such measures were introduced to the Security Council.[46] It is because of the absence of the specific authorisation for the use of force in UNSCR 688 that the legal foundation of the air exclusion zones was questionable under international law.

The legality of the air exclusion zones enforcement was also questionable on the grounds of whether it was concurrent with the authorisation for the use of force under UNSCR 678.[47] But even when the legality of this action is considered under the umbrella of legal humanitarian intervention, it seems clear this basis for intervention "would have limited the operation to air drops and other non-forcible assistance of a humanitarian character".[48] In addition to these issues, any potential justification of self-defence as a means of legitimising enforcement in the air exclusion zones was also questionable "since the argument depends on coalition aircraft having the right to fly over Iraq in the first place".[49] Therefore, under international law the legal foundation for the US position on air exclusion zones was absent and simply highlights the willingness of the United States to nullify the provisions in the Treaty of Westphalia on the ground of humanitarian concerns.

The Clinton administration's support for the air exclusion zones, which were clearly inherited from the previous Bush administration, proved to be a contentious issue and a dividing factor within the Security Council. The decision by Clinton in September 1996 to extend the southern air exclusion zone to the 33rd parallel was in response to Hussein's attack on Irbil on 31 August 1996.[50] France did not support this change in policy and did not commit its forces to patrolling the extended area of the no-fly zone.[51] But on 27 December 1996, France withdrew its involvement from Operation Northern Watch, as it no longer found there to be a humanitarian requirement to justify its continued participation. The US took a contrary position and continued to enforce the air exclusion zone, which undoubtedly served to further aggravate the emerging divisions on the Security Council up until late 1997. France's participation in Operation Southern Watch was suspended on 16 December 1998, due to the commencement of Operation Desert Fox by the United States and the United Kingdom.

It is therefore clear that the Clinton administration's participation in the Iraqi air exclusion zones was a factor that ultimately served to heighten tensions within the multilateral coalition. The Clinton administration's commitment of its forces to enforce the southern and northern air exclusion zones within Iraq was a policy which, although grounded on humanitarian considerations, did not possess legal legitimacy in the eyes of the international community and under international law. The significance of US support and enforcement of the Iraqi air exclusion zones is that whilst they demonstrated a US commitment towards the humanitarian predicament of the oppressed Kurdish and Shi'ite population areas, it was a policy that served to undermine the integrity of the multilateral international coalition. With heightened divisions in the Security Council, most notably from 1996–1998, the French withdrawal from the northern air exclusion zone and disagreement over the US decision to extend the southern air exclusion zone would have undoubtedly served to further challenge this integrity.

Strategic Policy: Regime Change

The safe haven in northern Iraq not only served the function of providing humanitarian relief, but it was also intended to stem the flow of Kurdish refugees into Iran and Turkey.[52] In addition it provided a secure base of operation for opposition movements as part of covert US efforts to promote an insurgency which would have weakened Saddam's regime and thus made it more susceptible to an internal *coup d'état*.[53] It was following the establishment of the northern safe haven in 1991 that the opposition movements were able to unite under the umbrella organisation of the Iraqi National Congress (INC). The CIA then began supporting the INC covertly as part of the regime change strategy.[54] The CIA sent small quantities of armaments, money and supplies to the constituent parts of the INC, as part of US covert efforts to promote an insurgency which would have weakened Saddam's regime and thus made it more susceptible to an internal *coup d'état*.[55]

Although the official position of the Clinton administration was geared towards the upholding of UN resolutions through multilateral sanctions, the overall strategy has been suggested by David Wurmser as having covertly altered towards the objective of regime change from 1995.[56] The truth of the matter is actually quite different as there is evidence to support the position that a strategic policy continuation from the preceding Bush administration actually occurred, which means that US policy was officially geared towards the objective of regime change since 1991. In an interview by the author with Anthony Lake, he clarified the situation thus:

> The problem was that we could not, at that time, state explicitly that the purpose of our policy was the overthrow of the regime . . . because if that became explicitly stated at that time it would blow apart the coalition, as such a goal did not fall explicitly within the terms of the UN resolutions. Although when we argued that there needed to be full compliance with all the resolutions passed in the wake of the first Gulf War, in effect, that was calling for [Saddam Hussein's] overthrow because, if he observed the provisions calling for an end to repression, then his regime would fall.[57]

Therefore, Lake's remarks underline that containment was viewed by the administration as a tactical means of achieving its over-arching strategic objective of regime change. However, in considering the implementation of this strategic policy of regime change it is necessary to provide an examination of CIA operations, and those involving opposition groups, undertaken by the Clinton administration towards Iraq.

In terms of opposition groups, the Clinton administration continued to support the INC as a means of bringing about a "democratic and pluralist government in Iraq that can live in peace with its neighbors and its own people".[58] Washington saw the INC as a useful tool for fostering a degree of domestic opposition to the Iraqi regime, but not as a direct threat to it.[59] Indeed, Lake commented that "the institution that could actually overthrow Saddam was the Iraqi military".[60] Thus, the administration did not believe groups such as the INC were going to actually unseat Saddam Hussein.

In March 1995 however, the INC launched a military offensive against Iraqi military forces and admittedly made advances against them. With a sizeable number of defections having occurred to the INC, it seemed that a real threat was being posed to the regime of Saddam Hussein.[61] For Washington, however, the advances posed the problem that a victory by the INC forces would have potentially threatened the territorial integrity of Iraq due to the major role of Kurdish separatist movements in mounting the insurgency. But given that it would have likely had a bearing on the stability of neighbouring states, its success would have been contrary to the US strategic interests of an unhindered flow of hydrocarbon resources from the region.[62]

In light of the threat posed to the territorial integrity of Iraq by a potential INC victory during March 1995, the US withdrew its support for the insurrection.[63] The decision to withdraw all support is reported as having come directly from the White House.[64] The unwillingness to support the INC in this effort was a departure of policy by the Clinton administration as US policy towards the INC stipulated:

> We are also providing stronger backing for the Iraqi National Congress (INC) as a democratic alternative to the Saddam Hussein regime. The INC has succeeded in broadening its base to encompass representatives of all three major communities in Iraq: Sunni, Shi'ite and Kurd. It is committed, as are we, to maintaining the territorial integrity of Iraq and to adhering to Iraq's international responsibilities. We are now urging others in the region to accord the INC the recognition and support it deserves.[65]

Although Washington clearly supported the insurgency activities of the INC as a means of promoting domestic opposition within Iraq, the Clinton administration reneged on its policy position by not supporting the INC as a replacement to Saddam's regime. It has been speculated that the Clinton administration's reversal in policy was on account of their unwillingness to get embroiled in an INC-orchestrated military engagement,[66] which could have placed unwanted pressure on the territorial integrity of Iraq that was contrary to US interests.

The withdrawal of US support for the March 1995 insurgency resulted in the fragmentation of the Kurdish coalition and also in the failure of the INC offensive,[67] and the INC's ability to mount any effective opposition to Baghdad ceased.[68] More importantly though, it marked the failure of CIA covert operations in northern Iraq and damaged US credibility with the Kurdish factions and those remaining in the INC.[69]

Washington subsequently opted to focus its insurgency efforts on the newly emerging Iraqi National Accord (INA).[70] The INA, headed by Iyad Allawi, who was a former Iraqi intelligence official, consisted mainly of military officers from the Sunni core of the Iraqi regime. Unlike the INC, which offered regime change through military confrontation, the INA had the potential to bring about an internal *coup d'état*. Importantly, an internal *coup d'état* was seen as unlikely to pose the same threats to the territorial integrity of Iraq as a military insurgency by the INC. Washington saw an internal coup as the most feasible and also the most politically expedient way of achieving regime change. Assistant Secretary of State Robert Pelletreau aptly commented "the only way you were going to succeed in unseating the existing regime was through an internal military coup against it".[71] The defection of Hussain Kamal al-Majeed and General Nizar al-Khazraji[72] undoubtedly demonstrated to Washington that Saddam's inner circle was disloyal, fragmenting and thus conducive to undertaking an internal coup.

The key problem with the INA as an opposition movement, however, was that it had been "heavily penetrated by Iraqi security".[73] With the vast majority of the defections to the INA having come from the Iraqi military and Saddam's own inner circle, it was likely that many bogus defections would have occurred to provide disinformation and carry out counter-intelligence operations. This would have served to not only hamper the operations of the INA, but also to undermine and prevent any coup attempts against Saddam.

The infiltration of the INA by Iraqi intelligence proved to be the root cause of the failure of the INA as an insurgency movement. In 1996 an INA coup operation was thwarted by Iraqi intelligence and resulted in the execution of several hundred CIA-backed conspirators within Iraq.[74] The lack of success of the INA's operation understandably placed Saddam in a more secure position and underlined the inability of the INA to initiate a coup. Although Washington continued to support the INA after 1996, it is only reasonable to conclude that the significant infiltration of the INA by Iraqi intelligence made its effectiveness and the future likelihood of it successfully carrying out a coup *very unlikely*.

The Clinton administration's strategic insurgency and covert regime change policy had, therefore, ultimately failed in fulfilling its objectives, and by 1996, was a policy option rendered ineffectual. Although the United States overtly premised its policy on Iraq's full and complete compliance with UN resolutions, it covertly continued the Bush administration's official strategy of supporting insurgency movements within Iraq towards the ultimate objective of initiating regime change. Indeed, the pursuit of this strategy demonstrates the duplicitous nature of Clinton's policy as it was officially premised on a destruction of Iraq's prohibited weapons leading to reconciliation, whilst the true objective was regime change.

The support for the INC by Clinton was initially effective in serving the purpose of uniting the Kurdish factions and in fostering general opposition towards Saddam's regime. However, by 1995, the administration's unwillingness to militarily support the INC had resulted in the failure of the offensive and the collapse of the CIA-sponsored insurgency in northern Iraq. The regime change strategy of the administration can therefore be split into two parts: firstly, using the INC as a means of weakening Saddam's regime and thus making it more susceptible to a coup; and secondly, switching its focus in 1995 towards the INA as a means of instigating a coup. In sum, this demonstrates that regime change through internal means had been pursued as a strategic objective since 1991.

The Failure of Tactical Containment

In the aftermath of the liberation of Kuwait in 1991, the Iraqi domestic economic infrastructure virtually collapsed. As a consequence, the Iraqi people faced a humanitarian predicament and the government was not in a position to alleviate it. UNSCR 687 incorporated provisions that exempted food and medicine from the embargo, and eased the restrictions on Iraqi assets for use in purchasing such supplies. Security Council Resolution 706, passed on 15 August 1991, was a direct response to these needs. It gave Iraq the ability to sell up to US$1.6 billion in oil over a six month period using an escrow account, which could be used to purchase food and medicine, and to compensate Kuwait.[75] For Saddam, this UN initiative posed a threat to his rule as the control of revenue and provision of supplies would fall to the UN which would consequently be seen as an alternative authority within Iraq.[76] As compliance with the humanitarian relief provisions of UNSCR 687 and 706 challenged the rule of Saddam, Baghdad's response was to adopt a self-sufficiency programme rather than cooperating and utilising the provisions the UN had provided.[77]

During the first Clinton administration, the humanitarian situation within Iraq weakened support amongst the international community, most notably among Arab states, for the multilateral sanctions mandate. In response to these concerns, the United States proposed UNSCR 968 on 14 April 1995, dubbed the 'oil-for-food' programme, which greatly expanded the oil sales Iraq could use for purchasing humanitarian provisions.[78]

Despite the introduction of this programme, 'sanctions fatigue' amongst UN member states was clearly growing and being fostered by Iraq.[79] Iraq realised that the most effective method of having the sanctions lifted was to divide the will of the Security Council on the sanctions and inspections processes. Apart from highlighting the humanitarian impact of the sanctions, Baghdad proactively engaged in discussions with Russia and France on lucrative oil and trade agreements. Although the State Department attempted to refute Iraq's claims on the effect of sanctions, it had little impact.[80] In addition to this, it is reasonable to believe that both France and Russia had a vested interest in seeing the sanctions lifted, as Iraq owed them US$4 billion and US$8 billion respectively.[81] Indeed, Russian Foreign Minister Yevgeny Primakov commented that "[w]ithout sanctions, the Iraqis would sell oil and pay us; with sanctions, they sell oil and use the sanctions as an excuse not to pay us".[82] This situation was used by Iraq to make these countries support the lifting of sanctions due to their own national economic interests. Therefore Washington's emphasis and reliance on a concerted multilateral response to Iraq was unravelling due to the humanitarian effects of the sanctions policy and the resolute efforts by Iraq to further divisions within the international community.

The oil-for-food programme was subsequently further expanded[83] in order to reduce the opposition to sanctions, which was occurring mainly through humanitarian concerns. For Washington, however, the policy of maintaining multilateral international support for sanctions by providing backing for increased Iraqi oil sales for humanitarian supplies was in essence a double-edged sword. The US had to support the oil-for-food programme, but this strategy resulted in the weakening of the strict nature of sanctions on Iraq. Mary O'Connell comments:

> The agreement contained in UN Security Council Resolution 1153 more than doubled the cash Iraq would receive every six months. In fact, it potentially allowed Iraq to sell US$10.5 billion a year of oil, which compares to average Iraqi annual oil exports of US$11.5 billion (in 1998 dollars) during 1981–1989 . . . This compares with US$1.32 billion every six months under the prior agreement, or US$2.64 billion a year.[84]

Therefore, the Clinton administration's multilateral policy of containment through sanctions on Iraq was showing signs of deficiency and potential failure. Whilst Washington's support for easing the humanitarian crisis served the diplomatic purpose of revitalising its multilateral support base, thus strengthening the integrity of the multilateral coalition, at the same time it undermined the strict nature of the sanctions and provided a diplomatic success for Iraq through the increased revenue it had at its disposal.

Despite Iraq being found in breach of its obligations by the UN, Washington found that the international community's willingness to support UN sanctions indefinitely was increasingly wavering. Many saw the sanctions as having created a significant humanitarian predicament for the Iraqi people.[85] It appears, however, that the main cause of the humanitarian crisis was the deliberate withholding of humanitarian supplies by the Iraqi regime.[86] Saddam's regime withheld supplies in order to create a humanitarian crisis amongst the Iraqi population, which served the purpose of fostering divisions within the international community towards enforcing sanctions[87] and achieving its own purely political objectives.[88]

Iraq's strategy was undoubtedly effective in creating divisions in the Security Council. The increased debate as to the actual legality of UN sanctions towards Iraq further undermined the US position. The issue was whether sanctions were in line with both the legal principle of proportionality and with customary international humanitarian law standards.[89]

The regional political ramifications of the sanctions were viewed in terms of the humanitarian predicament of the Iraqi people. The humanitarian situation inflamed regional public opinion towards the US, and Secretary of State Albright found that the rulers of Qatar, Bahrain and Kuwait were deeply concerned over the plight of the Iraqi people. This impacted on their support for the US position towards Iraq.[90] Further compounding the loss of regional support was the slow pace of negotiations in the Arab–Israeli peace process following the election of Binyamin Netanyahu. These factors made the US policy of containment towards Iraq lose vital support from Arab states and the wider international community, which further served to encourage Saddam to defy the UN sanctions policy.

In light of the split in the international community, Iraq focused its energies on attempting to divide the Security Council, whilst continuing active non-cooperation during 1997–1998. With Russia and France both showing an unwillingness to resort to force in order to compel Iraq,[91] it was clear to Baghdad that it was succeeding in dividing the will of the international community and that determination to enforce UN resolutions was lacking. The concerted Iraqi effort to defy UN resolutions saw Iraq have four further UN Security Council Resolutions passed against it, as it was found to be in breach of its obligations.[92]

Domestic Political Factors in the United States
The continued Iraqi defiance of UN resolutions and the emerging divisions within the international coalition towards the sanctions were clear evidence of a failing US position. Members of the US Congress were openly critical of the situation vis-à-vis Iraq and the general mood in Congress was usefully summed up by the Chairman of the Congressional Committee on Energy and Natural Resources:

> [A]ctions by the administration and the UN particularly have rendered the effectiveness of the sanctions less than meaningful, and without effective sanctions the UN inspectors in my opinion will never be able to force Saddam to destroy his weapons of mass destruction.[93]

The immediate response given by Congress to Iraq's defiance was a ruling that Iraq was in material breach of its international obligations.[94] The Congressional dissatisfaction with the administration, and realisation that US policy towards Iraq had virtually failed, was heightened by the testimony of the former Chief of UNSCOM's Concealment and Investigation Unit, Scott Ritter. Ritter accused the Clinton administration of deliberately interfering in the operations of UNSCOM, with the express intention of preventing a confrontation from occurring.[95] The implication from Ritter's testimony was that the Clinton administration actively and deliberately impeded the weapons inspection processes in order to prevent a confrontation from occurring, which would have further divided the international coalition. Ritter specifically suggested that Secretary of State Madeleine Albright intervened in the independent inspection process by delaying the no-notice inspections on 6–9 August 1998. From Ritter's testimony, it was widely reported that this was a deliberate action by

Albright to prevent a confrontation.[96] Ritter also alleged that the CIA was using UNSCOM as a means of gathering intelligence. Former UNSCOM Chairman Richard Butler, however, convincingly rebutted Ritter's allegations that the US had interfered with the operations of UNSCOM on the dates in question.[97] Although Butler also denied that the CIA gathered intelligence through UNSCOM,[98] it subsequently transpired that this aspect of Ritter's allegation was accurate.[99] Indeed, not only did the CIA covertly participate in the inspection process and receive full briefings from UN weapons inspectors, they also were highly involved in providing intelligence to further the inspection mandate.[100]

Ritter's testimony had a damning effect on Congress's perception of the Clinton administration. Speaker of the House, Newt Gingrich, was scathing in his criticism by suggesting that the effect of the administration was to appease Iraq, and that its "tough rhetoric on Iraq has been a deception masking a real policy of weakness and concession".[101] In addition to this, Ritter gained international notoriety as a vocal critic of the Clinton administration's policy strategy[102] and, given his credentials as a former Chief Weapons Inspector, it was likely he had some influence on public opinions towards Clinton's foreign policy.

The stagnation of the US position towards Iraq during 1997–1998 led to a growing number of calls within Congress for increased efforts to overthrow Saddam Hussein's regime. Congress recognised that it was the regime of Saddam that posed the continuing threat to international peace and security and, through legislation in January 1998, urged the President "to work with Congress in furthering a long-term policy aimed at definitively ending the threat to international peace and security posed by the government of Iraq and its weapons of mass destruction programme".[103] The growing calls for direct action against the Iraqi regime ultimately resulted in Congress adopting the Iraq Liberation Act on 31 October 1998.[104] Proposed by Majority Leader Trent Lott and House International Relations Committee Chairman Benjamin Gilman, the Iraq Liberation Act specified that "[i]t should be the policy of the United States to support efforts to remove the regime headed by Saddam Hussain from power in Iraq and to promote the emergence of a democratic government to replace that regime".[105] The bill, which received bipartisan support and passed by a margin of 360–38, gave President Clinton the authority to allocate US$97 million in defence equipment to Iraqi opposition groups, and a further US$2 million for opposition groups' radio and television broadcasts. The adoption of this legislation clearly originated from the failure of the multilateral approach towards Iraq, and marked a decisive shift in Congressional pressure on US policy from containment towards overtly and officially pursuing regime change. Moreover, it is important to recognise that although this legislation came clearly from Congress, the administration viewed the new policy with some degree of scepticism[106] as it was seen to be hampering efforts to maintain the multilateral coalition towards the maintenance of sanctions. Nevertheless, the covert policy since 1991 of regime change had now become an official policy.

Continuing Iraqi Defiance

Only two months after Richard Butler had taken over from Rolf Ekeus as the Chairman of the UNSCOM inspection team, Iraq provoked a major crisis in an effort to shake off the inspections and sanctions. On 13 September 1997, the Iraqi regime refused the UN inspectors direct access to the military barracks in Tikrit. In this instance, UNSCOM was informed that the site they were planning on visiting was classed as a 'sensitive' site. Under an agreement in 1996 between Rolf Ekeus and the Iraqi government, only four UNSCOM personnel would conduct the inspection of such sites. The inspection team was initially denied access to the site, and despite an agreement that no vehicles could be used within the site or leave it, several did so. Moreover, the UNSCOM Chief Aerial Inspector was prevented by Iraqi officials from photographing the site, which was in clear breach of Iraq's legal obligations. When the inspectors finally gained access to the site after three hours, they found evidence that documentation had been removed from the site.[107]

Two days after the incident at Tikrit military base a similar incident occurred at the Sarabadi Republican Guard base.[108] Later that month, however, there was a stand-off over the inspection of the Iraqi Special Security Organisation (SSO) headquarters, and a major crisis unfolded. The inspectors were stopped in the vicinity of the SSO headquarters at gunpoint. Despite direct negotiations between Tariq Aziz and Butler, the UNSCOM inspectors were prevented from gaining access on the justification that the SSO headquarters were part of a presidential site. With the inspectors being held at gunpoint, they were withdrawn on account of fears for their safety.

UNSCOM Chairman Richard Butler formed the opinion that the arbitrary prevention of inspectors from accessing certain sites, and the lack of substantive cooperation, made it clear that the priority of Iraq was to maintain WMD stockpiles rather than to get a clean bill of health from the UN. Butler commented that:

> The claim that Saddam Hussain's regime wanted, above all, to rid Iraq of economic sanctions was false. Iraq's priority . . . had always been to retain weapons of mass destruction – and, perhaps in particular, a biological weapons capability. Because disarmament and relief of sanctions are tied together under international law, this means that Saddam's ability to hold on to such weapons is far more important to him than the welfare of 22 million ordinary Iraqis.[109]

Indeed, at face value, it is logical to conclude that given Iraq's failure to substantively comply with its obligations, its priority was to maintain an unconventional weapons programme. However, it also seems clear that Iraq had a real desire to rid itself of UN sanctions: therefore it seemed to many that Iraq's priority was to covertly maintain some form of WMD capabilities whilst also attempting to rid itself of the UN sanctions and the inspections mandate.

The response at the UN Security Council to Iraq's defiance was UNSCR 1134 of 23 October 1997. Whilst the resolution did not find Iraq in 'material breach' of its obligations, it did note with 'grave concern' Iraq's recent obstruction of the UN mandate. Unlike previous Security Council Resolutions, UNSCR 1134 was not adopted unanimously. Three permanent members of the Security Council – China, France and Russia abstained in the vote. It would have therefore been clear to Iraq that sanctions fatigue was taking effect at the Security Council.

With the tide of international opinion moving in its favour, Baghdad decided to up the stakes by barring US nationals from partaking in UNSCOM inspections.[110] In addition to this, Tariq Aziz also specified that American-provided U-2 flights must cease. Whilst the UN condemned Iraq's position, a stalemate "developed and the inspections process ground to a halt".[111] Although the Secretary-General of the United Nations, Kofi Annan, attempted to reach a political solution by sending UN Special Envoys to Baghdad, a solution was not forthcoming.[112]

A breakthrough in the stalemate came via Russian diplomatic offices on 20 November 1997. Tariq Aziz held talks with Russian Foreign

Minister Primakov and reached an agreement that Iraq would allow a resumption of the UNSCOM inspections with the provision that the inspection process would be conducted efficiently in order to usher in a speedy lifting of the sanctions.[113] Following this announcement, the representatives of the five permanent members of the Security Council met in Geneva to conclude a joint statement on the Iraq–Russia Agreement.

The Geneva Agreement saw the representatives of the permanent members of the Security Council endorse the unconditional return of the inspectors, however, it was conceded that there would be an effort to make UNSCOM more 'effective' in its operations as a means of seeing the sanctions speedily lifted.[114] Despite the positive outlook the Geneva Agreement provided, within a few months Iraq resorted to its former policy of disrupting the inspections process, which again indicated that it was trying to conceal a covert WMD programme. With this defiance as a backdrop, the United States and the United Kingdom continued to build up their military forces in the Persian Gulf, as a means of compelling Iraq to comply; this build up had begun before the Geneva Agreement.

Given the continued military deployment and Iraq's failure to comply with its obligations, by February 1998 there was notable concern within the United Nations that the crisis was spiralling out of control. Kofi Annan took it upon himself to reach a political solution to the crisis and travelled to Baghdad to meet with Saddam Hussein.[115] The UN-brokered agreement provided Iraq with a further opportunity to comply with its obligations with the provision that UN diplomats would accompany the inspection teams whenever they inspected Iraqi presidential sites. Whilst the United States was sceptical that the UN-brokered agreement would actually work, they nonetheless welcomed it as it provided for a resumption of the inspections.[116] The United States responded by sponsoring Security Council Resolution 1154, which provided, under Chapter VII of the UN Charter, the "severest consequences" for Iraq in the event of it violating its obligations under UNSCR 687. [117]

Operation Desert Fox and Stalemate

With Congress, and particularly the Republican members of Congress, applying pressure on the administration to adopt a more aggressive strategy towards Baghdad, Washington was forced to take a more proactive approach towards the enforcement of UN resolutions. Despite the UN-brokered agreement that had been concluded in February 1998, by August Iraq's Revolutionary Command Council and the Ba'ath Party Command halted their cooperation with UNSCOM and the IAEA on the basis that the oil embargo needed to be lifted and the composition of the UNSCOM and IAEA inspection teams should be reorganised. Iraq did, however, allow the monitoring as required by UNSCR 715 to continue. As a result of Iraq's defiance of its obligations under international law and its failure to honour the UN-brokered agreement of February 1998, the UN Security Council passed Resolution 1194 which ultimately condemned Iraq for its non-compliance.

However, when Clinton signed into law the Iraq Liberation Act on 31 October 1998, Iraq responded on the same day by terminating its cooperation with the inspectors. Clinton had been under pressure from the Republican-controlled Congress to take more forceful steps, and Iraq understandably viewed this policy adoption as a highly provocative and illegal action. Iraq's cessation of cooperation with the inspectors resulted in the adoption of UNSCR 1205 of 5 November 1998. This resolution condemned Iraq for having halted its cooperation indefinitely with UNSCOM and the IAEA.[118]

In the face of a divided international community, Iraq's cessation of the weapons inspection process proved to be the most significant test of the determination of the United States to enforce UN resolutions. On 14 November 1998 Clinton, along with British Prime Minister Blair, ordered air strikes on Iraq, but ultimately postponed them for twenty-four hours due to Iraqi concessions. With Iraq declaring it would fully and unconditionally comply with UN resolutions on 15 November, the air strikes were called off. It was made clear by Tony Blair that the United States and the United Kingdom would act militarily if Iraq withdrew its cooperation again.[119]

Despite the threat of force hanging over Iraq, Richard Butler informed the Security Council on 8 December that Iraq was continuing to hamper the inspections process. In his sobering report to the Secretary-General of the United Nations on 15 December 1998 Butler stated: "Iraq did not provide the full cooperation it promised on 14 November 1998".[120] With the very real likelihood of military action as a result of Butler's report, the UN removed its staff from the UNSCOM mission in Baghdad on 15 December. On the following day, whilst the UN Security

Council was in session and debating Butler's report, the United States and the United Kingdom carried out Operation Desert Fox, which involved concentrated air strikes on a variety of targets within Iraq.[121] The military strikes lasted for seventy-two hours, after which Clinton announced that the military objectives had been achieved.[122] Although the military air strikes were successful in degrading the military apparatus of Saddam's regime,[123] they did not prove successful in re-establishing Iraq's cooperation and compliance with UN resolutions and further reinforced divisions in the Security Council.[124]

The United States and the United Kingdom justified the legality of the air strikes under the provisions of UNSCR 1154 and 1205 under Chapter VII. The former stressed that Iraq must "accord immediate, unconditional and unrestricted access to the Special Commission and the IAEA in conformity with the relevant resolutions", and that "any violation would have [the] severest consequences for Iraq".[125] Resolution 1205 provided condemnation for an Iraqi violation through its suspension of cooperation with UNSCOM and the IAEA. Although the resolutions did not explicitly authorise the use of force, it was argued that they provided *implied authorisation.*[126] In addition to the reliance on implied authorisation, the US and UK argued that UNSCR 678 provided the authorisation[127] for the use of force, due to its provision that "Iraq comply fully with Resolution 660 and all subsequent relevant resolutions".[128] However, this argument is open to question under international law.[129] Therefore, the position taken by the United States and the United Kingdom in justifying Operation Desert Fox clearly demonstrated their departure from the multilateral doctrine as they carried out military action without the express authorisation of a Security Council Resolution.

Therefore, the shift in *official* US policy towards regime change occurred in 1998 as a result of Republican Congressional pressure on the basis that the multilateral effort had failed due to the unwillingness of the international community to enforce resolutions in the face of clear Iraqi defiance. Indeed, Clinton commented in 1998 that Saddam posed a threat to the whole world and that "[the] best way to end that threat once and for all is with a new Iraqi government".[130] Martin Indyk notably stated that:

> We have come to the conclusion, after more than seven years of effort at seeking Saddam's compliance with UN Security Council resolutions, that his regime will never be able to be rehabilitated or

reintegrated into the community of nations. This conclusion is based on what Saddam's record makes manifest – that he will never relinquish what remains of his WMD arsenal, and that he will never cease being a threat to the region, US interests, and his own people. It is based on Saddam's policies, not on any predetermined policy of our own. Thus, in November of last year, President Clinton announced a new policy with regard to Iraq: henceforth, we would contain Saddam Hussain until a new regime can govern in Baghdad.[131]

Clearly by 1998, Clinton's official policy strategy towards Iraq had completely changed. Importantly, he had ultimately come to officially accept the very same strategic understanding that his predecessor, President George H. W. Bush, had adopted towards Iraq: a normalisation of relations and the security of the Persian Gulf could not be ensured while Saddam was in power.

US Policy Post-Operation Desert Fox

In the aftermath of Operation Desert Fox, which lasted for only seventy-two hours, it seemed that the war objectives were geared towards not only debilitating Iraq's capability for threatening neighbouring states and its production of weapons of mass destruction, but also towards destabilising Saddam's regime. US Defense Secretary William Cohen and General Henry H. Shelton, the Chairman of the US Joint Chiefs of Staff, indicated that "American forces attacked not just the headquarters of Iraqi military intelligence, Special Republican Guard and Special Security Organization, but also barracks housing Republican Guard troops, while regular Army units were left alone".[132] It was reported that "[t]his aspect of the war plan served what military officials acknowledged was the larger, if undeclared, purpose of the air strikes: to weaken Saddam Hussain's hold on power by damaging his personal support structure and sowing unrest within the Iraqi military".[133] This was in addition to the stated objective of degrading Iraq's WMD capability, despite 'dual use' facilities not being targeted in order to avoid civilian casualties. Indeed, Sandy Berger recognised that in the aftermath of the bombing campaign, the only choices left for US policy were to ensure "total Iraqi compliance with UN Security Council demands, which is unlikely, or the downfall of Saddam Hussain, which is inevitable".[134]

Whilst the *official* position of the United States changed towards the promotion of regime change as a result of Congressional legislation, the multilateral containment approach came under strong criticism from France, Russia and China in the wake of the air strikes. Russian President Boris Yeltsin, who was under pressure from the Russian Duma and was potentially facing impeachment, used the air strikes as a means to deflect attention away from his domestic problems and ultimately withdrew the Russian Ambassadors temporarily from both Britain and the United States as a political gesture. Spurred by his domestic political concerns, Yeltsin highlighted the US and British air strikes as an illegal action and pressed for the lifting of UN sanctions towards Iraq.[135] Clearly, the US position of multilaterally containing Iraq through the United Nations had become virtually untenable in the aftermath of Operation Desert Fox.

With the unravelling of the sanctions policy in the United Nations, Saddam Hussein raised the stakes by declaring that he no longer recognised the northern and southern no-fly zones on the basis of their illegality under international law. Saddam's calculation resulted in a sustained war of attrition, which ultimately further degraded his air defence capability.[136]

The French Ambassador to the United Nations, Alain Dejammet, recommended altering the existing system, which required Iraq to account for its stockpiles, to one which prevented Iraq from acquiring new stockpiles of weapons of mass destruction.[137] The problem for the United States in accepting this position, according to State Department spokesman James P. Rubin, was that "Iraq should not be liberated from the sanctions until it rids itself of all weapons of mass destruction".[138] With the United States proving unwilling to lift sanctions until Iraq had verified the destruction of its weapons, the French proposal was not adopted. Similarly, Russia issued its own proposal on 15 January which stated that "the embargo could be lifted once the council receives a report from an assessment team on the status of Iraqi cooperation on disarmament and decides to start the monitoring system".[139] Clinton's counter-proposal, which proved equally unsatisfactory, was to "allow Baghdad to borrow against a UN escrow fund to buy food and medicine, encourage humanitarian contributions to Iraq, and strengthen UNICEF and other UN programs already on the ground".[140] The US proposal was in essence an extension of the oil-for-food programme. Iraq however rejected this proposal as Iraq's Trade Minister, Medhi Saleh, stated that "Iraq will not accept anything short of a comprehensive lifting of the unfair embargo".[141]

Given the conjecture already discussed regarding the unlikelihood that Iraq could actually account for its prohibited weapons, it seems that the French and Russian proposals were a more realistic means of containing Iraq's potential long-term threat whilst maintaining the international consensus towards Iraq. Therefore, whilst Clinton's decision to insist on Iraq fully accounting for its stockpiles before the sanctions could be lifted was, strictly speaking, a legitimate course of action in the light of Iraq's legal obligations, it was not a realistic policy position. However, given that the United States was committed to regime change, allowing the sanctions against Iraq to be lifted would have increased the regime's economic position, thus making it more secure. Therefore, in keeping with the US strategy of regime change towards Iraq, Washington demonstrated an unwillingness to lift sanctions regardless of whether Iraq could actually account for its prohibited weapons.

With the impasse in the Security Council and Baghdad's unwillingness to cooperate, UN inspections within Iraq remained suspended for the remainder of Clinton's second term of office. The strategic priority, however, clearly rested on the promotion of regime change. Under the terms of the Iraq Liberation Act, US$97 million was allocated to insurgent groups operating within Iraq, with the objective being to effect regime change. This policy was notably criticised by General Anthony Zinni, Commander of US Forces in the Persian Gulf, as not being a realistic policy option.[142] Zinni commented "I will be honest. I don't see an opposition group that has the viability to overthrow Saddam at this point".[143] Given the high number of competing opposition groups, it seems likely that Zinni's assessment was indeed correct. Martin Indyk's comments that "[i]t will take time and hard work", and that "a lot more will be done behind the scenes than will be noticeable publicly, at least at first" seem an accurate assessment of the situation. [144]

The Clinton administration refrained from providing the opposition groups with military help as, according to James Rubin, the United States was "not prepared to take action that is premature or that puts people's lives needlessly at risk . . . [t]here are a number of steps that have to be taken before we're in a position to provide lethal assistance".[145] Indeed, by the end of the second Clinton administration, just under US$2 million of the allocated amount had been spent by the Pentagon. It was only in the final week of the Clinton administration that a plan for distributing a US$25 million Congressional aid package to further the efforts of opposition movements was formulated. This was an aid package in addition to the US$97 million provided for under the Iraq Liberation Act, of which only US$5 million had been allocated. The Clinton administration was obligated into formulating a distribution plan for the US$25 million aid package as Congress had incorporated it into the federal aid budget:[146]

> As a reflection of continued congressional support for the overthrow effort, a provision of the FY2001 foreign aid appropriation (H.R. 4811, P.L. 106-429, signed November 6, 2000) earmarked US$25 million in ESF for "programs benefiting the Iraqi people," of which at least: US$12 million was for the INC to distribute humanitarian aid inside Iraq; US$6 million was for INC broadcasting; and US$2 million was for war crimes issues. According to the appropriation the remaining US$5 million could be used to aid the seven groups eligible to receive assistance under the ILA.[147]

The Republican Congress was thus clearly pressing for Iraqi opposition groups to be assisted in order to effect regime change within Baghdad. Therefore, on a domestic political level, the George W. Bush administration came to power with strong political support within Congress for the terms of the Iraq Liberation Act to be fulfilled.

Overall, given the impasse at the United Nations, Clinton's tactical policy of intrusive inspections and sanctions, whilst pursuing a regime change strategy, lay in tatters. Multilateral support for the sanctions had virtually disappeared in the aftermath of Operation Desert Fox. The continued application of sanctions, which were a highly watered down version of their original form, only remained active through the safeguard of a potential US veto. Although Clinton's policy had *officially* reverted to regime change, given the fractured state of the opposition movements (which was to a certain extent a product of Clinton's unsuccessful covert efforts at inducing regime change), the prospect of a credible armed insurgency was remote indeed.

Summary Assessment

Clinton's official policy towards Iraq up until 1998 was for the application of sanctions until a full compliance with UN resolutions was achieved: this was seen to allow for potential reconciliation once the sanctions had been lifted. This policy, however, served the US national interest as it allowed for a multilateral containment of Iraq which catered for Persian Gulf security. Comparatively, the strategy of George H. W. Bush's administration towards Iraq differed by way of being centred on containment as a means of controlling potential threats *until regime change had occurred*, ruling out any prospect of reconciliation. Whilst the pursuit of regime change was a policy option, it was nevertheless strategically incompatible with the reconciliation through containment approach.

It was not until October 1998, with the signing into law of the Iraq Liberation Act, that US policy *officially* reverted to the strategy of the previous Bush administration: *containment until regime change occurred*. Given the covert pursuit of regime change prior to this and its incompatibility with the containment leading to reconciliation path, the question of what exactly Clinton's strategy was towards Iraq prior to October 1998 is clearly justified.

Clinton's policy towards Iraq has almost uniformly been described as pursuing inconsistent and incompatible objectives. Indeed, Henry Kissinger accuses Clinton's policy towards Iraq of having lacked strategic clarity. This study has shown this perspective to be wanting as Clinton's duplicitous strategy of striving for incompatible objectives was more politically and strategically sophisticated than the current body of scholarship would have us believe. As already discussed, Clinton did not conceive a normalisation of relations with Iraq as being possible while Saddam Hussein was in power but, nevertheless, had to balance the logic of pursuing an official regime change strategy against the long-term need for the maintenance of international support for the multilateral sanctions-based policy. The problem facing Clinton was that the adoption of an official regime change policy would have most likely fractured the support base of the multilateral sanctions-based policy, rendering it wholly ineffective. Indeed, Robert Kagan comments that the "rehabilitation and reintegration of Saddam Hussain's Iraq" was precisely what most of Washington's allies in Europe sought.[148] Clinton's strategy was, therefore, sophisticated in that it catered for this disparity by being officially committed to reconciliation[149] after a full Iraqi compliance with UN resolutions had occurred, whilst covertly pursuing regime change. Clinton's duplicitous strategy thus received the benefit of international legitimacy through multilateralism whilst a classic *realpolitik* strategy, reflecting the US national interest, was pursued covertly. Indeed, it has been shown that Clinton refrained from supporting an armed military insurgency to unseat Saddam Hussein, preferring an internal *coup d'état*, as a result of the potential risks it may have had on the territorial integrity of Iraq and the geopolitical stability of the Persian Gulf. Therefore, Clinton's strategy was for regime change, but not at the expense of an armed insurgency or military invasion, which could have impacted upon US strategic interests in the wider Persian Gulf.

The uprisings in 1991 and the continual stream of defections that followed made an internal coup seem likely. Clinton continued the application of multilateral containment in order to control the threat Iraq posed to regional security. With Iraq facing the key issue of verifying the destruction of its prohibited weapons, the prospect of a long-term necessity for sanctions was realistic. However, the sanctions also served the tactical role of weakening the regime of Saddam Hussein, both economically and militarily, and making it more susceptible to a *coup d'état*.

The strategic objective of the Clinton administration towards Iraq was therefore premised on regime change from the offset, and its duplicitous commitment towards Iraq's compliance with UN resolutions was very much a tactical policy geared towards the continual multilateral containment of Iraq. The significance of this is that the US *strategy* towards Iraq during the Clinton administrations did not alter from its original inception in the previous Bush administration in 1991. Kissinger and others are therefore mistaken to assume that Clinton's strategy towards Iraq lacked clarity: it was in fact a policy which maintained a consistent strategic objective and was sophisticated in that it used tactical measures as a means of achieving a greater degree of international legitimacy. Moreover, it used containment as a means of controlling the threat posed by Saddam until a *coup d'état*, which was favourable to Washington, had occurred.[150]

Therefore, it was with the adoption of the Iraq Liberation Act and the collapse of the multilateral containment after Operation Desert Fox that Clinton's tactical and covert strategic policies ultimately failed by December 1998, resulting in the forced reversion by Congress to the Bush administration's official policy of regime change. By January 2001, Clinton's policy towards Iraq throughout his two terms of office had thus been consistent in its overall strategic objective of pursuing regime change through the only politically viable method of achieving this result: a *coup d'état*. There was also the strategic failure to achieve Gulf security by regime change, not as a result of a policy mistake by Clinton, but rather as a product of the effectiveness of Iraq's security forces and the inability of the Western intelligence agencies to effectively operate within Iraq. Nevertheless, it was this very policy position and strategic context that was inherited by George W. Bush.

NOTES

1 The uprisings in Iraq followed a speech given by President Bush in which he called on the people of Iraq to overthrow Saddam Hussein. Although Bush's speech gave no indication that the US would provide direct support for any uprising, it was widely interpreted within Iraq that a subsequent invasion or provision of direct support was imminent.

2 Don Oberdorfer, "US Had Covert Plan to Oust Iraq's Saddam, Bush Adviser Asserts; Effort to Remove Leader Came 'Pretty Close'", *Washington Post* 20 Jan. 1993: A1.

3 Madeleine Albright and William Woodward, *Madam Secretary: A Memoir* (London: Macmillan, 2003) 275.

4 Lake, "Confronting Backlash States" 48.

5 Dan Rather, "President Interviewed by Dan Rather," *CBS* 24 Mar. 1993, 12/07/04 <http://www.clintonfoundation.org/legacy/032493-president-interviewed-by-dan-rather.htm>.

6 The coalition's military action to liberate Kuwait from Iraqi forces was authorised by UNSCR 678 of 29 Nov. 1990 under Chapter VII of the UN Charter.

7 Iraq was obligated under UNSCR 687, Sect. C, to fulfil its obligations to the Protocol for the Prohibition of the Use in War of Asphyxiating, Poisonous or Other Gases, and of Bacteriological Methods of Warfare, which was signed by Iraq on 17 Jun. 1925 in Geneva.

8 UNSCR 687 of 3 Apr. 1991, Sect. C, Par. 8 (a).

9 W. Seth Carus and Joseph Bermudez, "Iraq's Al-Husayn Missile Programme: Part 1", *Jane's Intelligence Review* 2.5 (1990): 204-09; and W. Seth Carus and Joseph Bermudez, "Iraq's Al-Husayn Missile Programme: Part 2", *Jane's Intelligence Review* 2.6 (1990): 242–48.

10 UNSCR 687 of 3 Apr. 1991, Sect. C, Par. 8 (b).

11 UNSCR 687 of 3 Apr. 1991, Sect. C, Par. 11..

12 Kenneth M. Pollack, *The Threatening Storm: The Case for Invading Iraq* (New York: Random House, 2002) 53.

13 Pollack, *The Threatening Storm* 53.

14 UNSCR 699 of 17 Jun. 1991 and UNSCR 715 of 11 Oct. 1991.

15 United Nations, International Atomic Agency, *First Semi-Annual Report on the*

Implementation of UNSCR 687, (S/23295), (Vienna: IAEA, 5 Dec. 1991) 6pp. 18/07/02 <http://www.iraqwatch.org/un/IAEA/s-23295.htm>.

16 United Nations, UNSCOM, *First Report by the Executive Chairman of the Special Commission Pursuant to the Implementation Security Council Resolution 687 (1991)*, (S/23165), (New York: United Nations, 25 Oct. 1991) 29pp. 18/07/02 <http://www.iraqwatch.org/un/UNSCOM/687/s23165.htm>.

17 United Nations, UNSCOM, *Fourth Report by the Executive Chairman of the Special Commission Pursuant to the Implementation Security Council Resolution 687 (1991)*, (S/24984), (New York: United Nations, 17 Dec. 1992) 22pp. 18/07/04 <http://www.iraqwatch.org/un/UNSCOM/687/s-24984.htm>.

18 United Nations, Secretariat, *Third Report under UNSCR 715 by the Secretary-General on the Activities of the Special Commission*, (S/25620), (New York: United Nations, 19 Apr. 1993) 8pp. 12/05/03 <http://www.iraqwatch.org/un/UNSCOM/715/s25620.pdf>.

19 United Nations, UNSCOM, *Ninth Report by the Executive Chairman of the Special Commission Pursuant to the Implementation Security Council Resolution 687 (1991)*, (S/1995/494), (New York: United Nations, 20 Jun. 1995) 10pp. 18/07/03 <http://www.iraqwatch.org/un/UNSCOM/687/s-1995-0494.htm>.

20 United Nations, *Fourth Report by the Executive Chairman of the Special Commission Pursuant to the Implementation Security Council Resolution 687 (1991)*.

21 Anthony H. Cordesman, *Iraq and the War of Sanctions: Conventional Threats and Weapons of Mass Destruction* (Westport: Praeger, 1999) 127–28.

22 United Nations, *Ninth Report by the Executive Chairman of the Special Commission Pursuant to the Implementation Security Council Resolution 687 (1991)*.

23 William J. Clinton, *Public Papers of the Presidents of the United States 1994: William J. Clinton (Bk. 1)*, Washington D.C.: GPO, 1995. 07/01/04 <http://frwebgate.access.gpo.gov/cgi-bin/getpage.cgi?dbname=1994_public_papers_vol1_misc&page=1046&position=all >.

24 United Nations, *Ninth Report by the Executive Chairman of the Special Commission Pursuant to the Implementation Security Council Resolution 687 (1991)*.

25 United Nations, Secretariat, *Seventh Report under UNSCR 715 by the Secretary-General on the Activities of the Special Commission*, (S/1995/284), (New York: United Nations, 10 Apr. 1995) 36pp. 12/08/03 <http://www.iraqwatch.org/un/UNSCOM/715/s-1995-284.htm>.

26 They defected to Jordan along with several members of their family and their wives who were Saddam Hussein's daughters.

27 Amatzia Baram, *Building toward Crisis: Saddam Husayn's Secret Strategy for Survival* (Washington, DC: Washington Institute for Near East Policy, 1998) 8–17.

28 United Nations, *First Semi-Annual Report on the Implementation of UNSCR 687*.

29 United Nations, *Ninth Report by the Executive Chairman of the Special Commission Pursuant to the Implementation Security Council Resolution 687 (1991)*.

30 United Nations, *Seventh Report under UNSCR 715 by the Secretary-General on the Activities of the Special Commission*.

31 Ibid.

32 Ibid.

33 Ibid.

34 United Nations, *Ninth Report by the Executive Chairman of the Special Commission Pursuant to the Implementation Security Council Resolution 687 (1991)*

35 Approved on 27 Mar. 1996, the Resolution was adopted unanimously and was sponsored by France, Germany, Italy, the United Kingdom and the United States.

36 United Nations, UNSCOM, *Fourth Report by the Executive Chairman of the Special Commission Pursuant to the Implementation Security Council Resolution 1051 (1996)*, (S/1997/774), (New York: United Nations, 6 Oct. 1997) 41pp. 25/09/03 <http://www.iraqwatch.org/un/UNSCOM/1051/sres97-774.htm>.

37 Iraq's failure to cooperate with UNSCOM and the IAEA 1996–1998, saw the international community condemn Iraq through UNSCR 1060 of 12 Jun. 1996, UNSCR 1115 of 21 Jun. 1997, UNSCR 1134 23 Oct. 1997, UNSCR 1137 of 12 Nov. 1997 and UNSCR 1205 of 5 Nov. 1998.

38 United Nations, Secretariat, *Memorandum of Understanding between the Secretariat of the United Nations and the Government of Iraq on the Implementation of Security Council Resolution 986 (1995)*, (S/1996/356), (New York: United Nations, 20 May 1996) 10pp. 04/11/04 <http://www.meij.or.jp/text/Gulf%20War/mouunirq1996. htm>.

39 United Nations, UNSCOM and IAEA, *Interview Transcript with Hussain Kamel in Amman*, Sensitive classification note for file, (New York: United Nations, 22 Aug. 1995) 15pp. 12/07/03 <http://www.casi.org.uk/info/unscom950822.pdf>.

40 Ibid.

41 Ibid.

42 George H. W. Bush, "Statement from Baghdad: A Cruel Hoax", Comments to the American Association for the Advancement of Science, Washington, D.C.: GPO, 15 Feb. 1991. 20pp. 13/07/03 <http://dosfan.lib.uic.edu/erc/briefing/dispatch/1991/html/Dispatchv2no07.html >.

43 UNSCR 688 of 5 Apr. 1991. Par. 6.

44 George H. W. Bush, "US Expands Kurdish Relief Efforts", Opening statement at White House news conference, Washington, D.C.: GPO, 16 Apr. 1991. 38pp. 15/07/03 <http://dosfan.lib.uic.edu/erc/briefing/dispatch/1991/html/Dispatchv2no16.html>.

45 Christine Gray, "From Unity to Polarization: International Law and the Use of Force against Iraq", *European Journal of International Law* 13.1 (2002): 9.

46 Simon Chesterman, *Just War or Just Peace? Humanitarian Intervention and International Law* (Oxford; New York: Oxford University Press, 2001) 200.

47 Ibid. 203.

48 Ibid. 205.

49 Ibid. 200.

50 Robert H. Pelletreau, "Developments in the Middle East", US Department of State Dispatch, 5.41, Washington, D.C.: GPO, 30 Sept. 1996. 33pp. 13/06/03 <http://dosfan.lib.uic.edu/erc/briefing/dispatch/1996/html/Dispatchv7no40.html>.

51 William J. Perry, *Report of the Assessment of the Khobar Towers Bombing*, (Washington, D.C.: GPO, 30 Aug. 1996) 2pp. 13/06/03 <http://www.au.af.mil/au/awc/awcgate/khobar/downing/downltr.htm>.

52 Bush, "US Expands Kurdish Relief Efforts".

53 David Wurmser, *Tyranny's Ally: America's Failure to Defeat Saddam Hussain* (Washington, D.C.: AEI Press, 1999) 13.

54   Ibid. 14.
55   Daniel Byman, et al., "Coercing Saddam Hussain: Lesson from the Past", *Survival* 40.3 (1998): 136.
56   David Wurmser, *Tyranny's Ally* 10–18.
57   Anthony Lake, Telephone Interview with Author, 27 Sep. 2004.
58   Robert H. Pelletreau, *Developments in the Middle East*, 4 Oct. 1994 <http://dosfan.lib.uic.edu/ERC/briefing/dispatch/1994/html/Dispatchv5no41.html >.
59   Ibid.
60   Lake, Telephone Interview with Author.
61   Wurmser, *Tyranny's Ally* 14–15.
62   Pelletreau, *Developments in the Middle East*.
63   Wurmser, *Tyranny's Ally* 14–15.
64   Jim Hoagland, "How CIA's Secret War on Saddam Collapsed", *Washington Post* 26 June 1997: A21.
65   Martin Indyk, *The Clinton Administration's Approach to the Middle East*, 18 May 1993 .
66   Hoagland, "How CIA's Secret War on Saddam Collapsed", A21.
67   Ibid. A21.
68   John Burgess and David Ottway, "Iraqi Opposition Unable to Mount Viable Challenge", *Washington Post* 12 Feb. 1998: A2.
69   Ewan Thomas, et al., "How the CIA's Secret War in Iraq Turned into Utter Fiasco", *Newsweek* 23 Mar. 1998: 5
70   Wurmser, *Tyranny's Ally* 20–25.
71   Wurmser, *Tyranny's Ally* 21.
72   Nizar al-Khazraji was a former Iraqi Chief of Staff who defected to the INA in 1996.
73   Cordesman, *Iraq and the War of Sanctions* 27.
74   Wurmser, *Tyranny's Ally* 21.
75   UNSCR 706 of 15 Aug. 1991, Para. 1.
76   Pollack, *The Threatening Storm* 60.
77   Dilip Hiro, *Neighbors, Not Friends: Iraq and Iran after the Gulf Wars* (London; New York: Routledge, 2001) 25–67.
78   United Nations, *Memorandum of Understanding between the Secretariat of the United Nations and the Government of Iraq on the Implementation of Security Council Resolution 986 (1995)*.
79   Mary E. O'Connell, "Debating the Law of Sanctions", *European Journal of International Law* 13.1 (2002): 69–71.
80   See United States, Department of State, *Saddam Hussain's Iraq*, (Washington, D.C.: GPO, 1999) 1–29.
81   Kenneth Katzman, "Iraq: International Support for US Policy", *CRS Issue Brief for Congress*, (98-114F), (Washington D.C.: Congressional Research Service, Library of Congress: GPO, 19 Feb. 1998) 10pp, 12/08/03 <http://www.globalsecurity.org/wmd/library/report/crs/98-114.htm>.
82   Albright and Woodward, *Madam Secretary* 275.
83   Its provisions were expanded by UNSCR 1143 of 4 Dec. 1997 and UNSCR 1158 of 28 Mar. 1998.
84   O'Connell, "Debating the Law of Sanctions" 270.
85   Geoff Simons, *Imposing Economic Sanctions: Legal Remedy or Genocidal Tool?*

(London: Pluto, 1999) 173–80; Geoff Simons, *Targeting Iraq: Sanctions and Bombing in US Policy* (London: Saqi Books, 2002) 63–85; and Eric Rouleau, "America's Unyielding Policy Towards Iraq", *Foreign Affairs* 74.1 (1995): 59–74.

86 Pollack, *The Threatening Storm* 125–44.

87 Cordesman, *Iraq and the War of Sanctions* 269–71.

88 Pollack, *The Threatening Storm* 125–44.

89 O'Connell, "Debating the Law of Sanctions" 269–74.

90 Albright and Woodward, *Madam Secretary* 278.

91 O'Connell, "Debating the Law of Sanctions" 227.

92 UNSCR 1115 of 21 Jun. 1997, UNSCR 1134 of 23 Oct. 1997, UNSCR 1137 of 12 Nov. 1997 and UNSCR 1205 of 5 Nov. 1998.

93 Qtd. in Katzman, "Iraq: International Support for US Policy" 4.

94 Barton Gellman, "Gingrich Opens File on White House Iraq Policy", *Washington Post* 29 Aug. 1998: A2.

95 Burgess and Ottway, "Iraqi Opposition Unable to Mount Viable Challenge" A2.

96 Cordesman, *Iraq and the War of Sanctions* 271.

97 Richard Butler, *Saddam Defiant: The Threat of Weapons of Mass Destruction and the Crisis of Global Security* (London: Phoenix, 2001) 193–98.

98 Ibid. 197–98.

99 Barton Gellman, "US Spied on Iraqi Military Via UN", *Washington Post* 2 Mar. 1999: A2.

100 Bob Woodward, *Plan of Attack* (New York: Simon & Schuster, 2004) 245.

101 Gellman, "Gingrich Opens File on White House Iraq Policy".

102 Scott Ritter, "An Ineffective Policy toward Baghdad", *International Herald Tribune* 17 Aug. 1999: 5.

103 United States, Senate, *Condemning Iraq's Threat to International Peace and Security*, 105th Cong., 2nd Sess., Res 711988 (Washington, D.C.: GPO, 21 Jan. 1998) 2pp. 17/12/03 <http://weblog.theviewfromthecore.com/2004_02/ind_003148.html>.

104 United States, House, *Iraq Liberation Act of 1998*, H.R. 466, P.L. 105-338, (Washington, D.C.: GPO, 31 Oct. 1998) 8pp. 17/12/03 <http://www.iraqwatch.org/government/US/Legislation/ILA.htm>.

105 Ibid. Sect. 3.

106 Kenneth Katzman, "Iraq: US Efforts to Change the Regime", *CRS Report for Congress*, (RL31339), Washington, D.C.: Congressional Research Service, Library of Congress, 22 Mar. 2002, 16pp, 23/10/03 <http://www.casi.org.uk/info/usdocs/crs/020322rl31339.pdf>.

107 Butler, *Saddam Defiant* 96–97.

108 Ibid. 97.

109 Ibid. 100.

110 Judy Aita, "UNSCOM Suspends Operations in Iraq", *United States Information Agency* 29 Oct. 1997, 12/03/03 <http://www.fas.org/news/iraq/1997/10/97102902_npo.html>.

111 United Nations, Security Council, *United Nations Security Council Statement on Iraq*, (New York: United Nations, 29 Oct. 1997) 2pp. 25/10/03 <http://www.fas.org/news/iraq/1997/10/97102904_npo.html>.

112 Judy Aita, "Iraq Rejects United Nations Overtures to Resume Co-Operation

with UNSCOM", *United States Information Agency* 7 Nov. 1997, 12/06/02 <http://www.fas.org/news/iraq/1997/11/97110701_npo.html>.

113 Government of Iraq, *Joint Communique from the Iraqi and Russian Governments*, 20 Nov. 1997, http://www.fas.org/news/iraq/1997/11/iraq_un_97_11_20.htm.

114 Wendy Lubetkin, "Secretary of State: Perm Five Unity Brings Apparent Reversal in Iraq", *United States Information Agency* 20 Nov. 1997, 26/09/03 <http://www.fas.org/news/iraq/1997/11/97112006_tpo.html>; Albright and Woodward, *Madam Secretary* 280–81; and Butler, *Saddam Defiant* 120.

115 Butler, *Saddam Defiant* 140–68.

116 Albright and Woodward, *Madam Secretary* 283–84.

117 UNSCR 1154 of 2 Mar. 1998, Par. 3.

118 Iraq's Revolutionary Command Council and the Ba'ath Party Command halted their cooperation with UNSCOM and the IAEA on 5 Aug. 1998, and the government of Iraq terminated its cooperation on 31 Oct. 1998.

119 Cordesman, *Iraq and the War of Sanctions* 366–67.

120 United Nations, UNSCOM, *UNSCOM Chairman's Letter to the Security Council*, (New York: United Nations, 15 Dec. 1998) 9pp. 12/08/03 <http://www.iraqwatch.org/un/UNSCOM/s-1998-1127.htm >.

121 Alfred B. Prados and Kenneth Katzman, "Iraq: Former and Recent Military Confrontations with the United States", *CRS Issue Brief for Congress*, (IB94049), Washington, D.C.: Congressional Research Service, Library of Congress, 16 Oct. 2002) 18pp, 04/11/04 *<http://fpc.state.gov/documents/organization/14836. pdf>*.

122 Prados and Katzman, "Iraq: Former and Recent Military Confrontations with the United States".

123 William Arkin, "The Difference Was in the Details", *Washington Post* 17 Jan. 1999: B1.

124 Colum Lynch, "UN Arms Inspectors Will Not Return to Iraq", *Washington Post* 24 Sept. 1999: A22.

125 UNSCR 1154 of 2 Mar. 1998, Par. 3.

126 Gray, "From Unity to Polarization: International Law and the Use of Force against Iraq" 12.

127 Ibid.

128 UNSCR 687 of 3 Apr. 1991, Par. 1.

129 Gray, "From Unity to Polarization: International Law and the Use of Force against Iraq" 12–13.

130 Albright and Woodward, *Madam Secretary* 287.

131 Martin Indyk, "Indyk Says US Is Committed to a Better Future for the Middle East," Indyk remarks at New York Council on Foreign Relations, New York: GPO, 23 Apr. 1999. 12pp. 13/05/03 <http://www.usembassy-amman.org.jo/4Ind.html>.

132 Bradley Graham, "The Big Military Question: What's Next?", *Washington Post* 24 Dec. 1998: A5.

133 Ibid.

134 Thomas W. Lippman, "Two Options for US Policy", *Washington Post* 20 Dec. 1998: A2.

135 David Buchan, "Europeans Rally to Allies' Cause", *Financial Times* 19 Dec. 1998: 59.

136 Steven Komarow, "Saddam's Ouster Is Goal Now, US Officials Say", *USA Today* 21 Dec. 1998: 01A; and Barbara Slavin, "UNSCOM Unlikely to Return to Iraq", *USA Today* 21 Dec. 1998: 18A.

137 The Associated Press, "France Offers Plan to Lift Iraqi Embargo", *USA Today Online* 13 Jan. 1999, 12/02/03 <http://www.usatoday.com/news/index/iraq/iraq549.htm>.

138 The Associated Press, "French Proposal Leads to Talks on Iraq", *USA Today Online* 14 Jan. 1999, 12/02/03 <http://www.usatoday.com/news/index/iraq/iraq550.htm>.

139 The Associated Press, "US Rejects Russian Solution on Iraq", *USA Today Online* 15 Jan. 1999, 12/02/03 <http://www.usatoday.com/news/index/iraq/ iraq553. htm>.

140 Ibid.

141 Ibid.

142 The Associated Press, "Top General Criticizes US Policy on Iraq", *USA Today Online* 28 Jan. 1999, 12/02/03 <http://www.usatoday.com/news/index/iraq/iraq567.htm>.

143 Ibid.

144 David Ensor, "US to Intensify Work with Iraqi Opposition Groups", *CNN Online* 16 Nov. 1998, 12/02/03 <http://edition.cnn.com/US/9811/16/saddam.overthrow/>.

145 Harry Dunphy, "US Will Aid Iraqi Opposition", *Associated Press* 25 May 1999, 15/04/03 <http://www.iraqcmm.org/cmm/clari-990525.html>.

146 United States, House, *Foreign Operations, Export Financing, and Related Programs Appropriations Act*, H.R. 4811, P.L. 106-429, (Washington, D.C.: GPO, 19 Dec. 2000) 45pp. 17/09/03 <http://clinton4.nara.gov/OMB/legislative/7day/12-19-00.pdf>.

147 Katzman, "Iraq: US Efforts to Change the Regime".

148 Robert Kagan, *Of Paradise and Power: America and Europe in the New World Order* (New York: Knopf, 2004) 44.

149 Clinton's commitment to a multilateral containment of Iraq provided a legal commitment, and thus official position, of being premised on a continuation of sanctions *until* Iraq had complied with its international obligations.

150 Notwithstanding an armed invasion of Iraq to enact regime change, containment was seen as a requirement by Washington as a means of controlling the threats Iraq potentially posed to the region until either regime change or its full compliance with UN resolutions was achieved.

PART 3

THE UNITED STATES AND THE PERSIAN
GULF IN THE WAR ON TERROR

6

Iraq and the War on Terror: Untangling Tactical and Strategic Policy

"The United States has adopted a new policy, a forward strategy of freedom in the Middle East. This strategy requires the same persistence and energy and idealism we have shown before. And it will yield the same results. As in Europe, as in Asia, as in every region of the world, the advance of freedom leads to peace."

George W. Bush
November 2003

At the very first meeting of the Principals of the National Security Council on 30 January 2001, Secretary to the Treasury, Paul O'Neill, reported that the focus of the administration was clearly on effecting regime change within Iraq.[1] Secretary of State Powell saw a clear need to revamp Clinton's failed sanctions regime to achieve regime change through a tactical policy of seeking Iraq's compliance with UN resolutions. Powell commented that the sanctions are "not endearing us to the Iraqi people, whose support we're hoping to elicit . . . to help overthrow this regime".[2] The summary of the State Department's strategy towards Iraq at the National Security Council meeting on 1 February 2001 stated:

> Our overall objective would be to prevent Iraq from threatening its neighbors or the national security more broadly on the basis of continued control of Iraqi revenue, [a] ban on military and WMD related imports and weapons inspections. This approach has two tracks which are mutually reinforcing and which we would pursue concurrently; one track is to intensify sanctions enforcement and the other is to implement UN Security Council resolution 1284.[3]

As with the Clinton administration, the strategic objective of regime change continued, and the use of sanctions as a tactical policy for promoting the conditions required to effect regime change was applied. The use of military force – in terms of an invasion – was reportedly *never* specifically discussed at the NSC meeting on 1 February 2001, and was not seen as a prudent policy option at that time. However, the need to rekindle the military coalition of the 1991 Gulf War was seen as a suitable way of coercing Saddam to comply with Security Council Resolutions. The Bush administration's strategy was therefore premised on a policy continuation from the Clinton administration.

It was, however, in the period between 31 May and 26 June 2001 that the Deputy National Security Advisor, Stephen J. Hadley, held discussions at the Deputies' Subcommittee level to formulate the Principals' strategic framework into an official policy strategy.[4] The official policy strategy towards Iraq was eventually presented to the Principals at the National Security Council on 1 August 2001. Entitled "A Liberation Strategy",[5] the Top Secret document "proposed a phased strategy of pressuring Saddam and developing the tools and opportunities for enhancing that pressure, and how to take advantage of the opportunities. It relied heavily on the Iraqi opposition".[6] The strategy did not call for a military invasion but was a revitalised version of the policy that was undertaken during the Clinton era. Bob Woodward writes that:

> The paper had classified attachments that went into detail about what might be done diplomatically – economic sanctions and U.N. weapons inspectors; militarily with the no-fly zones and the contingencies if a pilot were shot down; and what the CIA or others might do to support, strengthen and empower the Iraqi opposition.[7]

Although this was a policy continuation from the Clinton years, the willingness of the administration to use military force to achieve a foreign policy objective was seen as being in marked contrast to the general reluctance present within the Clinton presidency. Indeed, Paul O'Neill found that "[t]hose present who had attended NSC meetings of the previous administration – and there were several – noticed a material shift [in the willingness to use military force]" and that the "prohibition [for using military force] was clearly gone . . . that opened options, options that hadn't been opened before".[8] Indeed, the most notable advocate for the use of military force against Iraq was Paul Wolfowitz, the Deputy Secretary of Defense.[9] His views were exceptionally hawkish – he had notably been calling for a military solution towards Iraq even before he had taken office in the Bush administration.

Although the willingness to use military force was present and being touted by Wolfowitz, contextually little had changed since the Clinton administration. The general willingness to use military force, short of an invasion, could most realistically be explained by the different intellectual beliefs held by those in Bush's foreign policy circle, specifically, its neo-conservative character and outlook on international affairs. Nevertheless, the actual policy towards Iraq in the Bush administration prior to 11 September 2001 should be characterised as a policy continuation from the Clinton era, but with the caveat that there was a substantive change in the administration's willingness to use military force, even though a military invasion was *not* part of the administration's policy towards Iraq at that time.

In accordance with Bush's election pledges and the administration's policy framework, efforts were made at attempting to rebuild the multilateral coalition towards Iraq from the onset. Secretary of State Powell sought regional support from within the Middle East for 'smart sanctions' that would ease the flow of humanitarian and civilian goods to Iraq, whilst tightening restrictions on Iraqi illicit imports and exports.[10] Katzman explains Powell's stance:

> The smart sanctions plan represented an effort, articulated primarily by Secretary of State Colin Powell at the beginning of the Bush administration, to rebuild a consensus to contain Iraq. The US plan centered on a trade-off in which restrictions on the flow of civilian goods to Iraq would be greatly eased and, in return, Iraq's illicit trade with its neighbors would be brought under the oil-for-food program and its monitoring and control mechanisms.[11]

At the United Nations, Washington was successful in having UN Security Council Resolution 1409 adopted. This resolution eased the restrictions on Iraqi civilian and humanitarian imports. But within the Middle East, the smart sanctions proposal did not receive the crucial backing from Middle Eastern countries. In spite of this, Powell claimed that the policy was a success as "[w]e have kept him contained, kept him in his box".[12] Thus whilst Washington's smart sanctions strategy did cater for the demands being levied by France, China and Russia for a broad easing of sanctions, it was generally unsuccessful in tightening the restrictions on Iraq's illicit imports and exports.

To fulfil Bush's pledge to uphold the terms of the Iraq Liberation Act of 1998, the level of contact between Washington and Iraqi opposition groups was increased. However, the administration should not be seen as having made *substantive progress* towards the implementation of the Iraqi Liberation Act. Although the administration did carry out the distribution of economic support funds in accordance with the plan devised by Clinton in his final week of office, no funds were distributed as part of the Iraq Liberation Act itself. The reason for this was that the State Department suspended the distribution of funds by the Pentagon until a financial audit of the INC was carried out.[13] The suspension was based on the suspected financial mismanagement of funds by the INC. This suspension of the allocation of funds continued until shortly after Bush's January 2002 State of the Union speech.

Since 1991, successive administrations had categorised Iraq as a hostile state which posed a threat to the United States through unconventional weapons. Iraq was presumed to be in possession of such weapons because of its inability or unwillingness to verify the destruction of all of its prohibited weapon stockpiles. But it is important to recognise, however, that even if Iraq was in a position to verify the destruction of its entire prohibited weapons stockpile, it would have continued to be seen as a threat to the United States. Specifically, since 1991, an Iraq under the regime of Saddam Hussein was viewed as being intent on rekindling its unconventional weapon programmes if the sanctions and inspection mandates were ever lifted because of the presumed intent of Saddam Hussein to acquire such weaponry.

Given this contextual situation, the options available to the newly incumbent Bush administration can be summarised as:

1. A continual application of UN sanctions until both Iraq had verified the destruction of its prohibited weapon stockpiles and Saddam Hussein's regime had been internally deposed from power;[14]
2. A military invasion of Iraq to oust Saddam Hussein's regime from power;
3. An abandonment of the containment strategy, opting instead for engagement and reintegration.

Although the third option was a theoretical possibility, it would not have been a realistic policy option until the United Nations was able to rule that Iraq had *fully* complied with its obligations.[15] But, as has already been discussed, Iraq cannot be regarded as having been *able* to verify the destruction of all of the prohibited weapons the UN inspectors had calculated were outstanding, and thus would have technically remained in contravention of UN resolutions. Therefore, at the most basic level, the policy decision facing the Bush administration was either the application of UN sanctions until an internal regime change had occurred, or a military invasion to achieve regime change. In either case the endgame strategic objective had remained consistent since 1991: regime change.

In the following analysis, the Bush administration will be shown to have been consistent in its application of US foreign policy towards Iraq that it inherited from the Clinton administration up until the 9/11 attacks. The analysis will demonstrate that the 9/11 attacks resulted in a fundamental break from the consistent US policy approach that had been applied since 1991. The manner in which the 9/11 attacks altered the contextual situation vis-à-vis Iraq was through the definition of the threat facing the United States in the newly emerged grand strategic era of the War on Terror.

Specifically, the attacks prompted the definition of threat to not only include state sponsors of terrorism such as Afghanistan, but to also include countries hostile to the United States that were producing, or intent on producing, unconventional weapons.[16] In other words, Iraq was seen to pose a future threat as Saddam's regime was ultimately seen as intent on manufacturing unconventional weapons which could be used against the United States. By categorising Iraq in this manner, the *preventive* use of force was deemed to be applicable.

On a wider level however, the new grand strategic era also had a direct bearing on the definition of Persian Gulf security: the balance of power doctrine, coupled with the tactical use of containment and deterrence as a means of safeguarding the security of the GCC, was wholly rejected. The strategy was seen by the Bush administration as preventing the widespread adoption of liberal democracy, but crucially, in the advent of the War on Terror era this was interpreted by Bush's neoconservative foreign policy team as being the root cause of politically-inspired Islamic terrorism epitomised by al-Qa'ida. In addition, the spread of liberal democracy was seen by neoconservatives as providing stability to the region as peaceful relations are, admittedly, the norm amongst like-minded liberal democracies. With the acceptance of this neoconservative pillar, the road map towards both ensuring Persian Gulf security and countering the root causes of international Islamic terrorism were seen as achievable through the successful spread of liberal democracy throughout the Middle East.

With Persian Gulf security resting on the need to re-engineer the political landscape of the Middle East, a change in US policy towards Iraq occurred. The following analysis will show that the Bush administration saw the most effective means of achieving its objectives in the Middle East, and on a wider level towards its global counterterrorism campaign, through implementing regime change in Iraq via a military invasion. Specifically speaking, an invasion of Iraq was seen as allowing for nation building, on a par with post-Second World War West Germany, which would ultimately serve as a beacon for democracy throughout the region thereby creating unassailable pressures on its neighbouring states to democratise. Through doing so, the logic was that the overall dual strategic objectives of countering the root causes of international terrorism and safeguarding Persian Gulf security were attainable.

The following analysis will show that the Bush administration saw Iraq's failure to comply with its international obligations as providing a *casus belli*. It will be argued that this was used as a tactical means to provide public justification for the war, as the strategic goals of spreading democracy as a counterterrorism initiative and preventing Iraq from *potentially* manufacturing unconventional weapons was not widely seen as a legitimate legal and political justification for invading Iraq.

The tactical policy road map to launching an invasion of Iraq is characterised as:

1. Arguing that Iraq possessed unconventional weapons, and was actively producing them in violation of international law;
2. Arguing that although Iraq had the capability to peacefully resolve the situation, it had no intention of doing so;
3. Showing that Saddam Hussein's regime had ties with al-Qa'ida-linked terrorist groups, and could potentially supply them covertly with unconventional weapons;
4. To demonstrate that if the United States provided Iraq with an ultimatum to comply with its international obligations which it failed to heed, the United States would be justified to enforce UN resolutions to prevent the national security of the United States being potentially threatened by terrorists armed with the 'smoking gun' of an unconventional weapon.

These tactical justifications will be shown to be insufficient to warrant the use of force against Iraq, and consequently it is possible to infer that the Bush administration knowingly overstated the risk as a means of garnering legitimacy for this policy. Nevertheless, this will serve to underline that the official policy towards Iraq was tactical, and masked the true strategic reasoning behind the invasion of Iraq in March 2003.

The structure of the following analysis of US foreign policy will be twofold: firstly, an analysis of the official policy in the prelude of the invasion of Iraq in March 2003 will show that it did not adequately explain the foreign policy decision to depart from the post-Cold War containment policy towards Iraq. Secondly, an analysis of alternative factors will be provided in order to demonstrate that following the 9/11 attacks, the official policy in the prelude to the invasion of Iraq was a tactical means of achieving a strategic objective that ultimately resulted from the context of the War on Terror.

Tactical Foreign Policy Towards Iraq

According to Bob Woodward, it was within days of the 9/11 attacks that Donald Rumsfeld and Paul Wolfowitz began advocating military action against Iraq.[17] This is corroborated by the former Treasury Secretary, Paul O'Neill, who recalled that Wolfowitz raised the prospect of military action against Iraq at the National Security Council meeting on 13 September 2001 as part of the administration's response to the 9/11 attacks.[18] Whilst this is evidence of the internal debate on the appropriate response to the terrorist attacks, the actual manifestation of this aspect of the Bush Doctrine that saw Iraq encompassed as part of the War on Terror was unveiled in the 2002 State of the Union Address.

Following the 2002 State of the Union Address, Bush administration officials continued making the case for the inclusion of rogue states as part of the War on Terror on account of the risk from unconventional weapons. Although such a threat is conceivable, it arguably overstates the risk in that the modus operandi of terrorist groups should more accurately be associated with conventional weapons.[19] But within the post 9/11 context, an attack by terrorists armed with unconventional weapons was generally accepted as the sum of all fears. By highlighting this potential threat, a domestic political will to extend the War on Terror to encompass Iraq was being fostered.

To actually encompass Iraq into the rubric of the War on Terror, the White House began a twofold strategy which aimed to establish that Iraq was in possession of unconventional weapons and that it had links with al-Qa'ida. Members of Bush's foreign policy team made several references to the risk of Iraq's smoking gun being a 'nuclear cloud' appearing over an American city that would effectively dwarf the scale of the 9/11 attacks. Indeed, such reports played on the already present perception of a linkage: according to a poll by *Newsweek* in late July 2002, 72% of people in the United States believed that Iraq was involved with aiding al-Qa'ida to acquire unconventional weapons.[20] This was significant in that, by fostering the perception of threat, the ultimate risk of terrorists using an unconventional weapon against the United States became ever more real.

With the Bush administration referring to Iraq's potential smoking gun as a 'nuclear cloud' over an American city if UN resolutions were not enforced, the fears of the average American were being unjustly played upon, as the IAEA inspectors had effectively rendered harmless Iraq's nuclear programme during the Clinton administration. Importantly, the Bush administration would have known this to have been the case. As Iraq simply did not have a nuclear capability or an active nuclear programme at the time, the use of such phraseology was effectively scaremongering.

In terms of establishing a connection between the two, the Bush administration highlighted the presence in Iraq of the al-Qa'ida linked group Ansar al-Islam.[21] The implication was that Ansar al-Islam's presence in Iraq was evidence of some form of substantive cooperative agreement with al-Qa'ida. But again, it was misleading of the Bush administration to have highlighted this. Ansar al-Islam was operating in the Kurdish area which was not under the control of Saddam Hussein. Although Saddam would have indirectly benefited from Ansar al-Islam's attacks on the Kurds,[22] it is important to recognise that the group was also hostile to Saddam's regime. Indeed, the prospect of a cooperative agreement was rejected by the leader of Ansar al-Islam as he saw Saddam's regime as operating "outside the Islamist zone".[23] Therefore, the implication of the Bush administration that Saddam's regime was connected to al-Qa'ida through Ansar al-Islam is a misrepresentation of the facts. But more importantly, it is inconceivable that this would not have been known by the US intelligence community. In some respects however, this was reflected in the administration's comments as a linkage was only *implied*, and not *categorically stated*. There appears to be a degree of justification to conclude that stating the link in this way was done deliberately to allow for Iraq's inclusion into the rubric of the War on Terror.

In addition to this, it was reported that the lead hijacker of the 9/11 attacks, Mohamed Atta, met with Iraqi intelligence in Prague in June 2000 and April 2001.[24] Although these reports were subsequently rejected by the Czech police,[25] it is important to recognise that with the Bush administration citing such information, the public perception of a linkage between Iraq and al-Qa'ida would have been fostered. But in terms of whether there is substance to the overall view that Saddam's regime had links with al-Qa'ida, both the 9/11 Commission and the Duelfer reports have given little currency to these allegations.[26] Although the 9/11 Commission did find evidence that al-Qa'ida had repeatedly approached Iraq, they found no evidence to support the conjecture that any real cooperation had existed.[27] Therefore, there is a clear question: why did the administration infer from its intelligence data that Iraq had substantial linkages to al-Qa'ida when a post-invasion reassessment suggested the contrary?

In terms of translating this perception to Congress, the White House's alarming pronouncements saw Iraq steadily evolve as a key political issue in the War on Terror. Congress had clearly favoured regime change since 1998, but the issue of unconventional weapons falling into the hands of al-Qa'ida had altered the definition of threat that Iraq posed. The Senate Committee on Foreign Relations met at the end of July 2002 to discuss the threats posed by Iraq; it was clear from the testimony of several of the witnesses that the administration's fears were warranted.[28] With much of the substance of the Senate committee having confirmed the administration's position, this newly defined threat was given political credibility on a bipartisan level.

Of equal importance, however, was the nature of the intelligence released by the CIA to members of Congress. With the CIA confirming that Iraq possessed such weapons and had links with al-Qa'ida, there appeared to be a clear political case which justified the executive's position. Indeed, in advance of the Congressional debate on the authorisation of the use of force against Iraq, the CIA released excerpts of a closed Congressional hearing held on 2 October 2002. The excerpts left little doubt that Iraq had long-standing ties to al-Qa'ida and posed a threat through its undeclared stockpiles of unconventional weapons.[29] With the executive and the intelligence community confirming that Iraq posed a threat to the United States through such linkages, the political climate within Congress shifted towards an acceptance of the position of the executive. Crucially, this allowed the executive to implement a substantive foreign policy change towards Iraq.

With regard to Iraq's unconventional weapons programmes, the intelligence community was correct to highlight that Iraq had the *theoretical capability* to be in possession of the weapons that the UN Special Commission saw as outstanding. However, as has already been shown, the intelligence community should have analytically known that this was *highly unlikely* and any suggestion to the contrary was misleading. According to the 2005 Commission on the Intelligence Capabilities of the United States Regarding Weapons of Mass Destruction, "[t]he intelligence community was dead wrong in almost all of its pre-war judgments about Iraq's weapons of mass destruction. This was a major intelligence failure".[30] Although there was a clear failure of intelligence, there is also the possibility that the intelligence data was 'politicised' by way of it being selectively used as a tactical means of providing the *casus belli* against Iraq.

The clear case was thus made that Iraq had failed to comply with its obligations and that it continued to possess a prohibited unconventional weapons stockpile. By adding the terrorist linkage, US foreign policy was able to provide a level of justification, on the grounds of safeguarding US national security, to issue an ultimatum to Iraq. But, as already discussed, the policy response to this *potential* threat was the adoption of the doctrine of anticipatory self-defence. So, if Iraq failed to adhere to its obligations, the Bush administration maintained that it reserved the right to use 'pre-emptive' action against Iraq as per its rules of engagement.

A key issue was whether the Bush administration should resort to the United Nations as part of its tactical strategy. Bush acknowledged that "[t]here were certain people in the administration that were hopeful we could solve this diplomatically. And there were some that basically said we can't solve it diplomatically."[31] Colin Powell has been portrayed as a notable advocate within the administration for resorting to the United Nations as a means of providing a wider diplomatic footing; but as Secretary of State it was only reasonable to expect that someone in such a position would advocate this. Although this was accepted by the administration, Cheney's views on the United Nations route leading to a "never-ending process of debate, compromise and delay"[32] seemed to capture the essence of the view held by the White House. It was recognised, however, that the active participation of the United Kingdom was required for political legitimacy if it could not be provided through the United Nations. Whilst the administration would conceivably not have felt a domestic political need for the specific authorisation of the Security Council in the same manner as the United Kingdom, some form of international legitimacy was still required. Robert Kagan rightly highlights that although the Bush administration did not require the active participation of British forces to invade Iraq "[i]t was the patina of international legitimacy Blair's support provided – a legitimacy the American people wanted and needed, as the Bush officials well understood".[33] The conclusion was to place the emphasis on the need for the United Nations to enforce its own resolutions and, failing that, there would be a case for the United States to act without a specific UN sanction along with a 'coalition of the willing'. Moreover, by resorting to the United Nations in the first instance, the spectre of international legitimacy was afforded by the United Kingdom to the United States.

On 12 September 2002, Bush declared in a speech in the United Nations that it was the responsibility of the international community to enforce UN resolutions on Iraq. Bush sent the clear message to the United Nations that if it failed to enforce the relevant UN Security Council resolutions the United States would be forced into action. Bush stated:

> My nation will work with the UN Security Council to meet our common challenge. If Iraq's regime defies us again, the world must move deliberately, decisively to hold Iraq to account. We will work with the UN Security Council for the necessary resolutions. But the purposes of the United States should not be doubted. The Security Council resolutions will be enforced – the just demands of peace and security will be met – or action will be unavoidable.[34]

In accordance with the Bush Doctrine, this immediate threat had to be dealt with multilaterally if possible, but pre-emptively and in a unilateral fashion if the UN route proved ineffective.[35] A few days later on 17 September 2002 the Bush administration released its National Security Strategy. As has already been discussed, it controversially adopted the preventative use of force doctrine as a key method of preventing rogue states developing unconventional weapons which could be provided to terrorist groups. In terms of Iraq, this basically set out the political 'rules of engagement' whereby launching an invasion of Iraq would occur if the United Nations failed to enforce its own resolutions.

On a domestic level, Congress provided authorisation for the use of force against Iraq in October 2002. This sent a clear statement to the world that the United States was prepared to act if Iraq failed to comply with UN resolutions. This, in addition to Bush's speech to the UN General Assembly, prompted revised diplomatic attempts at the United Nations to have the inspectors returned to Iraq.

It was following these developments that the Security Council unanimously passed UNSCR 1441 on 8 November 2002. The resolution recognised that Iraq had been in material breach of a series of previous UN resolutions, but nonetheless accorded Iraq a final opportunity to comply with the will of the international community. Iraq was required to provide a full and complete declaration of its unconventional weapons programmes and missile technology within thirty days. The resolution made clear that if Iraq failed to comply with the terms of the resolution, it would face "serious consequences".[36] But under international law, this did not amount to an authorisation for the use of force unless the case of Kosovo is interpreted as providing the customary international legal justification required for the use of force, without specific authorisation from the Security Council.

It is worth recognising at this point, that in the Security Council discussions on Resolution 1441 it was recognised that the resolution did not contain the authorisation for the use of force, and that any authorisation to do so would require an additional resolution. The United States Ambassador to the United Nations, John Negroponte, said:

> As we have said on numerous occasions to Council members, this Resolution contains no 'hidden triggers' and no 'automaticity' with respect to the use of force. If there is a further Iraqi breach, reported to the Council by UNMOVIC, the IAEA, or a member state, the matter will return to the Council for discussions as required in paragraph 12.[37]

The recognition that Resolution 1441 did not contain the authorisation for the use of force against Iraq was also confirmed by the British permanent representative to the United Nations, Jeremy Greenstock:

> We heard loud and clear during the negotiations the concerns about 'automaticity' and 'hidden triggers' . . . Let me be equally clear in response, as one of the co-sponsors of the text we have adopted. There is no 'automaticity' in this Resolution. If there is a further Iraqi breach of its disarmament obligations, the matter will return to the Council for discussion as required in operational paragraph 12.[38]

Therefore, Resolution 1441 was adopted on the provision given by its sponsors, the United States and the United Kingdom, that the resolution *did not* contain the authorisation for the use of force, even in the event of an Iraqi non-compliance.

Iraq resumed its cooperation with the IAEA and the UN special commission on 27 November and provided a 12,000-page declaration to the United Nations in early December. Iraq's declaration amounted to a statement that it was no longer in possession of unconventional weapons as it had unilaterally destroyed them.[39] Hans Blix described the declaration as consisting of "reprints of declarations that had been sent to UNSCOM in the years before the inspectors left at the end of 1998".[40] But, for the United States, the declaration amounted to a material breach as it did not include declarations on everything it believed to be outstanding. Nevertheless, the United States did not aim to bring the crisis to a close and allowed the inspections process to continue.

With the inspection process continuing, both the United States and the United Kingdom released intelligence dossiers on Iraq's WMD capabilities in order to bolster domestic support against Iraq. The CIA's and British Joint Intelligence Committee's (JIC) dossiers asserted that Iraq was continuing its unconventional weapon programmes and was in possession of actual weapons. The British government's assessment stated that, based on UNSCOM reports, Iraq had failed to declare the following materials:

> Up to 360 tonnes of bulk chemical warfare agent, including 1.5 tonnes of VX nerve agent; up to 3,000 tonnes of precursor chemicals, including approximately 300 tonnes which, in the Iraqi chemical warfare programme, were unique to the production of VX; growth media procured for biological agent production (enough to produce over three times the 8,500 litres of anthrax spores Iraq admits to having manufactured); over 30,000 special munitions for delivery of chemical and biological agents.[41]

It is important to recognise here that the JIC's assessment highlighted not only the quantities of precursor materials Iraq had not accounted for, but also the quantities of actual biological and chemical weaponries Iraq was believed to be in possession of. But this estimate was misleading: it was the maximum potential of Iraq's capability, and did not account for the production wastage of precursors during manufacture; the actual shelf life of such weapons; or even potential stockpiles destroyed during bombing raids.

In the aftermath of the apparent suicide of the British government's weapons expert, Dr David Kelly, the Hutton Inquiry examined the intelligence data which was included in the JIC's dossier on Iraq. A key finding was that Downing Street wanted a compelling case to be made in the dossier and that this influenced the language used by the JIC. Lord Hutton's report stated that this "may have subconsciously influenced . . . members of the JIC to make the wording of the dossier somewhat stronger than it would have been if it had been contained in a normal JIC assessment".[42] Overall, the dossier contained language that permitted a degree of misrepresentation of Iraq's capability; the dossier was therefore arguably construed towards serving the political purpose of bolstering legitimacy for launching an invasion. In essence, the Hutton Report underlined that the intelligence data had been potentially politicised to serve the tactical policy of invading Iraq to effect regime change.

The US and the United Kingdom interpreted Iraq's actions after the inspection process resumed as constituting a material breach.[43] Following the rhetoric and military deployments which indicated that an invasion was likely, numerous large-scale antiwar protests occurred across the world. By themselves, such protests had little bearing on altering US policy, but they did fuel the antiwar position of several countries, in particular France and Germany. This had a bearing on US foreign policy because it affected the viability of a second resolution being passed by the United Nations, classifying Iraq as being in material breach and providing specific authorisation for the use of force. As has already been discussed, whilst this would not necessarily have prevented the United States from invading Iraq, it was significant for US policy because of the effect it had on the United Kingdom's ability to partake in an invasion. The problem was very much whether a credible case could be made at the United Nations to overcome the widespread domestic opposition to any potential war against Iraq.

President Bush promised compelling evidence in his January 2003 State of the Union Address to allay doubts over Iraq's possession of prohibited weapons. The administration provided this through a public presentation of intelligence data by Secretary Powell at the United Nations in early February 2003. This was the culmination of efforts by the United States to provide a clear-cut case of the need to bring Iraq into compliance with UN resolutions. The presentation was very reminiscent of Secretary Adlai Stevenson's performance during the Cuban Missile Crisis. Powell's photographic and audio data indicated that Iraq was actively concealing and deceiving UNMOVIC. Although it was widely hailed within the United States as a compelling case it was also subject to a great degree of scepticism.[44] Indeed, Hans Blix noted that the presentation contained inaccuracies and was by no means a clear-cut case.[45] Russia, France and China shared this scepticism and were unwilling to accept the British and American position that it provided a *casus belli* against Iraq. They took the position that the inspectors should be accorded more time before a judgement was formulated, and thus a second resolution finding Iraq in material breach and authorising the use of force was seen as premature. However, *on face value*, Powell's presentation did seem convincing and it is reasonable to conclude that it had some effect on swaying public opinion in favour of the need to launch punitive action against Iraq.

However, with Hans Blix's report to the United Nations on 6 March 2003 which specified a catalogue of unresolved disarmament issues,[46] the United Kingdom and the United States saw clear justification for a second resolution finding Iraq in material breach and authorising the use of force. Despite the findings in Blix's report, Russia and France expressed their unwillingness to authorise the use of force and their willingness to use their veto at the Security Council. Crucially, Jacques Chirac stated that "France will vote no to a new UN resolution on Iraq whatever the circumstances".[47] This was important in that it ended any possibility of a vote being taken at the Security Council and implied that this would be the case even if Iraq was in clear breach of its obligations. Chirac's position, however, in effect gave political justification for the use of force without the specific authorisation of the Security Council. This proved to be a key issue which aided Tony Blair in receiving the authorisation from the British Parliament, as resolving the issue through the United Nations was no longer seen as a viable option. Therefore, France's position gave a degree of legitimacy to the use of force without specific authorisation for the use of force from the Security Council, and thus nullified any restraints the United Nations could have had over preventing an invasion from taking place.

With the United Nations route effectively closed off, US policy was able to function with a greater degree of latitude. This culminated in an ultimatum being issued to Iraq. Without the ability to refer to the United Nations, the United States and a 'coalition of the willing' subsequently launched an invasion on 20 March 2003. Allegations were widespread at the US subjugation of international law and political unilateralism. Although the invasion was not sanctioned by a specific resolution, it arguably relied on the customary principle of international law set by the case of Kosovo where both the EU and the United States acted without specific authorisation for the use of force; admittedly, this is by no means a resolved issue under international law. In terms of the allegation of unilateralism, the United States did act with several other countries including the United Kingdom, Poland, Italy and Spain, and it is therefore incorrect to refer to the invasion as a unilateral undertaking. Indeed, Robert Kagan is correct to highlight that France and Germany's accusation of unilateralism more aptly stems from their loss of influence over US policy.[48] Nevertheless, it was by no means a policy undertaking that received full support from the international community.

It is clear that the 9/11 attacks resulted in a tactical shift in US policy which resulted in a military invasion to achieve the US strategic objective of regime change that had been applied unchanged since 1991. However, it has been shown that the official justifications for launching the invasion were lacking. This underscores the fact that the United States had applied the doctrine of anticipatory self-defence and had used Iraq's failure/inability to comply with UN resolutions as a *casus belli*. Nevertheless, it is important to recognise that, on a wider level, the grand strategic premise of the United States was to promote democracy and liberalism as a means of countering extremist political Islam and terrorism. As will be shown in the next section, this was a key strategic objective which was arguably of more importance than the perceived need to act preventatively against Iraq.

Strategic Foreign Policy Towards Iraq

Under the rubric of the Bush Doctrine, the potential threat posed by an Iraq in possession of unconventional weapons should not be interpreted as mandating pre-emptive action in the form of regime change through a military invasion: theoretically, it would only have become a requirement once *all* diplomatic channels had been exhausted. However, although the United States made clear its belief that Iraq possessed such weapons, and was in a position to comply with its international obligations, the truth of the matter is more sobering: Iraq's unilateral destruction of its prohibited weapons prior to 1995 placed it in a position whereby it was not capable of fully complying with its obligations, despite the Bush administration's position that Iraq was capable of doing so.[49]

Nevertheless, it is reasonable to conclude that given Iraq's failure to comply with its international obligations since 1991, the Bush administration would have taken the position that there was little or no realistic prospect of a *willing* Iraqi compliance, without the threat of a subsequent invasion hanging over it like the sword of Damocles. But of more importance, given the nature of the intelligence data, is the difficulty in seeing how the administration could have seen a full and complete compliance with UN resolutions as anything but a marginal possibility. When the factor of verifying weapons destroyed in the allied bombing campaigns was taken into account, or the possibility that Iraq had indeed unilaterally destroyed some of its weapons that were past their shelf life, even a conservative interpretation of the data which was publicly released leads to the conclusion that a strict Iraqi compliance with UN resolutions was not possible. In addition to this, the intelligence data, which was mainly provided by opposition groups, was circumstantial and laced with qualifiers. Therefore, it is justifiable to conclude that the logical product of the administration's foreign shift after the 9/11 attacks was the realisation that the decision to give Iraq an ultimatum would almost certainly require a subsequent invasion.[50]

According to Richard Hass, after a discussion with Condoleezza Rice in early July 2002, he was left with little doubt that a decision to go to war had already been made. Hass commented that:

> Condi and I have regular meetings, once every month or so – she and I get together for thirty or forty-five minutes, just to review the bidding. And I raised this issue about were we really sure that we

wanted to put Iraq front and center at this point, given the War on Terrorism and other issues. And she said, essentially, that that decision's been made, don't waste your breath. And that was early July [2002].[51]

From Hass's remarks, it is reasonable to conclude that the administration recognised that compliance by Iraq would not be forthcoming, or was not possible, and therefore it was in effect planning for an invasion against Iraq. This serves to underline the argument that the Bush administration had changed its tactical policy towards achieving the unchanged strategic objective of regime change.

In addition to this, a secret memo was leaked to the press in the run up to the British general election in May 2005 which confirmed Hass's remarks. The internal Downing Street memo listed the minutes from a meeting the Prime Minister held with senior cabinet members and intelligence personnel on 23 July 2002. The minutes reported the following from the head of the British Secret Intelligence Service after holding talks with counterparts in Washington:

> There was a perceptible shift in attitude. Military action was now seen as inevitable. Bush wanted to remove Saddam, through military action, justified by the conjunction of terrorism and WMD. But the intelligence and facts were being fixed around the policy. The [US National Security Council] had no patience with the UN route, and no enthusiasm for publishing material on the Iraqi regime's record. There was little discussion in Washington of the aftermath of military action.[52]

The significance of the leaked Downing Street memo is that it confirms that the Bush administration had decided to invade Iraq for strategic reasons and had embarked on a tactical policy that would almost certainly result in an invasion. Indeed, this tactical policy hinged around misleading the general public through the selective use of intelligence data to justify the invasion.

With there being a clear use of tactical foreign policy to justify the invasion of Iraq the key issue is what was the strategic objective which underpinned the policy change? As already highlighted, the root cause of Islamic terrorism was seen by Bush's neoconservative foreign team as stemming from the absence of liberal democracy in Middle

Eastern countries. Therefore the universal adoption of liberal democracy throughout the Middle East would form the basis of a long-term counterterrorism strategy.[53] Iraq, however, was seen as the key to a wider geostrategic vision of democratising the wider Middle East area. Indeed, Bush commented in February 2003 that:

> A liberated Iraq can show the power of freedom to transform that vital region, by bringing hope and progress into the lives of millions. America's interests in security, and America's belief in liberty, both lead in the same direction: to a free and peaceful Iraq.[54]

This approach departed from the traditional notion of the maintenance of Persian Gulf security by way of supporting pro-Western autocratic regimes.

With the neoconservative interpretation of the post-9/11 context, the need to achieve a democratisation throughout the Middle East was a pressing concern. The manner in which this assessment tied in with US foreign policy towards Iraq was via the impact a democratised Iraq would arguably have on the greater Middle East area.[55] The logic behind the line of thought was that following an invasion of Iraq, the post-war reconstruction effort, which would necessarily include the establishment of democratic governmental institutions, would result in unassailable pressures on neighbouring authoritarian countries to indigenously democratise. The net effect would be that the establishment of a liberal democratic regional system within the Middle East would safeguard US national security by countering the base-level conditions that result in Islamic terrorist movements. In essence, the grand strategic era of the War on Terror dictated the *primacy of national security*, and the widespread adoption of liberal democracy was seen as providing this in the long term.

Although it is a moot point, it is highly dubious that democracy *can* be imposed through military force in a secure and sustainable manner while also promoting moves towards democratisation in neighbouring authoritarian states.[56] Indeed, the Vietnam debacle showed this to be the case. However, it does seem clear that this was the key strategic objective of the Bush administration's policy calculations towards Iraq.[57] The unveiling of the Middle East Partnership Initiative (MEPI) in December 2002 underlined the administration's commitment to the promotion of economic, political and educational reform across the Middle East through the provision of developmental assistance. Although the investment, training and support programmes that are encompassed in MEPI appear a benign political initiative, in the long term they would arguably provide the United States with more political influence as a result of its economic investments. Moreover, the educational and political reform initiatives would conceivably result in gradual socio-political changes occurring across the Middle East. Here suffice it to say that their adoption underlines the argument that the War on Terror has resulted in an abandonment of the concept of containment and balance of power approach in favour of a widespread overhaul of the Middle East on a socio-political level as a means of countering terrorism. It also underscores that post-9/11 US grand strategy was being driven by a crusading moralism akin to President Johnson's view which drove the United States into Vietnam. Therefore, the invasion of Iraq because of its failure/ inability to comply with its international obligations as a justification for war was a tactical foreign policy initiative geared towards achieving this wider strategic objective.

Post-Invasion of Iraq: Strategic Opportunity or Quagmire
The military campaign to unseat Saddam Hussein's regime is accurately described by Timothy Garden as having "no formal conclusion".[58] Bush declared on 1 May 2003 that "[m]ajor combat operations in Iraq have ended" and that "our coalition is engaged in securing and reconstructing that country".[59] Bush was correct that the Iraqi regime had been toppled and the Iraqi army had been defeated but providing security for post-war reconstruction was to be a greater task than many in the administration had envisaged.

The Coalition Provisional Authority (CPA), headed by L. Paul Bremer III, was charged with the political administration of Iraq until the formal transfer of authority on 28 June 2004. Resulting in the main from the Bush administration's miscalculation and unwillingness to commit the level of forces required for Iraqi security needs, a guerrilla-style insurgency grew unabated.[60] In the initial period after the toppling of Saddam Hussein's regime the Iraqi economy virtually collapsed and the country was plagued with widespread looting, lawlessness and insecurity. Given that US strategy was for Iraq to be reconstructed as a functional and pluralistic democracy in order to foster a move within the region towards democratic polity, the insecurity within Iraq was a clear barrier.

The administration's initial strategy towards the post-war reconstruction of Iraq was for it to remain under US control. The US was not prepared to cede control of Iraq to the UN but, nevertheless, saw it as a useful vehicle for soliciting financial aid.[61] However, the growing insurgency had underlined that the US forces were insufficient to restore security to Iraq. This was compounded by the active-duty troop strength of the US which indicated it required some form of third party participation by early 2004 or it would need to extend the tour of duty period. These factors prompted a change in tactic from the Bush administration in early September as it began to seek a UN resolution that would provide for an internationalised military force which was comparable to that employed in Kosovo.[62]

Within the context of this policy change, two car bomb attacks struck the UN compound in Baghdad in late August and early September. The former resulted in the death of Sergio Vieira de Mello, the UN Special Representative for Iraq. This raised questions within the UN over whether it was targeted as a result of a perceived linkage with the United States.[63] With the second bombing in September, the assessment was made by the UN that the security situation was too dangerous to warrant a significant commitment of personnel.[64] By October the UN began to significantly downsize its deployment in Iraq and this hampered the US efforts to garner support for an internationalised force.

The downsizing of the UN deployment in October 2003 made the prospect of the UN assuming a greater role an unrealistic option. Simon Chesterman and David Malone aptly comment:

> The idea that the United Nations can somehow quaff the poisoned chalice is delusional. The present US policy reversal and UN staff concerns place the secretary general in a difficult position. Until security improves, [Kofi Annan] cannot in good conscience send civilian staff into harm's way. But security will only improve when the United States looks less like an occupying power. Many analysts therefore think that Iraq is going to get worse before it gets better.[65]

In sum, the post-invasion strategic context saw the United States descend into a situation where it was seen to be acting more and more unilaterally without the legitimacy afforded by the United Nations. In some respects, a parallel can be drawn with the Vietnam War where the US faced a similar form of insurgency and was acting without a comfortable level of multilateral legitimacy. The guerrilla warfare that began to develop from 2003 in the aftermath of the invasion was small when compared to the scale of attacks witnessed in subsequent years. Nevertheless, the key challenge the post-invasion scenario presented to the United States was how long it would take for the security situation to be addressed and for a functional democratic government to take power. A true assessment of the strategic impact of this aspect of US policy on Persian Gulf reform issues will necessarily require a medium- to long-term retrospective study.

Concluding Observations

The 9/11 attacks were highly significant for US policy towards the Persian Gulf in that the neoconservative vision of how the threat of terrorism should be countered had a direct bearing on US strategy towards achieving Persian Gulf security. Since 1991 a policy of dual containment had been applied in order to maintain a balance of power and thus ensure regional security. The Bush administration's response to the 9/11 attacks saw the promotion of liberal democracy as the over-arching means of countering the root causes of international terrorism. This made the traditional balance of power approach in the Persian Gulf no longer viable. Indeed, it was seen as being a contributory factor to the development of Islamic terrorism. Therefore, there was a need for political, economic and educational reforms to be applied across the Persian Gulf as part of the long-term goal of democratisation which would provide security and stability for the Persian Gulf.

The invasion of Iraq served this strategic objective in that the post-war reconstruction would allow nation building on a par with post-Second World War West Germany, making way for the adoption of democratic governance. More significantly, a fully functioning democratic Iraq was believed to hold the potential for spreading democracy throughout the region as the position of authoritarian rulers would become untenable.

Whilst this was a key strategic objective in the rationalisation behind the invasion of Iraq, the Bush Doctrine also saw a potential future threat arising from Iraq through the perceived commitment by

Saddam Hussein's regime to the production of unconventional weapons in the future. The prospect of such weapons being used directly or asymmetrically against the United States was taken as justification in itself for the preventative use of force.

It has been suggested that the reason why these strategic objectives were not stated as the actual *casus belli* for mounting an invasion against Iraq stemmed from their perceived illegitimacy in the eyes of the international community. Indeed, this would have posed practical difficulties in that it might well have jeopardised the formation of a coalition to launch the invasion. Even so, Iraq was a unique case in that it was unable to fully comply with UN resolutions. This gave the United States the opportunity to premise the invasion on the basis of an enforcement of UN resolutions. US policy therefore used the case for an enforcement of UN resolutions as a tactical means of achieving its dual objectives that stemmed from the post-9/11 international context. The case for enforcement was therefore used as a clear fait accompli.

NOTES

1 Ron Suskind, *The Price of Loyalty: George W. Bush, the White House, and the Education of Paul O'Neill* (New York: Simon & Schuster, 2004) 29.
2 Ibid. 74.
3 Suskind, *The Price of Loyalty* 84.
4 Bob Woodward, *Plan of Attack* (New York: Simon & Schuster, 2004) 21.
5 Ibid.
6 Ibid.
7 Woodward, *Plan of Attack* 21.
8 Suskind, *The Price of Loyalty* 75.
9 Woodward, *Plan of Attack* 21.
10 Kenneth Katzman, "Iraq: Oil-for-Food Program, International Sanctions, and Illicit Trade", *CRS Report for Congress*, (RL30472), Washington, D.C.: CRS, Congress, 19 May 2003, 24pp., 17/06/04 <http://fpc.state.gov/documents/organization/21122.pdf>.
11 Ibid.
12 United States, Department of State, *Briefing En Route to Cairo, Egypt* (23 Feb. 2001) 3pp. 23/08/04 <www.state.gov/secretary/rm/2001/931.html>.
13 Elizabeth J. Lake, "State Department Audit to Delay Aid for INC", *Washington Times* 11 Jun. 2001: 11.
14 It is reasonable to conclude that a succession by one of his sons upon his death would have been equally unacceptable to the United States as the sons would

have likely been seen as having the same intent that Saddam had in terms of rekindling Iraq WMD programmes.

15 Given that the Bush administration allowed a resumption of relations with Libya after it renounced its intent to procure weapons of mass destruction, coupled with an inspections regime which was able to verify the destruction of its stockpiles, it is theoretically possible that if Iraq has been able to verify the destruction of such weapons, this *might* have been a policy option.

16 Vice President Cheney was instrumental in extending the definition of the terrorist threat to encompass 'rogue states' that were proliferating in weapons of mass destruction. See: Woodward, *Plan of Attack* 29.

17 Bob Woodward, *Bush at War* (New York: Simon & Schuster, 2002) 49, 83–85.

18 Suskind, *The Price of Loyalty* 188.

19 John Gearson, "Terrorism in Historical Perspective", *The Goodenough–Chevening Conference on Terrorism* (London: unpublished, 2003).

20 Spenser Ackerman, "The Weakest Link: Why the Bush Administration Insists against All Evidence on an Iraq–Al Qaeda Connection", *Washington Monthly* Nov. 2003, 23/08/04 <http://www.findarticles.com/p/articles/mi_m1316/is_11_35/ai_111027164>.

21 Johnathan Schanzer, *Ansar Al-Islam: Iraq's Al-Qa'ida Connection*, 2003, The Washington Institute for Near East Policy, 2pp. 10 Aug. 2004 http://www.frontpagemag.com/Articles/Printable.asp?ID=5571.

22 Schanzer, *Ansar Al-Islam*.

23 *Uncovered: The Whole Truth About the Iraq War*, Dir. Robert Greenwald, DVD, The Disinformation Company Ltd., 2004.

24 Fred Barnes, "Mohamed Atta Was Here and Met with Saddam Hussain's Man in Prague", *Weekly Standard* 8 Dec. 2002, 12/06/03 <http://www.weeklystandard.com/content/public/articles/000/000/001/539dozfr.asp>.

25 Peter Green, "Iraq Link to Sept 11 Attack and Anthrax Is Ruled Out", *Telegraph Online* 18 Dec. 2001, 12/01/02 <http://www.telegraph.co.uk/news/main.jhtml?xml=/news/2001/12/18/wirq18.xml>.

26 National Commission on the Terrorist Attacks upon the United States, *The 9/11 Commission Report: The Full Final Report of the National Commission on Terrorist Attacks upon the United States*, (Washington, D.C.: GPO, 2004) 567pp. 12/01/05 <http://www.9-11commission.gov/report/index.htm>; and Charles Duelfer, *Comprehensive Report of the Special Advisor on Iraq's WMD: Chemical and Biological Weapons*, (Washington, D.C.: CIA, 2004) 350pp. 02/03/05 <http://www.cia.gov/cia/reports/iraq_wmd_2004/>.

27 National Commission on the Terrorist Attacks Upon the United States, *The 9/11 Commission Report: The Full Final Report of the National Commission on Terrorist Attacks upon the United States*.

28 United States, Senate. Committee on Foreign Relations, *Threats, Responses and Regional Considerations Surrounding Iraq*, 107th Cong. 2nd Sess., (Washington, D.C.: GPO, 31 Jul. 2002) 279pp. 16/06/03 <http://frwebgate.access.gpo.gov/cgi-bin/getdoc.cgi?dbname=107_senate_hearings&docid=f:81697.pdf>.

29 George J. Tenet, "CIA Letter to Senate on Baghdad's Intentions", *New York Times Online* 9 Oct. 2002, 10/10/02 <www.nytimes.com/2002/10/09/international/09TTEX.html>.

30 United States, Commission on the Intelligence Capabilities of the United States Regarding Weapons of Mass Destruction, *Commission on the Intelligence Capabilities of the United States Regarding Weapons of Mass Destruction: Report to the President* (GPO, 2005) 618pp. 04/04/05 <http://www.wmd.gov/report/>.

31 Woodward, *Plan of Attack* 153.

32 Ibid. 157.

33 Robert Kagan, *Of Paradise and Power: America and Europe in the New World Order* (New York: Knopf, 2004) 150.

34 George W. Bush, "President's Remarks to the United Nations General Assembly", Remarks by the President in Address to the United Nations General Assembly, New York: GPO, 12 Sept. 2002 5pp. 17/02/02 <http://www.whitehouse.gov/news/releases/2002/09/20020912-1.html>.

35 United States, House, *Authorization for the Use of Force against Iraq*, H.R. 114, P.L. 102–1, (Washington, D.C.: GPO, 10 Oct. 2002) 8pp. 17/12/03 <http://www.iraqwatch.org/government/US/Legislation/ILA.htm>.

36 UNSCR 1441 of 8 Nov. 2002, Para. 13.

37 United States, Mission to the United Nations, *Explanation of Vote by Ambassador John D. Negroponte*, (New York: United States, GPO, 8 Nov. 2002) 2pp. 12 Jul 2003 <http://www.un.int/usa/02print_187.htm >.

38 United Kingdom, Mission to the United Nations, *Explanation of Vote by Jeremy Greenstock*, (New York: United Nations, 8 Nov. 2002) 1pp. 12/07/03 <http://www.un.org/webcast/unitedkingdom110802.htm>.

· 39 Hans Blix, *Disarming Iraq* (London: Bloomsbury, 2004) 99–102.

40 Ibid. 107.

41 United Kingdom, 10 Downing Street, *Iraq's Weapons of Mass Destruction: The Assessment of the British Government*, (ID114567), (London: The Stationery Office, 24 Sep. 2002) 55pp. 20/10/03 <http://www.number-10.gov.uk/output/Page271.asp >.

42 United Kingdom, House of Commons, *Report of the Inquiry into the Circumstances Surrounding the Death of Dr David Kelly C.M.G.*, (HC247), (London: The Stationery Office, 28 Jan. 2004) 473sect. 25/10/04 <http://www.the-hutton-inquiry.org.uk/content/report/>.

43 United Nations, UNMOVIC, *An Update on Inspection*, (New York: United Nations, 27 Jan. 2003) 9pp. 19/06/04 <http://www.un.org/Depts/unmovic/Bx27.htm>.

44 Glen Rangwala, "Blix and Elbaradei Vs Powell", *Middle East Reference* 14 Feb. 2003, 10/11/04 <http://middleeastreference.org.uk/un030214.html>.

45 Blix, *Disarming Iraq* 152–57.

46 United Nations, UNMOVIC, *Unresolved Disarmament Issues: Iraq's Proscribed Weapons Programmes*, (New York: United Nations, 6 Mar. 2003) 175pp. 13/06/04 <http://www.un.org/Depts/unmovic/documents/6mar.pdf>.

47 Anonymous, "France Will Use Iraq Veto", *BBC News Online* 10 Mar. 2003, 11/05/03 <http://news.bbc.co.uk/1/hi/world/middle_east/2838269.stm>.

48 Kagan, *Of Paradise and Power* 105–58.

49 There is no evidence to support the view that any US administration since 1991 actually believed Iraq was not in possession of unconventional weapons, and therefore incapable of diplomatically complying with its obligations. To suggest

that the Bush administration knew its intelligence data was *incorrect*, rather than simply based on *inferences and circumstantial evidence*, would equate to the charge that it was guilty of the federal felony of misleading Congress.

50 Admittedly, the United States had been consistent in its position that Saddam Hussein would have rekindled his unconventional weapons programme if the sanctions were lifted. Therefore, although it can be argued that it would have made little substantive difference if Iraq had indeed complied with UN resolutions, the prospect of the United States leading an invasion of Iraq if it had indeed fully complied with its international obligations, is unlikely to have been a politically expedient option.

51 Nicholas Lemann, "How It Came to War", *New Yorker* 31 Mar. 2003, 13/09/04 <http://www.newyorker.com/printable/?fact/030331fa_fact>.

52 Matthew Rycroft, "The Secret Downing Street Memo", *Times Online* 1 May 2005, 02/05/05 <www.timesonline.co.uk/article/0,2087-1593607,00.html >.

53 The widespread adoption of liberal democracy is widely highlighted as fostering more peaceful relations between countries.

54 George W. Bush, "President Bush Presents Vision of Middle East Peace", Remarks by the President at the American Enterprise Institute Annual Dinner, Washington, D.C.: GPO, 26 Feb. 2003. 6pp. 15/09/04 <http://tokyo.usembassy.gov/e/p/tp-20030228a1.html>.

55 Marina Ottway, et al., "Democratic Mirage in the Middle East", *Critical Mission: Essays on Democracy Promotion*, ed. Thomas Carothers (Washington, D.C.: Brookings Institution Press, 2002) 229–32.

56 Ibid. 230–36.

57 Thomas Carothers, "Promoting Democracy and Fighting Terror", *Critical Mission: Essays on Democracy Promotion*, ed. Thomas Carothers (Washington, D.C.: Brookings Institution Press, 2003) 63–74.

58 Timothy Garden, "Iraq: The Military Campaign", *International Affairs* 79.4 (2003): 701.

59 George W. Bush, "President Bush Announces Major Combat Operations in Iraq Have Ended" (Washington, D.C.: GPO, 1 May 2003) 3pp. 05/05/03 <http://www.whitehouse.gov/news/releases/2003/05/iraq/20030501-15.html>.

60 Larry Diamond, "What Went Wrong in Iraq", *Foreign Affairs* 83.5 (2004): 34–56.

61 Steven R. Weisman and Felicity Barringer, "US Abandons Idea of Bigger UN Role in Iraq Occupation", *New York Times* 19 Aug. 2003: A1.

62 David E. Sanger, "Bush Looks to UN to Share Burden on Troops in Iraq", *New York Times* 3 Sept. 2003: A1.

63 Thalif Deen, "UN Bombed for Perceived US Link, Experts Say", *Inter-Press Service* 19 Aug. 2003, 03/04/04 <http://www.globalpolicy.org/security/issues/iraq/after/2003/0819unbombed.htm>.

64 Edith M. Lederer, "Annan Won't Send UN Staff Back to Iraq", *Associated Press* 18 Oct. 2003, 12/03/04 <http://www.globalpolicy.org/security/issues/iraq/after/2003/1018annan.htm>.

65 Simon Chesterman and David Malone, "The Iraq Tragedy: It's Too Late for the UN to Help Much", *International Herald Tribune Online* 8 Dec. 2003, 10/12/03 <http://www.iht.com/articles/120574.html>.

7

Iran: Proliferation, Preventative Use of Force and Regime Change

---

"The United States has joined with our EU partners and Russia to pressure Iran to meet its international obligations and provide objective guarantees that its nuclear program is only for peaceful purposes. This diplomatic effort must succeed if confrontation is to be avoided."

George W. Bush
March 2006

With the onset of the Bush administration in January 2001, one may have been tempted to assume that its connections with the oil industry would have resulted in a softening of policy towards Iran.[1] This was not to be the case. Condoleezza Rice argued in an article in *Foreign Affairs* during the 2000 election campaign that "[a]ll in all, changes in US policy toward Iran would require changes in Iranian behaviour".[2] In essence she articulated a policy continuation as there was little scope for an alternative to the policy of containment. As had been found by the Clinton administration, the key obstacle to a change in relations rested with the Iranians. The structural impediments to Tehran taking advantage of overtures from the United States, in addition to the unwillingness to moderate Iranian foreign policy, made the prospect of a rapprochement a distant goal.

During the initial months of the Bush presidency up until the 9/11 attacks, US policy can be characterised as a continuation from the Clinton era while a policy review was undertaken.[3] But on a wider contextual level, little had altered to justify a substantive shift in foreign policy. By August 2001, the ILSA (Iran–Libya Sanctions Act) was up for renewal and the Bush administration renewed it with the caveat recommendation that it should be reviewed on a more periodical basis. Specifically, Colin Powell was reported as seeking a two-year extension rather than the normal five-year period. This was ultimately rejected by Congress and it was renewed for a full five years on a 96–2 vote in the Senate.[4]

Although the White House was clearly attempting to garner some flexibility in its diplomacy towards Iran through its recommendation, the sponsor of the bill, Senator Charles Schumer of New York, argued that even though President Khatami had been elected, a moderation in Iran's sponsorship for terrorist movements had not occurred.[5] It can be argued that the reason why Congress voted against this stems from the manner in which AIPAC effectively mobilised support within Congress against any potential policy review. Indeed, by March 2001, AIPAC had gathered upwards of 180 co-sponsors in the House for the renewal of ILSA before the White House had publicly issued its policy position. It was only by June 2001 that the White House took the official position of seeking only a two-year extension and this position was subjected to a great deal of criticism: "[I]f ILSA was a good policy, then why extend it for only two years, and if it was a bad policy, why extend it at all?"[6]

On a wider level, however, in June 2001 a United States federal court issued indictments for fourteen men, alleged to be members of Hezbollah, for the 1996 bombing at Khobar Towers. Crucially, the indictment implicated the Iranian government as being behind the bombing.[7] Although this did not have a clear effect on the executive branch, it is likely that this served to underline the case being made by AIPAC within Congress for a renewal of ILSA.

The onset of the War on Terror was the unlikely conduit whereby bilateral relations were developed through shared geopolitical interests. Discussions on Afghanistan had taken place prior to the 9/11 attacks under the auspices of the United Nations' 'six-plus-two' talks.[8] The Iranians were fervent opponents of the Taliban and al-Qa'ida, and during the Clinton era they had aimed to solicit the active help of the United States to directly target them. However, US policy at that time had other priorities and thus no substantive cooperative agreement was achieved. The 9/11 attacks fundamentally changed this contextual situation.

The presence of Osama bin Laden, and the refuge being provided to his organisation by the Taliban, gave a renewed sense of importance to US policy towards Afghanistan under the rubric of the War on Terror. In order to facilitate discussion being held in the six-plus-two talks, a subgroup was created which included Italy and Germany for political cover. The group held meetings in Geneva, and as American action in Afghanistan served Iran's geopolitical interests, agreement was reached for it to provide logistical, intelligence and operational support for Operation Enduring Freedom.[9] For Tehran, it would have been clear that the United States was going to take military action regardless of whether it cooperated but, given its interests in deposing the Taliban, it is likely that Khamene'i[10] saw this cooperation as a necessary evil.

With the end of war in Afghanistan, Iran became an active partner in the United Nations post-war conference held in Bonn, Germany. Khamene'i was pragmatic in his decision to cooperate with the post-reconstruction effort. Indeed, Iran had a vested interest in the United States succeeding in Afghanistan: Kenneth Pollack is correct to argue that a successful post-war reconstruction effort would have prevented a repeat of the instability caused by the Soviet withdrawal in 1989.[11] By providing assistance and being an active partner for the United States, Iran was in effect securing its own national interests.

With these shared geopolitical interests, it is only reasonable to speculate that the opportunity for confidence-building measures towards a rapprochement would have been rife. However, it is important to recognise that the over-arching contextual issue had become terrorism. With the State Department listing Iran as a leading state sponsor of terrorism, it is questionable to what extent the Bush administration could have actually moved beyond containment without a substantive change in Iran's policies towards US-designated terrorist groups. Moreover, with the central premise of the War on Terror being the spread of democracy and freedom, the Iranian regime was viewed within this context. Therefore a rapprochement without substantive reforms, which would have effectively resulted in a complete political transformation within Iran, would not have been viable and any cooperation the Bush administration was having with Iran was arguably *tactical*. So whilst cooperation based on geopolitical interests was important, it is doubtful it could have overcome the issue of Iranian links with terrorism.

Unravelling the New Strategic Dynamic

Relations with Iran were being steadily built up through shared geopolitical interests, but all of this was undone on 3 January 2002 when Israel intercepted a ship, the *Karine A*, carrying an arsenal of weaponry from Iran. The ship was captained by an officer in the Palestinian Authority's Navy and contained "[k]atyusha rockets, mortars, rifles, machine guns, sniper rifles, ammunition, antitank mines, rocket-propelled grenades, and 2.5 tons of explosives".[12] The weapons were manufactured in Iran and had been loaded onto the ship within Iranian territorial waters.[13] Israel and the United States found it to be a compelling case that Iran was guilty of illicitly supplying weapons. Powell commented that:

> I think he [Arafat] ought to acknowledge, as the first step toward moving forward, that this has happened and they bear some responsibility for it happening, and give the international community, and especially the Israelis, some assurance that this kind of activity is going to stop. And do it in a way that will be persuasive and convincing and allow us to move forward.[14]

Whilst this did have a ramification on US diplomatic relations with the Palestinian Authority, it also had an impact on US foreign policy towards Iran. Within the newly emerged context of the War on Terror, Iran's provision of illicit armaments was seen by the White House and Congress as clear evidence of Iran's intention to derail the peace process through terrorism. Indeed, Pollack highlighted the fact that the US intelligence community was convinced that Iran was "stepping up its support to HAMAS and PIJ to attack the right-wing Israeli government of Ariel Sharon".[15] But of more importance were the reports that came to light alleging that Iran had allowed senior al-Qa'ida operatives to flee into Iran. This was in marked contrast to its initial clampdown and official position. With this coming to light only months after the 9/11 attacks, the political response in the United States to this was predictable and undid the 'good will' developed from the shared interests in the overthrow of the Taliban. Indeed, Condoleezza Rice stated that "Iran's direct support of regional and global terrorism, and its aggressive efforts to acquire weapons of mass destruction, belie any good intentions it displayed in the days after the world's worst terrorist attacks in history".[16]

Bush's 2002 State of the Union Address identified Iran as being part of an 'axis of evil' with Iraq and North Korea. According to Bob Woodward, both Rice and Stephen Hadley advised against Iran's inclusion in the speech as part of an 'axis' as it had a fledgling democratic movement.[17] Nevertheless, Bush insisted that Iran be included as he saw Iran, along with North Korea and Iraq, as the biggest threat to the world in terms of terrorism and the procurement of unconventional weapons.[18]

As has already been discussed, the Bush Doctrine saw the combination of these two factors as the greatest threat facing US national security; thus Iran's alleged involvement in both of these spheres resulted in it being categorised in this manner. For Iran, equating it with Iraq and North Korea was highly provocative and was greeted with condemnation by the hardliners as evidence of US provocation. Iran withdrew for a short period of time from the Geneva Group in protest, but later rejoined when it became clear that Iraq was to be targeted, as the Group was useful as a conduit of information on US Gulf policy.

With the onset of Operation Iraqi Freedom in March 2003, Iran refrained from hampering US policy, but was widely regarded as not having provided the same level of assistance that it had accorded the United States in its Afghanistan campaign. However, it is interesting to note that, according to Kenneth Pollack, Iran began moving intelligence personnel into Iraq from May 2003. He argues that an intelligence network was built up: "all of Iran's various intelligence and covert action organizations were represented in Iraq – the IRGC (including its Quds Forces), Hizballah, the MOIS, Lebanese Hizballah, and assorted others."[19] But crucially, according to Pollack, this intelligence apparatus was *not operational* and thus not involved in hampering US activities in post-war Iraq.[20] Pollack speculates that the reason for not activating this network was Iran's interest in seeing a successful post-war recovery in Iraq. More importantly, he also suggests that it was a tactical means by which Iran could achieve leverage against the United States if the Bush administration decided to take any preventative action against Tehran.[21] In other words, the Bush administration was facing a veiled threat from the hardliners in Iran through their ability to provoke varying degrees of instability within Iraq.

Contextual Issue: Support for Terrorism

Despite the United States having shared interests with Iran in both Afghanistan and Iraq, the main obstacle which was creating friction was Iran's perceived involvement with terrorism. The United States alleged that the al-Qa'ida attacks within Saudi Arabia on 12 May 2003, which saw three truck bombs detonated in a Western compound in Riyadh, killing twenty people, were actually planned in Iran. According to the United States, senior al-Qa'ida operatives were active in eastern Iran and had directed the attacks from a terrorist cell within Saudi Arabia. At face value, the United States saw Iran as complicit in these attacks as it had allowed known terrorists to freely operate within its territory. A more sober analysis, however, shows that these operatives were in an area of Iran which did not have a good governmental presence and consequently it is possible to see why al-Qa'ida was able to function in Iran. Nevertheless, the perception by many within Congress and in media circles was that links somehow existed between al-Qa'ida and Iran's Sh'ia theocracy.

Compounding this, Iran had allowed al-Qa'ida operatives, who were involved in the attacks of 11 September 2001, free movement across Iranian territory. Indeed, the 9/11 Commission Report indicated that Tehran had informed its immigration officials to refrain from stamping their passports.[22] Whilst the reports do not amount to evidence of some form of substantive agreement, they are significant in that they made any form of cooperation based on mutual interests a politically charged option for the White House.

As has already been highlighted, Iran was viewed by the US government as having long-standing ties to terrorist groups opposed to the existence of Israel and the whole concept of the peace process. Despite the newly emerged contextual situation which was characterised by a determined opposition to terrorism, Iran did not alter its policy towards such groups. In June 2002, reports came to light that Hezbollah, Hamas, the Popular Front for the Liberation of Palestine, and Islamic Jihad had convened under the auspices of the Iranian government in Tehran.[23] This was significant as it indicated that a more coordinated effort on behalf of the opposition groups was being promoted by Iran. As this occurred within the context of the War on Terror, the prospect of engagement occurring without a clear change in Iran's policies was a distant prospect, and underlines how Iran's policies undermined its relationship with the United States.

The terrorist bombing of the Western compound in Riyadh in May 2003 was especially significant for the United States as seven out of the twenty fatalities were American citizens. With a link being established in the aftermath of the attacks with al-Qa'ida personnel in Iran, the United States sought their extradition. Iran's response was essentially a quid pro quo in that it requested that the *Mujahedin-eKhalq* (MEK) operatives in Iraq, who were near the Iranian border, be extradited. Iran's request was, at least on face value, perfectly reasonable in that the United States had designated the MEK as a terrorist organisation and had detained 3,800 MEK fighters in the immediate aftermath of the invasion of Iraq. The detention of the MEK fighters was actually a product of bilateral negotiations before the March 2003 invasion of Iraq and was agreed on in order to secure Iranian cooperation in search and rescue missions in addition to securing the border with Iraq.

Although the United States had detained MEK operatives, the wider contextual situation which implicated Iran in the *Karine A* illicit arms shipment to the Palestinian Authority, in addition to widespread allegations about Iran's failure to arrest al-Qa'ida operatives on its territory, resulted in the Bush administration refusing Iran's extradition request as part of a quid pro quo. This highlights a degree of hypocrisy on the part of the Bush administration in that it was refusing to extradite operatives of a group it had designated as an active terrorist organisation to the country where they had carried out their attacks. However, it is more telling on US policy towards Iran under the overall framework of Persian Gulf security: Iran's ties with terrorism precluded mutual interests being built upon bilaterally with the United States.

Iran's Nuclear Programme

Although Iran's nuclear ambitions can be traced back to the purchase of a research reactor from the United States in 1959, the central issue for the United States has been whether Iran was seeking the production of a nuclear weapon despite it being a signatory to the Nuclear Non-Proliferation Treaty of 1968. Construction of Iran's nuclear power station at Bushehr was begun in 1974 by German contractors but was suspended in 1979. Iran signed an agreement with Russia on 8 January 1995 to complete the construction of the 1,000 MW light water power station. As has already been highlighted, Iran maintained that it required this alternative source of energy as a result of rising oil and gas prices which it sought to sell rather than use domestically. Nevertheless, within the context of Iran's perceived involvement in international terrorism, the United States has regarded Iran's domestic nuclear programme as being ultimately geared towards the acquisition of a nuclear weapon, despite Iran being entitled to a domestic nuclear power capability under international law.

Although Iran's nuclear programme had been viewed with suspicion by the Clinton administration, there had been no evidence to support the conjecture that Iran was developing an illicit nuclear programme. This situation altered dramatically in August 2002 following the announcement by the National Council of Resistance of Iran (NCRI) that two secret nuclear facilities had been constructed in Natanz and Arak.[24] The NCRI claimed that a nuclear production plant and a research laboratory had been constructed in Natanz, and a heavy water production plant had been constructed in Arak. Crucially these facilities had not been declared to the IAEA. According to White House Press Secretary Ari Fleischer, the covert nature of the facilities underscored the administration's view that Iran was seeking a nuclear weapon capability. Indeed, he clarified the administration's overall view on Iran's nuclear programme in December 2002 as being that "there is no economic gain for a country rich in oil and gas, like Iran, to build costly indigenous nuclear fuel cycle facilities . . . Iran flares off more gas every year than the equivalent power it hopes to produce with these reactors".[25]

Within the context of the War on Terror and under the rubric of the Bush Doctrine, Iran's presumed illicit development of nuclear weapons was seen to pose a grave threat to the national security of the United States. Moreover, Iran's perceived involvement in international terrorism placed it in the unenviable position of having the potential to supply unconventional weapons asymmetrically to terrorist groups. For Iran, it had genuine strategic reasons for wanting a nuclear weapon, despite rejecting such a proposal officially. With the US having a sizeable military presence in the Persian Gulf, Afghanistan and Iraq, and also the US having close ties with Turkey, Iran felt that it was effectively surrounded. Moreover, with the US supporting the MEK, the Iranian perception was that the US was a state sponsor of terrorism and when this was viewed in the context of US support for Israel, the Iranian leaders commonly described Washington as a flagrant violator of UN resolutions. Compounding this was Bush's rhetoric which encompassed Iran as part of an axis of evil; and when US grand strategy is understood as spreading liberal democracy, it was clear that Bush's strategic objective towards Iran was for its theocracy to be replaced with a democratic alternative: in essence regime change for US national security interests in the War on Terror.

Under the Bush Doctrine, the preventative use of force was justifiable once all diplomatic avenues had been exhausted. It is important, however, to recognise that in spite of the comprehensive nature of US sanctions towards Iran, the scope for diplomacy remained. In essence, the United States could not realistically impose any further punitive sanctions on Iran, so its options were essentially twofold:

1. Use incentives as a means of achieving a moderation in Iran's nuclear policy;
2. Rely on the good offices of other countries to negotiate a change in Iran's policies.

While the options available were limited, it is important to recognise that Iran's covert nuclear programme became public in August 2002, at which point the administration was firmly committed to achieving regime change in Iraq through an invasion. With the United States engaged in Afghanistan and committed to an invasion of Iraq, it is reasonable to conclude that a military option towards Iran would not have been viable at that time.

Given this contextual situation, the Bush administration appears to have had little choice but to premise its foreign policy towards Iran on non-military means. But on the other hand, an easing of US unilateral sanctions as part of a quid pro quo would have been a hard option politically for the White House. Indeed, within the context of the War on Terror, the rubric of the Bush Doctrine, and the presidential election campaign in 2004, it would have been politically difficult for the Bush administration to reduce sanctions towards Iran as an incentive for a moderation in Tehran's policies. Therefore, the Bush administration had little choice but to opt for the policy route which relied on the European Union and other countries as a means by which a diplomatic solution could be achieved. Indeed this point was conceded by Bush in December 2004 when he commented "[w]e're relying upon others, because we've sanctioned ourselves out of influence with Iran . . . in other words, we don't have much leverage with the Iranians right now".[26] In essence, United States foreign policy was in a position of stalemate as it did not have credible diplomatic options available to it, and was constrained in its ability to act punitively against Tehran. US foreign policy had, therefore, succumbed to the position of being essentially dependent on a *unilateral* modification of Iran's own policies, or the achievement of a diplomatic resolution commensurate with US policy objectives by the European Union.

There was clear scope for diplomacy over Iran's nuclear programme but, given Iran's continual progress, it was a time-contingent strategy which would test the very basis of the Bush Doctrine. As discussed already, a key pillar of the Bush Doctrine was the preventative use of force against a hostile nation deemed intent on producing unconventional weapons. Here, the position of the Bush administration was premised on a zero-sum game: the state in question would have to abandon its programme or ultimately would face military intervention. Any consequences of military action were theoretically seen to be less than the risks of a hostile state in possession of such weapons. So the key question over Iran's nuclear programme was at what stage would a decision need to be made on whether military force should be used as a last resort? At what point does diplomacy give way to a military option?

When one examines the nature of Iran's nuclear programme it is telling that it has two potential ways in which it could produce a nuclear warhead: enrichment for a uranium warhead or reprocessing towards a plutonium-based one. The former comes from enriching uranium through centrifuge technology. The latter comes from reprocessing the uranium fuel rods in an active reactor after they have been there for a minimum of four to five months. Through both of these avenues, Iran held the potential to produce a nuclear warhead if it so chose.

The central dilemmas for the Bush administration were: in what form would Iran's nuclear programme pose an acceptable proliferation risk, and how much diplomatic time could be allowed for Iran to comply with US concerns before it progressed to a stage when a military option needed to be decided on? Certainly, a nuclear power programme can never be proof of proliferation: the ease with which a state could withdraw from the Nuclear Non-Proliferation Treaty and manufacture a weapon or even produce one covertly when it has an operative nuclear programme is instructive. For the United States, it is questionable whether any form of Iranian nuclear capability would be deemed acceptable under the guise of the War on Terror. Since Iran's presidential elections in 2005, which saw the conservative Mahmoud Ahmadinejad elected, relations with the United States have worsened. Riding on a tide of populist sentiment, Ahmadinejad has placed his domestic platform squarely in opposition to the United States' position over Iran's nuclear

programme. Compounding this, he has made a number of inflam-
matory remarks about the state of Israel. Here the problem is that
Ahmadinejad and his neoconservative government are actually reinforcing the view within Washington that Iran simply cannot be trusted to be
a nuclear power.

Given this domestic political situation in Iran, it is possible to see
through a strict reading of the Bush Doctrine, as enshrined in the
National Security Strategies of 2002 and 2006, that the threat of a
nuclear-armed Iran is something which will be seen as too great a risk
under the rubric of the War on Terror. In essence, it is a threat which
would justify the preventative use of force: in essence military air strikes
if a satisfactory resolution through diplomacy is not achieved. The
geopolitical dilemma facing the Persian Gulf is, therefore, whether the
Bush administration will see the consequences of air strikes, direct or
by proxy, as being too great to justify. In either case, without Iran
capitulating to US demands or a clear compromise somehow being
reached, Iran's nuclear programme is likely to test the application of the
Bush Doctrine: it has the potential to test the pillar of the preventative
use of force or indeed spell its death through failure of application in the
face of ongoing Iranian defiance.

Summary Assessment

US foreign policy towards Iran at the start of the War on Terror was
both the nadir and the pinnacle of bilateral relations since 1993. The
alignment of the Taliban and al-Qa'ida brought Afghanistan into the
forefront of US foreign policy in the immediate aftermath of the 9/11
attacks. By virtue of geopolitics, Iran and the United States had shared
national interests in the success of the Bush administration's first phase
in the War on Terror. As a direct result of this contextual situation, the
Bush administration achieved direct negotiations on a wide scope of
issues with the Iranians. This was highly significant in that this had
historically eluded the United States. This situation arguably held the
potential for bilateral differences to be resolved similarly to differences
with Libya in December 2003.

Despite this political opportunity having so unexpectedly arisen,
Iran did not refrain from undertaking policies which were simply provocative to the United States. Indeed, within the newly emerged context of the

War on Terror, Iran's provision of armaments to the Palestinian Authority and inability to implement effective counterterrorism measures against al-Qa'ida operatives in Iran's eastern region was viewed by the executive and Congress as evidence of a simple unwillingness on behalf of Tehran to work with the United States. Iran's actions in this sphere undid the 'good will' that had grown up in the immediate aftermath of the 9/11 attacks. This prompted the United States to reject Iran's application for an extradition of MEK operatives and thus reignited the spectre of mutual antagonism and recriminations.

With the uncovering of Iran's nuclear facilities at Arak and Natanz, the long-term suspicion that Iran was intent on illicitly producing a nuclear weapon came to the fore. Although such facilities are permissible under the Nuclear Non-Proliferation Treaty of 1968, Iran's concealment of them, coupled with its failure to declare several components and materials which can be used to manufacture a nuclear weapon, provided sufficient reason to conclude that Iran was indeed embarked on a programme to produce nuclear weapons.

Given these revelations and the manner in which the United States became engaged in Afghanistan and subsequently in Iraq, the scope for punitive action or a relaxing of US policy as a diplomatic incentive were no longer viable options. Any diplomatic movement could conceivably only occur from a unilateral initiative on behalf of Iran, or through a negotiated settlement via the European Union. Therefore, despite the bilateral relationship showing a degree of promise from shared geo-political national interests, Iran's failure to abstain from policies which were highly provocative to the United States resulted in a diplomatic stalemate.

NOTES

1 Kenneth M. Pollack, *The Persian Puzzle: The Conflict between Iran and America* (New York: Random House, 2004) 343.
2 Condoleezza Rice, "Campaign 2000: Promoting the National Interest", *Foreign Affairs* 79.1 (2000): 6.
3 Pollack, *The Persian Puzzle* 343–45.
4 Alison Mitchell, "Senate Extends Sanctions on Libya and Iran", *New York Times* 26 Jul. 2001: A6.
5 Ibid. A6.

6 Iranians for International Cooperation, "ILSA Mistakes in Retrospect", *Payvand's Iran News* Aug. 2001, 12/11/02 <http://www.payvand.com/news/01/aug/1177.html>.

7 Anonymous, "Khobar Towers Indictments Returned", *CNN Online* 22 Jun. 2001, 28/08/02 <http://archives.cnn.com/2001/LAW/06/21/khobar.indictments/>.

8 The countries involved in the 'six-plus-two' talks were the six neighbouring countries to Afghanistan plus the United States and Russia.

9 Ayatollah Ali Khamene'i became Supreme leader in Iran in 1989. Prior to this he was Iran's President from 1981–1989.

10 Pollack, *The Persian Puzzle* 345–49.

11 Ibid. 349.

12 Ibid. 350–51.

13 James Bennet, "Seized Arms Would Have Vastly Extended Arafat Arsenal", *New York Times* 12 Jan. 2002: A5.

14 United States, Department of State, *Powell Says Arafat Needs to Acknowledge Karine A Incident*, (2002: United States Mission to the European Union, 13 Apr. 2002) 6pp. 12/05/03 <http://www.useu.be/Categories/GlobalAffairs/Jan2502PowellArafatKarine.html>.

15 Pollack, *The Persian Puzzle* 351.

16 Ibid. 351.

17 Bob Woodward, *Plan of Attack* (New York: Simon & Schuster, 2004) 87–88.

18 Ibid. 88.

19 Pollack, *The Persian Puzzle* 355.

20 Ibid. 352–58.

21 Ibid.

22 National Commission on the Terrorist Attacks upon the United States, *The 9/11 Commission Report: The Full Final Report of the National Commission on Terrorist Attacks upon the United States*, (Washington, D.C.: GPO, 2004) 567pp. 12/01/05 <http://www.9-11commission.gov/report/index.htm>.

23 Dennis Ross, "The Hidden Threat in the Middle East", *Wall Street Journal* 24 Jun. 2002: A14.

24 The Associated Press, "Group: Iran's Nuke Program Growing", *New York Times* 15 Aug. 2002: A3.

25 Glen Kessler, "Nuclear Sites in Iran Worry US Officials", *Washington Post* 14 Dec. 2002: A18.

26 Susan Rice, "We Need a Real Iran Policy", *Washington Post* 30 Dec. 2004: A27.

8

Conclusion

---

*"We shall not cease from exploring, and at the end of our exploration, we will
return to where we started, and know the place for the first time."*

T. S. Eliot
May 1943

The Persian Gulf is without doubt one of the most important geopolitical
regions in the world. Cradling substantial oil and gas reserves, it has been
considered of vital strategic interest to the United States since the Second
World War. The United States has by virtue of its national interest, opted
to forge close political, military and economic links with the Gulf States
and viewed potential challenges to US geopolitical influence with hostility. Following the British withdrawal from the region in 1971, the United
States' position towards the region has steadily evolved through changes
brought on from the international, regional and domestic contexts. All in
all, the general trend has been for increased US involvement in the Gulf to
the extent that its presence allows it to be considered as the hegemonic
player within the region.

On a regional geostrategic level, the United States' position
towards Persian Gulf security has historically been to achieve stability
through policies geared towards maintenance of the status quo. During
the Cold War era, the primary function under Nixon's 'twin-pillars'
approach was to prevent the encroachment of the Soviet Union. A
by-product of this was the bolstering of regional allies which served US
economic interests in a secure flow of hydrocarbon resources. Such geoeconomic interests were ultimately subordinate to the global strategic
threat from the Soviet bloc

The Redefined Concept of Security
Within the new grand strategic context of the War on Terror, the manner
in which the United States approaches international affairs differs in

[203]

fundamental respects from the past. With the United States having identified a clear global strategic threat under the guise of Islamic terrorism, the priority is now squarely on countering the root causes of this threat as part of a long-term policy strategy. As already discussed, the intellectual framework of political Islam and terrorism has found a resonance with American exceptionalism: in essence the understanding of universal moral maxims from the founding days of the republic. The very absence of such values is understood to be the reason why Islam is such an effective political mobilising agent in the region and also the cause of hostility towards the United States in general. The failure of the United States to historically uphold the pillars of freedom, democracy, equality and human rights across the region is widely seen as evidence of US double standards and hypocrisy. With US policy towards Persian Gulf security being historically dictated by Cold War maxims, and potential challenges to vital US economic interests, in hindsight we can see why external influence has contributed towards the political character of the region.

The challenge posed by Islamic extremism and finding means to counter it is instructive as to why the US has redefined its understanding of security in this vitally important region. Crucially, the long-standing maintenance of the status quo approach runs contrary to this new definition of countering the strategic threat of radical Islamism. For the Bush administration and many within Congress, a fundamental break from the past had become a national security necessity for the United States. Persian Gulf security had thus become subordinate to the maxims of the War on Terror and also intertwined with the universal moralism on which its pillars rested. For the United States, security in the Persian Gulf also came to be understood in the post-9/11 context as only achievable once the region had gone through a period of upheaval and moved towards the adoption of the very universal values on which the US republic was founded. As underlined earlier, the key point here is the often-touted truth that free representative democracies would not choose to engage in bloodshed against one another and would settle any disputes through arbitration or other legal process. The War on Terror has thus redefined security in this subregion as a conception resting on collective political and legal security.

Redefining Persian Gulf security in this regard poses fundamental and important questions for the international community. Here the key issue at hand is the manner in which the change to this benevolent goal is achieved. How will this change be managed and what impact will it have on a geopolitical level? What tactics employed by the West in achieving this objective will be counterproductive? Do the citizens in the oil-rich monarchies actually desire any changes to the political map for fear of losing the exceptional welfare benefits and standard of living that they enjoy? As already discussed, the key medium through which the United States and its close allies believed such change could be brought about was through the invasion of Iraq and the toppling of its despotic regime, despite the inevitable regional upheaval this would create. However, the manner in which near daily carnage and civil war has enveloped Iraq underlines that the benevolent goal of creating a beacon of freedom and democracy in the region is far from straightforward. Understanding the prospects for achieving this new definition of Gulf security thus revolves around the question of political reform in this region. The extent to which states reform themselves is thus the benchmark for the United States in judging how much progress has been made towards achieving this new regional order of security and countering the challenge posed by radical Islam in the long term. Security in the region has thus descended to the domestic political level in the individual Gulf countries.

Geopolitics and Security

The geopolitical consequences of Iraq's insecurity should not be underestimated when the long-term goal of political change in the region is considered. Here the highly charged political climate is fostering political activism and awareness amongst both pro-reformers and traditionalists. For many, the heightened level of insecurity within Iraq is now serving as a barrier to future reform – the complete opposite of what was intended by Washington. The pan-Arab satellite news media's graphic coverage of the carnage within Iraq is being increasingly cited by opponents to reform as an example of where reform will lead. The 'Western agenda' of democracy is commonly touted by critics as being equated with political and societal insecurity: this leads to a climate of fear and desire for caution within civil society with regards to the desirability of reform. In many respects this is a useful tool for the conservative elites of the Arabian Peninsula countries as they are able to convincingly argue that change should occur slowly and in a controlled fashion in order to ensure it does not backfire. The problem here is that this makes the likelihood of non-substantive liberalisation more likely and limits the prospects for true reform. This alters the balance of the power relationship which, on a theoretical level, is needed to counter the risks pertaining from radical political Islam.

Nevertheless, this highly charged geopolitical climate is also giving a new momentum to those who favour reform. It is encouraging political awareness within civil society of the question of political and social change and this is being compounded by the wider effects of globalisation. Key among these is the contemporary zeitgeist – historically tribalism has been the defining characteristic of the political order but the winds of change are now ushering in a new emphasis on the question of citizenship and the rights pertaining thereto. Gender politics are also increasingly proving to be an emerging issue across the region. The extension of universal suffrage, coupled with the participation of women in parliamentary elections in Kuwait and Bahrain as candidates, has served to challenge traditional conceptions of women's role in society and has served to break down social barriers. Of even more importance is the impact their participation as candidates has had on the wider region: it has served to inspire women in neighbouring countries and this change of attitude is likely to strengthen demands from civil society for a greater political voice for women. Change in this area is highly significant as the breakdown of social barriers will sow the seeds which will make such societies even more susceptible to the influence of globalisation.

As with the regional aftermath of Saddam's invasion of Kuwait, so too has the occupation of Iraq galvanised the views and activities of many within civil society on both sides of the political reform divide. However, democracy promotion is understandably not a risk-free strategy in the context of Western interests: the election victory of Hamas in Palestine is a case in point. Evidence seems to suggest that the promotion of reform in countries which lack a culture of social participation in a politically plural environment makes the likelihood of anti-Western Islamic parties gaining power that much more likely. With Islam having been the only alternative political mobilising agent not curtailed by the state apparatus across the Persian Gulf, liberalisation will likely see Islamic organisations play a prominent part in the elections for the advisory councils across the subregion. In many respects, the current encouragement afforded to civil society NGOs by the US and EU should be viewed as not necessarily having a tangible impact on driving further reform, but rather playing the key function of fostering a more politically plural civil society for when further top-down liberalisation is implemented. Indeed, the advantages of funding civil society organisations are likely only to be realised in the long term.

With Iraq having descended into a communal civil war between the Sunni and Shi'a factions, which is complicated by foreign Islamists and neighbouring states' intelligence operatives, the manner in which Iraq unfolds will likely be long-term and highly costly. Furthermore, given this rising sectarianism and insecurity, the prospect of Iraq maintaining its federal structure does not seem promising. An Iraq fragmented into possibly a two or three state structure will have clear geopolitical consequences on both neighbouring states and on a wider regional level given the instability. However, assessing Iraq as part of the strategic maxims of the War on Terror will probably only be truly possible in the very long term. However, what is clear is that even when the geopolitical area of Iraq stabilises in the long term and the states in the Persian Gulf subregion move towards an integration with the larger globalised community and transform themselves into more liberalised and democratic states, the key question will be whether the cost of this transformation was worth the price paid for it by a crusading moralism which saw upheaval as the quickest route to success.

Whilst the unfolding Iraqi geopolitical scenario has clear ramifications for the achievement of security in this region, what can be discerned is that the greatest potential challenge faced in the Persian Gulf revolves around the Islamic Republic of Iran. Iran is a geopolitical pivot in the region and if it were not for the presence of the United States, it would, along with Israel, be a clear regional superpower within the Middle East and in the Persian Gulf in particular. Under the current rubric of the Bush Doctrine, Iran and the United States are on a collision course over Tehran's nuclear programme. From a sober reading of the Bush Doctrine, Iran fulfils the criterion of a hostile state that is understood to be producing unconventional weapons. A clear dilemma that is now facing the region and the wider international community is whether Iran can be trusted to have non-military intentions. The development of a nuclear arsenal would, on a geopolitical level, clearly challenge the United States' dominance in the region and under the guise of the War on Terror poses an acute national security threat.

US foreign policy under this War on Terror mentality is premised, as highlighted earlier, on zero-sum calculations: a nuclear-armed hostile power cannot be allowed to arise and thus the preventative use of force is deemed justified. Therefore, the clearest policy challenge facing the United States with regard to the Persian Gulf is whether preventative action against Iran should be undertaken if time for diplomacy is considered to have run out. In essence the dilemma is: do the geopolitical consequences of using military force outweigh the risks of a nuclear-armed Iran? Of course, Israel too would necessarily see itself as having to make the same choice. Here suffice it to say that the question of Iran and its nuclear programme is likely to be the greatest geopolitical challenge in the short to medium term. It is not inevitable that military force will be seen as a necessary evil by Washington; after all a suitable compromise may be reached; but the current reading of the political chessboard does indicate that a nuclear-armed Iran is seen by the American political elite and by its key allies as the great risk on the horizon and one which should not be allowed to happen. The problem is whether both sides can realise that their failure to empathise with each other's concerns is actually fostering a 'fog of war' that will eventually lead them to a military confrontation that will have vast geopolitical costs.

Bibliography

Abrams, Elliot, et al. "Letter to Trent Lott and Newt Gingrich". Washington, D.C., 1998. (29 May). <http://www.newamericancentury.org/iraqletter1998.htm>.

Abrams, Elliott, et al. "Letter to President Clinton". Washington, D.C., 1998. (26 Jan.): Project for a New American Century. <http://www.newamericancentury.org/iraqclintonletter.htm>.

——. "Statement of Principles". Washington, D.C., 1997. (3 Jun.): Project for a New American Century. <http://newamericancentury.org/statementofprinciples.htm>.

Ackerman, Spenser. "The Weakest Link: Why the Bush Administration Insists Against All Evidence on an Iraq–Al Qaeda Connection". *Washington Monthly* Nov. 2003. 23/08/04 <http://www.findarticles.com/p/articles/mi_m1316/is_11_35/ai_111027164>.

Ahmed, Mumtaz, and I. William Zartman. "Political Islam: Can It Become a Loyal Opposition". *Middle East Policy* 5.1 (1997).

Aikman, David, and George W. Bush. *A Man of Faith: The Spiritual Journey of George W. Bush*. Nashville: W Publishing, 2004.

Aita, Judy. "Iraq Rejects United Nations Overtures to Resume Co-Operation with UNSCOM". *United States Information Agency* 7 Nov. 1997. 12/06/02 <http://www.fas.org/news/iraq/1997/11/97110701_npo.html>.

——. "UNSCOM Suspends Operations in Iraq". *United States Information Agency* 29 Oct. 1997. 12/03/03 <http://www.fas.org/news/iraq/1997/10/97102902_npo.html>.

Ajami, Fouad. *The Dream Palace of the Arabs: A Generation's Odyssey*. New York: Pantheon Books, 1998.

Al-Thani, Al-Hussain. "The Legality of Use of Force against Iraq in March 2003". Unpublished article. University of Durham, 2004.

Albright, Madeleine. "Albright Speech 6/17/98". Remarks at 1998 Asia Society Dinner Waldorf-Astoria Hotel New York. New York: GPO. 18 Jun. 1998. 4pp. 13/06/04 <http://www.aghayan.com/alb061798.htm>

Albright, Madeleine, and William Woodward. *Madam Secretary: A Memoir*. London: Macmillan, 2003.

Alikhani, Hossein. *Sanctioning Iran: Anatomy of a Failed Policy*. London; New York: I.B. Tauris, 2000.

Allison, Graham T. *Essence of Decision; Explaining the Cuban Missile Crisis*. Boston: Little, 1971.

——. "Conceptual Models and the Cuban Missile Crisis". *American Foreign Policy: Theoretical Essays*. Ed. G. John Ikenberry. 5th ed. New York: Georgetown University, 2005.

Allison, Graham T., and Morton H. Halperin. "Bureaucratic Politics: A Paradigm and Some Policy Implications". *World Politics* 24.2 (1972).

Almond, Gabriel A. *The American People and Foreign Policy*. Westport: Greenwood Press, 1977.

Amanpour, Christiane. "Transcript of Interview with Iranian President Mohammad Khatami". *CNN Online* 7 Jan. 1998. 12/07/04 <*http://www.cnn.com/WORLD/ 9801/07/iran/interview.html*>.

American Israeli Public Affairs Committee. *Comprehensive US Sanctions Against Iran: A Plan for Action*. Washington, D.C.: AIPAC, 1994.

Anonymous. "Khobar Towers Indictments Returned". *CNN Online* 22 Jun. 2001. 28/08/02 <*http://archives.cnn.com/2001/LAW/06/21/khobar.indictments/*>.

——. "France Will Use Iraq Veto". *BBC News Online* 10 Mar. 2003. 11/05/03 <*http:// news.bbc.co.uk/1/hi/world/middle_east/2838269.stm*>.

——. "A Review of US Unilateral Sanctions against Iran". *Middle East Economic Survey* 45.34 (2002).

——. "The Odd Couple". *Economist Online* 3 Feb. 2005. 12/02/05 <*http://www.economist. com/diversions/displaystory.cfm?story_id=3623386*>.

Anonymous, [George Kennan]. "The Sources of Soviet Conduct". *Foreign Affairs* 25.4 (1947).

Arkin, William. "The Difference Was in the Details". *Washington Post* 17 Jan. 1999.

Armitage, Richard. "Armitage: Afghan Vote to Show Democracy, Islam Compatible". Deputy Secretary of State interviewed by Italian newspaper. Washington, D.C.: GPO. 6 Oct. 2004. 4pp. 17/12/04 <*http://tokyo.usembassy.gov/e/p/tp-20041012-26. html*>.

Arnett, Peter. "March 1997 Interview with Osama Bin Laden". *CNN Online* March 2001. 12/07/04 <*http://news.findlaw.com/hdocs/docs/binladen/binladenintvw-cnn. pdf*>.

The Associated Press. "France Offers Plan to Lift Iraqi Embargo". *USA Today Online* 13 Jan. 1999. 12/02/03 <*http://www.usatoday.com/news/index/iraq/iraq549.htm*>.

——. "French Proposal Leads to Talks on Iraq". *USA Today Online* 14 Jan. 1999. 12/02/03 <*http://www.usatoday.com/news/index/iraq/iraq550.htm*>.

——. "Top General Criticizes US Policy on Iraq". *USA Today Online* 28 Jan. 1999. 12/02/03 <*http://www.usatoday.com/news/index/iraq/iraq567.htm*>.

——. "US Rejects Russian Solution on Iraq". *USA Today Online* 15 Jan. 1999. 12/02/03 <*http://www.usatoday.com/news/index/iraq/iraq553.htm*>.

——. "Group: Iran's Nuke Program Growing". *New York Times* 15 Aug. 2002.

Ayubi, Nazih N. M. *Political Islam: Religion and Politics in the Arab World*. London: Routledge, 1991.

Bacevich, Andrew J. *American Empire: The Realities and Consequences of US Diplomacy*. Cambridge: Harvard University Press, 2002.

Baker, James. "Peace, One Step at a Time". *New York Times* 27 Jul. 2000.

Baram, Amatzia. *Building Toward Crisis: Saddam Husayn's Secret Strategy for Survival.* Washington, D.C.: Washington Institute for Near East Policy, 1998.

Barnes, Fred. "Mohamed Atta Was Here and Met with Saddam Hussein's Man in Prague". *Weekly Standard* 8 Dec. 2002. 12/06/03 <*http://www.weeklystandard. com/content/public/articles/000/000/001/539dozfr.asp*>.

———. "God and Man in the Oval Office". *Weekly Standard* 17 Mar. 2003. 12/11/04 <*www.weeklystandard.com/Content/Public/Articles/000/000/002/335uuffd.asp*>.

Bendor, Jonathan, and Thomas H. Hammond. "Rethinking Allison's Models". *The American Political Science Review* 86.2 (1992).

Bennet, James. "Seized Arms Would Have Vastly Extended Arafat Arsenal". *New York Times* 12 Jan. 2002.

Bergen, Peter. *Holy War Inc.: Inside the Secret World of Osama Bin Laden.* London: Phoenix, 2002.

Blix, Hans. *Disarming Iraq.* London: Bloomsbury, 2004.

Blum, Bill. "The CIA's Intervention in Afghanistan: Interview with Zbigniew Brzezinski". *Le Nouvel Observateur* 15–21 Jan. 1998. 12/06/03 <*http://www. globalresearch.ca/articles/BRZ110A.html*>.

Bowles, Nigel. *The Government and Politics of the United States.* Comparative Government and Politics. Basingstoke: Macmillan, 1993.

Brady, David, and D. Sunshine Hillygus. "Assessing the Clinton Presidency: The Political Constraints of Legislative Policy". *The Clinton Riddle: Perspectives on the Forty-Second President.* Eds. Todd G. Shields, et al. Arkansas: University of Arkansas Press, 2004.

Brinkley, Douglas. "Democratic Enlargement: The Clinton Doctrine". *Foreign Policy* 106 (1997).

Bronson, Rachel. "The Reluctant Mediator". *Washington Quarterly* 25.4 (2002). 12/11/03 <*http://www.cfr.org/pub4967/rachel_bronson/the_reluctant_mediator.php*>.

Brumberg, Daniel. "Rhetoric and Strategy: Islamic Movements and Democracy in the Middle East". *The Islamism Debate.* Ed. Martin Kramer. Tel Aviv: The Moshe Dayan Center for Middle Eastern and African Studies, Tel Aviv University, 1997.

———. "Bush Policy or Bush Philosophy". *Washington Post* 16 Nov. 2003.

Bryson, Thomas A. *American Diplomatic Relations with the Middle East, 1784–1975: A Survey.* Metuchen: Scarecrow Press, 1977.

Brzezinski, Zbigniew. *The Grand Chessboard: American Primacy and Its Geostrategic Imperatives.* New York: Basic Books, 1997.

———. *The Choice: Global Domination or Global Leadership.* New York: Basic Books, 2005.

Brzezinski, Zbigniew, et al. *Iran: Time for a New Approach.* Washington, D.C.: Council on Foreign Relations, 2004.

———. "Differentiated Containment". *Foreign Affairs* 76.3 (1997).

Buchan, David. "Europeans Rally to Allies' Cause". *Financial Times* 19 Dec. 1998.

Burgat, François. "Ballot Boxes, Militaries and Islamic Movements". *The Islamism Debate*. Ed. Martin Kramer. Tel Aviv: The Moshe Dayan Center for Middle Eastern and African Studies, Tel Aviv University, 1997.

Burgess, John, and David Ottway. "Iraqi Opposition Unable to Mount Viable Challenge". *Washington Post* 12 Feb. 1998.

Burns, Nicholas. Department of State. "Daily Press Briefing". Washington, D.C.: GPO. 30 Sep. 1996. 19pp. 21/10/02 *<http://dosfan.lib.uic.edu/ERC/briefing/daily_ briefings/1996/9609/960930db.html>*.

Bush, George H. W. "Toward a New World Order". Address before a joint session of Congress. Washington, D.C.: GPO. 11 Sept. 1990. 27pp. 15/06/04 *<http:// dosfan. lib.uic.edu/erc/briefing/dispatch/1990/html/Dispatchv1no03.html>*.

——. "Statement from Baghdad: A Cruel Hoax". Comments to the American Association for the Advancement of Science. Washington, D.C.: GPO. 15 Feb. 1991. 20pp. 13/07/03 *<http://dosfan.lib.uic.edu/erc/briefing/dispatch/1991/html/ Dispatchv2no07.html>*.

——. "US Expands Kurdish Relief Efforts". Opening statement at White House news conference. Washington, D.C.: GPO. 16 Apr. 1991. 38pp. 15/07/03 *<http:// dosfan.lib.uic.edu/erc/briefing/dispatch/1991/html/Dispatchv2no16.html>*.

——. "President Bush Calls for New Palestinian Leadership". The Rose Garden. Washington, D.C.: 24 Jun. 2002. 3pp. 27/08/2002 *<http://www.whitehouse.gov/ news/releases/2002/06/20020624-3.html>*.

Bush, George W. "A Distinctly American Internationalism". Remarks at the Ronald Reagan Presidential Library. Simi Valley, California: FAS. 19 Nov. 1999. 8pp. 18/07/02 *<http://www.fas.org/news/usa/1999/11/991119-bush-foreignpolicy. htm>*.

——. "President's Remarks to the United Nations General Assembly". Remarks by the President in Address to the United Nations General Assembly. New York: GPO. 12 Sept. 2002. 5pp. 17/02/02 *<http://www.whitehouse.gov/news/releases/2002/ 09/20020912-1.html>*

——. "President Delivers State of the Union Address". The President's State of the Union Address. Washington, D.C.: GPO. 29 Jan. 2002. 20pp. 30/01/02 *<http://www. whitehouse.gov/news/releases/2002/01/20020129-11.html>*

——. "President, Vice President Discuss the Middle East". Remarks by the President and the Vice President Upon Conclusion of Breakfast. Washington D.C.: GPO. 21 Mar. 2002. 3pp. 19/02/03 *<http://www.whitehouse.gov/news/releases/2002/03/ 20020321-6.html>*

——. "West Point Commencement Speech". *America and the World: Debating the New Shape of International Politics*. Ed. Gideon Rose. New York: Council on Foreign Relations, 2002.

——. "President Bush Announces Major Combat Operations in Iraq Have Ended". Washington, D.C.: GPO. 1 May 2003. 3pp. 05/05/03 *<http://www.whitehouse. gov/news/releases/2003/05/iraq/20030501-15.html>*

——. "President Bush Discusses Freedom in Iraq and Middle East". Remarks by the

President at the 20th Anniversary of the National Endowment for Democracy. Washington, D.C.: GPO. 6 Nov. 2003. 6pp. 15/09/04 <*http://www.whitehouse. gov/news/releases/2003/11/20031106-2.html*>

——. "President Bush Presents Vision of Middle East Peace". Remarks by the President at the American Enterprise Institute Annual Dinner. Washington, D.C.: GPO. 26 Feb. 2003. 6pp. 15/09/04 <*http://tokyo.usembassy.gov/e/p/tp-20030228a1. html*>

——. "President Discusses the Economy with Small Business Owners". Remarks by the President in the Rose Garden. Washington, D.C.: GPO. 15 Apr. 2003. 4pp. 19/06/03 <*http://www.whitehouse.gov/news/releases/2003/04/20030415-2. html*>

——. "Remarks Prior to Discussions with Prime Minister". Remarks prior to discussions with Prime Minister Recep Tayyip Erdogan of Turkey. Ankara: GPO. 27 Jun. 2004. 1pp. 17/02/05 <*http://www.findarticles.com/p/articles/ mi_m2889/is_27_40/ ai_n6148652*>.

Butler, Richard. *Saddam Defiant: The Threat of Weapons of Mass Destruction and the Crisis of Global Security.* London: Phoenix, 2001.

Byman, Daniel, et al. "Coercing Saddam Hussein: Lesson from the Past". *Survival* 40.3 (1998).

Calabrese, John. "China and the Persian Gulf: Energy and Security". *Middle East Journal* 52. Summer (1998).

Carothers, Thomas. "The Clinton Record on Democracy Promotion". *Critical Mission: Essays on Democracy Promotion.* Ed. Thomas Carothers. Washington, D.C.: Brookings Institution Press, 2000.

——. "Democracy: Terrorism's Uncertain Antidote". *Critical Mission: Essays on Democracy Promotion.* Ed. Thomas Carothers. Washington, D.C.: Brookings Institution Press, 2003.

——. "Is Gradualism Possible? Choosing a Strategy for Promoting Democracy in the Middle East". *Critical Mission: Essays on Democracy Promotion.* Ed. Thomas Carothers. Washington, D.C.: Brookings Institution Press, 2003.

——. "Promoting Democracy and Fighting Terror". *Critical Mission: Essays on Democracy Promotion.* Ed. Thomas Carothers. Washington, D.C.: Brookings Institution Press, 2003.

Carus, W. Seth, and Joseph Bermudez. "Iraq's Al-Husayn Missile Programme: Part 1". *Jane's Intelligence Review* 2.5 (1990).

——. "Iraq's Al-Husayn Missile Programme: Part 2". *Jane's Intelligence Review* 2.6 (1990).

Chesterman, Simon. *Just War or Just Peace? Humanitarian Intervention and International Law.* Oxford; New York: Oxford University Press, 2001.

Chesterman, Simon, and David Malone. "The Iraq Tragedy: It's Too Late for the UN to Help Much". *International Herald Tribune Online* 8 Dec. 2003. 10/12/03 <*http://www.iht.com/articles/120574.html*>.

Chipman, John. *Strategic Survey 2001/2002.* Oxford: OUP, 2002.

——. *Strategic Survey 2002/2003*. Oxford: OUP, 2003.

——. *The Military Balance*. Ed. Christopher Langton. Vol. 2003–2004. Oxford: Oxford University Press, 2003.

Christopher, Warren. "Building Peace in the Middle East". Address at Columbia University, co-sponsored by the Council on Foreign Relations. New York: GPO. 20 Sep. 1993. 24pp. 13/09/01 <*http://dosfan.lib.uic.edu/erc/briefing/dispatch/1993/html/Dispatchv4no39.html*>.

——. "Progress on Resolving Israeli Deportation Issue". Excerpts from opening statement at a news conference at the US Mission to the United Nations. New York: GPO. 1 Feb. 1993. 24pp. 12/09/02 <*http://dosfan.lib.uic.edu/erc/briefing/dispatch/1993/html/Dispatchv4no07.html*>.

——. "Secretary Christopher Visits Europe and the Middle East". Opening statement at a news conference following a meeting with Syrian President Asad and Foreign Minister Shara. Damascus: GPO. 5 Dec. 1993. 26pp. 11/19/02 <*http://dosfan.lib.uic.edu/erc/briefing/dispatch/1993/html/Dispatchv4no50.html*>.

——. "America's Leadership, America's Opportunity". *Foreign Policy* 98 (1995).

Clarke, Richard A. *Against All Enemies: Inside America's War on Terror*. New York: Free Press, 2004.

Clinton, William J. "A New Covenant for American Security". Speech at Georgetown University. Washington, D.C.: GPO. 12 Dec. 1991. 3pp. 17/06/03 <*http://www.ibiblio.org/pub/docs/speeches/clinton.dir/c28.txt*>

——. *Public Papers of the Presidents of the United States 1993: William J. Clinton (Bk. 1)*. Washington, D.C.: GPO, 1993. 05/11/04 <*http://frwebgate.access.gpo.gov/cgibin/getdoc.cgi?dbname=1993_public_papers_vol1_misc&docid=f:pap_pre.htm#1993v1contents*>.

——. "Remarks on Signing the Religious Freedom Restoration Act of 1993". Washington, D.C.: GPO. 16 Nov. 1993. 1pp. 15/05/02 <*http://www.geocities.com/peterroberts.geo/Relig-Politics/WJClinton.html*>.

——. "Speech by President to the Jordanian Parliament". Remarks by the President to the Jordanian Parliament. Amman: GPO. 26 Aug. 1993. 2pp. 11/10/04 <*http://www.clintonfoundation.org/legacy/102694-speech-by-president-to-jordanian-parliament.htm*>

——. *Public Papers of the Presidents of the United States 1994: William J. Clinton (Bk. 1)*. Washington D.C.: GPO, 1995. 07/01/04 <*http://frwebgate.access.gpo.gov/cgi-bin/getpage. cgi?dbname=1994_public_papers_vol1_misc&page=1046&position=all*>.

——. *My Life*. New York: Knopf, 2004.

Clinton, William J., and Yitzak Rabin. "Strengthening US–Israeli Relations to Benefit America's Interests". Opening statements at a news conference released by the White House, Office of the Press Secretary. Washington, D.C.: GPO. 15 Mar. 1993. 17pp. 12/02/02 <*http://dosfan.lib.uic.edu/erc/briefing/dispatch/1993/html/Dispatchv4no12.html*>.

Coll, Steve. "CIA in Afghanistan: In CIA's Covert War, Where to Draw the Line Was Key". *Washington Post* 20 Jul. 1992.

Cook, Stephen. "The Right Way to Promote Arab Reform". *Foreign Affairs* 84.2 (2005).

Cordesman, Anthony H. *The Iran-Iraq War and Western Security 1984-87: Strategic Implications and Policy Options.* London: Jane's Publishing, 1987.

——. *Iraq and the War of Sanctions: Conventional Threats and Weapons of Mass Destruction.* Westport: Praeger, 1999.

Daalder, Ivo H., and James M. Lindsay. *America Unbound: The Bush Revolution in Foreign Policy.* Washington, D.C.: Brookings Institution, 2003.

——. "Bush's Foreign Policy Revolution". *The George W. Bush Presidency: An Early Assessment.* Ed. Fred I. Greenstein. Maryland: Johns Hopkins Press, 2003.

David, Stephen R. "Explaining Third World Alignment". *World Politics* 43.2 (1991).

Davies, Glyn. Department of State. "Daily Press Briefing". Washington, D.C.: GPO. 9 Apr. 1996. 11pp. 21/10/02 <http://dosfan.lib.uic.edu/ERC/briefing/daily_briefings/1996/9604/960409db.html>.

Deen, Thalif. "UN Bombed for Perceived US Link, Experts Say". *Inter-Press Service* 19 Aug. 2003. 03/04/04 <http://www.globalpolicy.org/security/issues/iraq/after/2003/0819unbombed.htm>.

Dekmejian, R. Hrair. "Islamic Revival: Catalysts, Categories, and Consequences". *The Politics of Islamic Revivalism: Diversity and Unity.* Ed. Shireen Hunter. Bloomington: Indiana University Press, 1988.

——. *Islam in Revolution: Fundamentalism in the Arab World.* 2nd ed. Syracuse: Syracuse University Press, 1995.

Denovo, John A. *American Interests and Policies in the Middle East, 1900–1939.* Minneapolis: University of Minnesota Press, 1963.

Diamond, Larry. "What Went Wrong in Iraq". *Foreign Affairs* 83.5 (2004).

Djerejian, Edward. "The US and the Middle East in a Changing World". Address at Meridian House International. Washington, D.C.: GPO. 2 Jun. 1992. 8pp. 04/05/02 <http://dosfan.lib.uic.edu/ERC/briefing/dispatch/1992/html/Dispatchv3no23.html>.

——. "US Policy in the Middle East". Statement before the Subcommittee on Europe and the Middle East of the House Foreign Affairs Committee. Washington, D.C.: GPO. 9 Mar. 1993. 17pp. 14/08/02 <http://dosfan.lib.uic.edu/erc/briefing/dispatch/1993/html/Dispatchv4no12.html>.

——. "US Policy on Recent Developments and Other Issues in the Middle East". Statement before the Subcommittee on Europe and the Middle East of the House Foreign Affairs Committee. Washington, D.C.: GPO. 27 Jul. 1993. 17pp. 24/10/02 <http://dosfan.lib.uic.edu/erc/briefing/dispatch/1993/html/Dispatchv4no32.html>.

——. "War and Peace: The Problems and Prospects of American Diplomacy in the Middle East". Address before the Los Angeles World Affairs Council. Los

Angeles: GPO. 30 Nov. 1993. 13pp. 20/08/02 <http://dosfan.lib.uic.edu/ERC/ briefing/dispatch/1993/html/Dispatchv4no21. html>.

Doran, Michael Scott. "Palestine, Iraq, and American Strategy". *Foreign Affairs* 82.1 (2003).

Duelfer, Charles. *Comprehensive Report of the Special Advisor on Iraq's WMD: Chemical and Biological Weapons.* Washington, D.C.: CIA, 2004. 350pp. 02/03/05 <http: //www.cia.gov/cia/reports/iraq_wmd_2004/>.

Dunphy, Harry. "US Will Aid Iraqi Opposition". *Associated Press* 25 May 1999. 15/04/03 <http://www.iraqcmm.org/cmm/clari-990525.html>.

Ehteshami, Anoushiravan. "The Delicate State of Muslim Democracy". *Global Agenda* 2004.

Eickelman, Dale F., and James P. Piscatori. *Muslim Politics.* Princeton, NJ: Princeton University Press, 2004.

Ensor, David. "US to Intensify Work with Iraqi Opposition Groups". *CNN Online* 16 Nov. 1998. 12/02/03 <http://edition.cnn.com/US/9811/16/saddam.overthrow/>.

Esposito, John L. "The Persian Gulf War, Islamic Movements and the New World Order". *The Iranian Journal of International Affairs* Spring (1991).

Esposito, John L., and James P. Piscatori. "Democratization and Islam". *Middle East Journal* 45.3 (1991).

Esposito, John L., and John O. Voll. "Islam and Democracy: Rejoinder". *Middle East Quarterly* 1.4 (1994).

——. "Islam's Democratic Essence". *Middle East Quarterly* 1.4 (1994).

——. *Islam and Democracy.* Oxford: OUP, 1996.

Evans, Malcolm D. *Blackstone's International Law Documents.* Blackstone's Statutes. 4th ed. London: Blackstone, 1999.

Fairbanks, Stephen C. "A New Era for Iran". *Middle East Policy* 5.3 (1997).

Farrands, Christopher. "Environment and Structure". *Understanding Foreign Policy: The Foreign Policy Systems Approach.* Eds. Michael Clarke and Brian White. Aldershot: Elgar, 1989.

Feickert, Andrew. "Iran's Ballistic Missile Program". *CRS Report for Congress.* (RS21548). Washington, D.C.: CRS, Congress, 23 Aug. 2004. 6pp. 12/02/05 <http://fpc.state.gov/documents/organization/39332.pdf>.

Ferguson, Niall. *Colossus: The Rise and Fall of the American Empire.* London: Allen Lane, 2004.

Fineman, Howard. "Bush and God". *Newsweek* 10 Mar. 2003.

Freedman, Robert O. "The Bush Administration and the Arab–Israeli Conflict: The Record of Its First Four Years". *The Middle East Review of International Affairs* 9.1 (2005). 27/03/05 <www.meria.ida.ac.il/journal/2005/issue1/jv9no1a4.html>.

Friedman, George. *America's Secret War: Inside the Hidden Worldwide Struggle between America and Its Enemies.* London: Little Brown, 2004.

Friedman, Thomas. "Clinton's Warning to Saddam: I'm Going to Judge You by Your Behaviour". *International Herald Tribune* 15 Jan. 1993.

Frum, David. *The Right Man: An Inside Account of the Surprise Presidency of George W. Bush*. New York: Random House, 2003.

Fukuyama, Francis. "The End of History?" *America and the World: Debating the New Shape of International Politics*. Ed. Gideon Rose. New York: W.W. Norton, 1989.

Fuller, Graham. "Islamism(S) in the Next Century". *The Islamism Debate*. Ed. Martin Kramer. Tel Aviv: The Moshe Dayan Center for Middle Eastern and African Studies, Tel Aviv University, 1997.

——. *The Future of Political Islam*. New York: Palgrave Macmillan, 2004.

Gaddis, John L. *We Now Know: Rethinking Cold War History*. Oxford: OUP, 1998.

——. "Bush's Security Strategy". *Foreign Policy* 133 (2002).

——. *Surprise, Security, and the American Experience*. Cambridge: Harvard University Press, 2004.

——. "Grand Strategy in the Second Term". *Foreign Affairs* 84.1 (2005).

Garden, Timothy. "Iraq: The Military Campaign". *International Affairs* 79.4 (2003).

Gause III, F. Gregory. *Oil Monarchies: Domestic and Security Challenges in the Persian Gulf States*. New York: Council on Foreign Relations, 1994.

——. "The Illogic of Dual Containment". *Foreign Affairs* 73.2 (1994).

——. "Getting It Back on Iraq". *Foreign Affairs* 78.3 (1999).

——. *US Policy toward Iraq*. Emirates Lecture Series. Vol. 39. Abu Dhabi: The Emirates Center for Strategic Studies and Research, 2002.

Gearson, John. "Terrorism in Historical Perspective". *The Goodenough–Chevening Conference on Terrorism*. London, 2003.

Gelb, Leslie. "A Reformed Iraq to Offset Iran? Forget It". *International Herald Tribune* 18 Jan. 1993.

Gelb, Leslie H., and Richard K. Betts. *The Irony of Vietnam: The System Worked*. Washington, D.C.: Brookings Institution, 1979.

Gellman, Barton. "Gingrich Opens File on White House Iraq Policy". *Washington Post* 29 Aug. 1998.

——. "US Spied on Iraqi Military Via UN". *Washington Post* 2 Mar. 1999.

Gerges, Fawaz A. *America and Political Islam: Clash of Cultures or Clash of Interests?* Cambridge: Cambridge University Press, 1999.

Gerner, Deborah J. "Foreign Policy Analysis: Exhilarating Eclecticism, Intriguing Enigmas". *International Studies Notes* 16.3 (1991).

——. "The Evolution of the Study of Foreign Policy". *Foreign Policy Analysis: Continuity and Change in Its Second Generation*. Eds. Laura Neack, et al. Englewood Cliffs: Prentice Hall, 1995.

Glad, Betty. "Bill Clinton: The Character Issue Revisited". *The Clinton Riddle: Perspectives on the Forty-Second President*. Eds. Todd G. Shields, et al. Arkansas: University of Arkansas Press, 2004.

Gordon, Phillip H. "Bush's Middle East Vision". *Survival* 45.1 (2003).

Graham, Bradley. "The Big Military Question: What's Next?". *Washington Post* 24 Dec. 1998.

Graubard, Stephen. *The Presidents: The Transformation of the American Presidency from Theodore Roosevelt to George W. Bush.* London: Penguin, 2005.

Gray, Christine. "From Unity to Polarization: International Law and the Use of Force against Iraq". *European Journal of International Law* 13.1 (2002).

Green, Peter. "Iraq Link to Sept 11 Attack and Anthrax Is Ruled Out". *Telegraph Online* 18 Dec. 2001. 12/01/02 <http://www.telegraph.co.uk/news/main.jhtml?xml=/news/2001/12/18/wirq18.xml>.

Greenstein, Fred I. "The Leadership Style of George W. Bush". *The George W. Bush Presidency: An Early Assessment.* Ed. Fred I. Greenstein. Maryland: Johns Hopkins Press, 2003.

Uncovered: The Whole Truth About the Iraq War. Dir. Greenwald, Robert. DVD. The Disinformation Company Ltd., 2004.

Hagan, Joe D. "Domestic Political Explanations in the Analysis of Foreign Policy". *Foreign Policy Analysis: Continuity and Change in Its Second Generation.* Eds. Laura Neack, et al. Englewood Cliffs: Prentice Hall, 1995.

Halberstam, David. *War in a Time of Peace: Bush, Clinton, and the Generals.* New York: Scribner, 2001.

Halper, Stefan A., and Jonathan Clarke. *America Alone: The Neo-Conservatives and the Global Order.* Cambridge: Cambridge University Press, 2004.

Harris, John F. "New Security Adviser Berger Is Known as Consensus Builder". *Washington Post* 6 Dec. 1996.

Hass, Richard N. "Fatal Distraction: Bill Clinton's Foreign Policy". *Foreign Policy* 108 (1997).

——. "The Clinton Administration's Approach to the Middle East". Remarks to the Foreign Policy Association. New York: GPO. 22 Apr. 2002. 7pp. 30/10/03 <http://www.state.gov/s/p/rem/9632.htm>.

Hatano, Yoshio. "Situation between Iraq and Kuwait". Statement by UN Security Council President Hatano. New York: US Department of State, 8 Jan. 1993. 12/08/02 <http://dosfan.lib.uic.edu/ERC/briefing/dispatch/1993/html/Dispatchv4no03.html>.

Heclo, Hugh. "The Political Ethos of George W. Bush". *The George W. Bush Presidency: An Early Assessment.* Ed. Fred I. Greenstein. Maryland: Johns Hopkins Press, 2003.

Helms, Jesse. "American Sovereignty and the UN". *National Interest* 62.Winter (2000).

Hiro, Dilip. *Neighbors, Not Friends: Iraq and Iran after the Gulf Wars.* London; New York: Routledge, 2001.

Hirsh, Michael. "Bernard Lewis Revisited: What If Islam Isn't an Obstacle to Democracy in the Middle East but the Secret to Achieving It?". *Washington Monthly* 45. Nov. (2004). 6pp. 13/12/04 <http://www.collectiveinterest.net/homepage/bernard_lewis%20revisited.pdf>.

Hoagland, Jim. "How CIA's Secret War on Saddam Collapsed". *Washington Post* 26 June 1997.

——. "How CIA's Secret War on Saddam Collapsed". *Washington Post* 26 June 1997.

Hollis, Rosemary. "Getting out of the Iraq Trap". *International Affairs* 79.1 (2003).

Holsti, Ole R. "Models of International Relations and Foreign Policy". *American Foreign Policy: Theoretical Essays*. Ed. G. John Ikenberry. 5th ed. New York: Georgetown University, 2005.

Hudson, Michael C. "To Play the Hegemon: Fifty Years of US Policy Towards the Middle East". *Middle East Journal* 50.3 (1996).

Huntington, Samuel. "Religion and the Third Wave". *National Interest* 24. Summer (1991).

——. "The Clash of Civilizations?". *Foreign Affairs* 72.3 (1993).

——. "American Ideals Versus American Institutions". *American Foreign Policy: Theoretical Essays*. Ed. G. John Ikenberry. 5th ed. New York: Georgetown University, 2005.

——. "The Lonely Superpower". *American Foreign Policy: Theoretical Essays*. Ed. G. John Ikenberry. 5th ed. New York: Georgetown University, 2005.

Ikenberry, G. John. "Conclusion: An Institutional Approach to American Foreign Economic Policy". 42.1 (1988).

——. "American Grand Strategy in the Age of Terror". *Survival* 43.4 (2001).

——. "The End of the Neo-Conservative Moment". *Survival* 46.1 (2004).

——. "America's Imperial Ambition". *American Foreign Policy: Theoretical Essays*. Ed. G. John Ikenberry. 5th ed. New York: Georgetown University, 2005.

——. "America's Liberal Grand Strategy: Democracy and National Security in the Post-War Era". *American Foreign Policy: Theoretical Essays*. Ed. G. John Ikenberry. 5th ed. New York: Georgetown University, 2005.

——. "Introduction". *American Foreign Policy: Theoretical Essays*. Ed. G. John Ikenberry. 5th ed. New York: Georgetown University, 2005.

Ikenberry, G. John, et al. "Introduction: Approaches to Explaining American Foreign Economic Policy". *International Organization* 42.1 (1988): 219–243.

Indyk, Martin. "The Clinton Administration's Approach to the Middle East". Address to the Soref Symposium. Washington, D.C.: Washington Institute for Near East Policy. 18 May 1993. 4pp. 12/07/03 <*http://www.washingtoninstitute.org/pubs/soreflindyk.htm*>.

——. "The Clinton Administration's Approach to the Middle East". Soref Symposium, Washington Institute, 18 May 1993.

——. "Indyk Reviews US Policy Towards Peace Process, Iran, Iraq and Maghreb". Remarks at House International Relations Committee. Washington, D.C.: GPO. 8 Jun. 1999. 12pp. 13/04/03 <*http://www.usembassy-israel.org.il/publish/peace/archives/1999/june/me0608a.html*>.

——. "Indyk Says US Is Committed to a Better Future for the Middle East". Indyk remarks at New York Council on Foreign Relations. New York: GPO. 23 Apr. 1999. 12pp. 13/05/03 <*http://www.usembassy-amman.org.jo/4Ind.html*>.

——. "Back to the Bazaar". *Foreign Affairs* 82.1 (2002).

Indyk, Martin, et al. "Symposium on Dual Containment: US Policy toward Iran and Iraq". *Middle East Policy* 3.1 (1994).

Iranians for International Cooperation. "ILSA Mistakes in Retrospect". *Payvand's Iran News* Aug. 2001. 12/11/02 <http://www.payvand.com/news/01/aug/1177.html>.

Iraq, Government of. "Joint Communique from the Iraqi and Russian Governments". Baghdad, 20 Nov. 1997. 20 Jun. 2003. <http://www.fas.org/news/iraq/1997/11/iraq_un_97_11_20.htm>.

Jervis, Robert. "Hypotheses on Misperception". *International Politics and Foreign Policy*. Ed. James N. Rosenau. New York: The Free Press, 1969.

——. *Perception and Misperception in International Politics*. Princeton, N.J.: Princeton University Press, 1976.

——. *American Foreign Policy in a New Era*. New York: Routledge, 2005.

——. "Understanding the Bush Doctrine". *American Foreign Policy: Theoretical Essays*. Ed. G. John Ikenberry. 5th ed. New York: Georgetown University, 2005.

Kagan, Robert. "Distinctly American Internationalism". *Weekly Standard* 29 Nov. 1999.

——. *Of Paradise and Power: America and Europe in the New World Order*. New York: Knopf, 2004.

Kagan, Robert, and William Kristol. "Clinton's Foreign Policy (cont.)". *Weekly Standard* 12 Mar. 2001.

Kaiser, Robert, and David Ottway. "Bush's Response Eased a Deep Rift on Mideast Policy; Then Came Sept. 11". *Washington Post* 10 Feb. 2002.

Katzman, Kenneth. "Iran: Military Relations with China". *CRS Report for Congress*. (96–572). Washington, D.C.: Congressional Research Service, Library of Congress: GPO, 26 Jun. 1996. 13pp.

——. "Iran: Arms and Technology Acquisitions". *CRS Report for Congress*. (97-474F). Washington, D.C.: Congressional Research Service, Library of Congress: GPO, 22 Jun. 1998. 6pp. 01/04/03 <http://www.globalsecurity.org/wmd/library/report/crs/97-474.htm>.

——. "Iraq: International Support for US Policy". *CRS Issue Brief for Congress*. (98–114F). Washington D.C.: Congressional Research Service, Library of Congress: GPO, 19 Feb. 1998. 10pp. 12/08/03 <http://www.globalsecurity.org/wmd/library/report/crs/98-114.htm>.

——. "Iran: Current Developments and US Policy". *CRS Report for Congress*. (IB93033). Washington, D.C.: Congressional Research Service, Library of Congress: GPO, 9 May. 2002.

——. "Iraq: US Efforts to Change the Regime". *CRS Report for Congress*. (RL31339). Washington, D.C.: Congressional Research Service, Library of Congress: GPO, 22 Mar. 2002. 16pp. 23/10/03 <http://www.casi.org.uk/info/usdocs/crs/ 020322rl31339.pdf>.

——. "Iraq: Oil-for-Food Program, International Sanctions, and Illicit Trade". *CRS Report for Congress*. (RL30472). Washington, D.C.: Congressional Research

Service, Library of Congress: GPO, 19 May 2003. 24pp. 17/06/04 <*http://fpc.
state.gov/ documents/organization/21122.pdf*>.

Katzman, Kenneth, et al. "The End of Dual Containment: Iraq, Iran and Smart
Sanctions". *Middle East Policy* 8.3 (2001).

Katzman, Kenneth, and Rinn-Sup Shinn. "North Korea: Military Relations with the
Middle East". *CRS Report for Congress*. (95–754F). Washington, D.C.:
Congressional Research Service, Library of Congress: GPO, 23 Jun. 1994. 19pp.

Kay, David A. "WMD Terrorism: Hype or Reality". *The Terrorism Threat and US
Governmental Response: Operational and Organisational Factors*. Eds. James M.
Smith and William C. Thomas. Colorado: USAF Institute for National Security
Studies, 2001.

Kelman, Herbert C. "Patterns of Personal Involvement in the National System: A
Social-Psychological Analysis of Political Legitimacy". *International Politics and
Foreign Policy*. Ed. James N. Rosenau. New York: The Free Press, 1969.

Kengor, Paul. *God and George W. Bush: A Spiritual Life*. New York: Regan Books, 2004.

Kennedy, Robert F. *Thirteen Days: A Memoir of the Cuban Missile Crisis*. Norwalk,
Connecticut: Easton Press, 1991.

Kessel, Jerrold. "Abu Mazen Confirmed as Palestinian Prime Minister". *CNN Online*
1 May. 2003. 17/08/04 <*http://www.cnn.com/2003/WORLD/meast/04/29/
palestinian.cabinet/*>.

Kessler, Glen. "Nuclear Sites in Iran Worry US Officials". *Washington Post* 14 Dec. 2002.

Kirkpatrick, Jeane. "Dictatorships and Double Standards". *Commentary* 68.Nov. (1979).

Kissinger, Henry. "Domestic Structure and Foreign Policy". *International Politics and
Foreign Policy*. Ed. James N. Rosenau. New York: The Free Press, 1969.

——. *The White House Years*. London: Weidenfeld & Nicolson, 1979.

——. *Diplomacy*. New York: Touchstone, 1995.

——. "Consult and Control: Bywords for Battling the New Enemy". *Washington Post*
16 Sept. 2002.

——. *Does America Need a Foreign Policy? Toward a Diplomacy for the 21st Century*. Rev.
ed. London: Free Press, 2002.

Komarow, Steven. "Saddam's Ouster Is Goal Now, US Officials Say". *USA Today* 21
Dec. 1998.

Kramer, Martin. "Islam Vs. Democracy". *Commentary* 95.Jan. (1993).

——. "The Mismeasure of Political Islam". *The Islamism Debate*. Ed. Martin Kramer.
Tel Aviv: The Moshe Dayan Center for Middle Eastern and African Studies,
Tel Aviv University, 1997.

——. "Coming to Terms: Fundamentalists or Islamists?" *Middle East Quarterly* 10.2
(2003).

Krasner, Stephen D. "Are Bureaucracies Important? (or Allison Wonderland)".
American Foreign Policy: Theoretical Essays. Ed. G. John Ikenberry. 5th ed. New
York: Georgetown University, 2005.

Krauthammer, Charles. "The Unipolar Moment". *Foreign Affairs* 70.1 (1990).

Kristol, Irving. *Neoconservatism: The Autobiography of an Idea*. New York: Free Press, 1995.

Laipson, Ellen, et al. "Symposium: US Policy Towards Iran: From Containment to Relentless Persuit". *Middle East Policy* 4.Sep (1995).

Lake, Anthony. "Conceptualizing US Strategy in the Middle East". Address to the Soref Symposium. Washington, D.C.: Washington Institute for Near East Policy. 17 May 1994. 4pp. 19/04/02 *<http://www.washingtoninstitute.org/pubs/sorefllake.htm>*.

——. "Confronting Backlash States". *Foreign Affairs* 73.2 (1994).

——. "From Containment to Enlargement". Remarks at Johns Hopkins University, School of Advanced International Studies. Washington, D.C.: Johns Hopkins University. 21 Sep. 1994. 11pp. 17/06/02 *<http://www.mtholyoke.edu/acad/intrel/lakedoc.html>*.

——. Former National Security Advisor to President Clinton. Telephone Interview with Author. 27 Sep. 2004.

Lake, Elizabeth J. "State Department Audit to Delay Aid for INC". *Washington Times* 11 Jun. 2001.

Lederer, Edith M. "Annan Won't Send UN Staff Back to Iraq". *Associated Press* 18 Oct. 2003. 12/03/04 *<http://www.globalpolicy.org/security/issues/iraq/after/2003/1018annan.htm>*.

Lemann, Nicholas. "How It Came to War". *New Yorker* 31 Mar. 2003. 13/09/04 *<http://www.newyorker.com/printable/?fact/030331fa_fact>*.

Lesch, David W. *The Middle East and the United States: A Historical and Political Reassessment*. Oxford: Westview, 1996.

Levy, Jack. "Declining Power and the Preventive Motivation for War". *World Politics* 40.Oct. (1987).

Lewis, Bernard. "Islam and Liberal Democracy". *Atlantic Monthly* 271.2 (1993).

——. *What Went Wrong?* London: Phoenix, 2002.

——. *The Crisis of Islam*. London: Phoenix, 2003.

Lippman, Thomas W. "To Islam, an Olive Branch". *Washington Post* 28 Dec. 1994.

——. "Hill Races White House to Get Tough with Iran". *Washington Post* 2 Apr 1995.

——. "Israel Presses U.S. To Sanction Russian Missile Firms Aiding Iran". *Washington Post* 25 Sept. 1997.

——. "Two Options for US Policy". *Washington Post* 20 Dec. 1998.

Lubetkin, Wendy. "Secretary of State: Perm Five Unity Brings Apparent Reversal in Iraq". *United States Information Agency* 20 Nov. 1997. 26/09/03 *<http://www.fas.org/news/iraq/1997/11/97112006_tpo.html>*.

Lynch, Colum. "UN Arms Inspectors Will Not Return to Iraq". *Washington Post* 24 Sept. 1999.

Mann, James. *Rise of the Vulcans: The History of Bush's War Cabinet*. New York: Viking, 2004.

Mansfield, Stephen. *The Faith of George W. Bush*. Lake Mary, Fla.: Charisma House, 2003.

Marty, Martin E. "Bush and God". *Newsweek* 10 Mar. 2003.

Maynes, Charles W. "A Workable Clinton Doctrine". *Foreign Policy* 93 (1993).

McNamara, Robert S., and James G. Blight. *Wilson's Ghost: Reducing the Risk of Conflict, Killing, and Catastrophe in the 21st Century*. New York: Public Affairs, 2003.

McNamara, Robert S., et al. *Argument without End: In Search of Answers to the Vietnam Tragedy*. New York: Public Affairs, 1999.

Mead, Walter Russell. *Special Providence: American Foreign Policy and How It Changed the World*. New York: Knopf, 2001.

——. *Power, Terror, Peace, and War: America's Grand Strategy in a World at Risk*. New York: Knopf, 2004.

Miller, Linda B. "The Clinton Years: Reinventing US Foreign Policy". *International Affairs* 70.4 (1994).

Mitchell, Alison. "Senate Extends Sanctions on Libya and Iran". *New York Times* 26 Jul. 2001.

Moon, Bruce E. "The State in Foreign and Domestic Policy". *Foreign Policy Analysis: Continuity and Change in Its Second Generation*. Eds. Laura Neack, et al. Englewood Cliffs: Prentice Hall, 1995.

Muravchik, Joshua. "The Bush Manifesto". *Commentary* 114.Dec. (2002).

National Commission on the Terrorist Attacks upon the United States. *The 9/11 Commission Report: The Full Final Report of the National Commission on Terrorist Attacks upon the United States*. (Washington, D.C.: GPO, 2004) 567pp. 12/01/05 <http://www.9-11commission.gov/report/index.htm>.

Nelan, Bruce W. "New Day Coming?". *Time* Jan. 19 1998.

Norton, Anne. *Leo Strauss and the Politics of American Empire*. New Haven: Yale University Press, 2004.

Nye, Joseph S. *The Paradox of American Power: Why the World's Only Superpower Can't Go It Alone*. Oxford: OUP, 2002.

O'Connell, Mary. E. "Debating the Law of Sanctions". *European Journal of International Law* 13.1 (2002).

Oberdorfer, Don. "US Had Covert Plan to Oust Iraq's Saddam, Bush Adviser Asserts; Effort to Remove Leader Came 'Pretty Close' ". *Washington Post* 20 Jan. 1993.

Ottaway, Marina, et al. "Democratic Mirage in the Middle East". *Critical Mission: Essays on Democracy Promotion*. Ed. Thomas Carothers. Washington, D.C.: Brookings Institution Press, 2002.

Pelletreau, Robert H. *Developments in the Middle East*. 04/10/94 <http://dosfan.lib. uic.edu/ERC/briefing/dispatch/1994/html/Dispatchv5no41.html>.

——. "Symposium: Resurgent Islam in the Middle East". *Middle East Policy* Fall (1994).

——. "Dealing with the Muslim Politics of the Middle East". Address to the Council on Foreign Relations. New York: GPO. 8 May 1996. 7pp. 15/09/02 <http:// dosfan.lib.uic.edu/ERC/bureaus/nea/960508PelletreauMuslim.html>.

——. "Developments in the Middle East". US Department of State Dispatch. 5.41.

Washington, D.C.: GPO. 30 Sept. 1996. 33pp. 13/06/03 <http://dosfan.lib.uic.edu/erc/briefing/dispatch/1996/html/Dispatchv7no40.html>.

Pelletreau, Robert H., et al. "Symposium: Resurgent Islam in the Middle East". *Middle East Policy* 2.2 (1994).

Perle, Richard, et al. "A Clean Break: A New Strategy for Securing the Realm". *A New Israeli Strategy Toward 2000 Study Group*. Jerusalem: Institute for Advanced Strategic and Political Studies. Jun. 1996. 6pp. 12/11/03 <http://www.israeleconomy.org/strat1.htm>.

Perlez, Jane. "Powell Backing Plan to Monitor Mideast Truce". *New York Times* 29 Jun. 2001.

Perlmutter, Amos. "Wishful Thinking About Islamic Fundamentalism". *Washington Post* 19 Jan. 1992.

Perry, William J. "Downing Assessment Task Force". Report of the Assessment of the Khobar Towers Bombing. Washington, D.C.: GPO. 30 Aug. 1996. 2pp. 13/06/03 <http://www.au.af.mil/au/awc/awcgate/khobar/downing/downltr.htm>.

——. *Downing Assessment Task Force*. 18 Sept. 1996. <http://www.defenselink.mil/news/Sep1996/b091996_bt544-96.html>.

Phillips, Kevin P. *American Dynasty: Aristocracy, Fortune, and the Politics of Deceit in the House of Bush*. New York: Viking Penguin, 2004.

Pillar, Paul R. *Terrorism and US Foreign Policy*. Washington, D.C.: Brookings Institution Press, 2001.

Pinto, Maria Do Céu. *Political Islam and the United States: A Study of U.S. Policy Towards Islamist Movements in the Middle East*. New York: Ithaca Press, 1999.

Pipes, Daniel. "There Are No Moderates: Dealing with Fundamentalist Islam". *National Interest* 41. Fall (1995).

——. "The Western Mind of Radical Islam". *The Islamism Debate*. Ed. Martin Kramer. Tel Aviv: The Moshe Dayan Center for Middle Eastern and African Studies, Tel Aviv University, 1997.

Pipes, Daniel, and Patrick Clawson. "Robert H. Pelletreau Jr.: Not Every Fundamentalist Is a Terrorist". *Middle East Quarterly* 2.3 (1995).

Piscatori, James P. "The Turmoil Within: The Struggle for the Future of the Islamic World". *Foreign Affairs Editors' Choice: The Middle East Crisis*. Ed. Gideon Rose. New York: Council on Foreign Relations, 2002.

Podhoretz, Norman. "Neoconservatism: A Eulogy". Washington, D.C., 1996. AEI Press. 10/08/05 2005. <http://www.aei.org/publications/pubID.18103/pub_detail.asp>.

Pollack, Kenneth. "Next Stop Baghdad?". *Foreign Affairs Editors' Choice: The Middle East Crisis*. Ed. Gideon Rose. New York: Council on Foreign Relations, 2002.

Pollack, Kenneth M. *The Threatening Storm: The Case for Invading Iraq*. New York: Random House, 2002.

——. *The Persian Puzzle: The Conflict between Iran and America*. New York: Random House, 2004.

Powell, Colin. "The US–Middle East Partnership Initiative: Building Hope for the Years Ahead". Remarks at the Heritage Foundation. Washington, D.C.: GPO. 12 Dec. 2002. 6pp. 15/01/03 <http://www.state.gov/secretary/former/powell/remarks/2002/15920.htm>.

Prados, Alfred B., and Kenneth Katzman. "Iraq: Former and Recent Military Confrontations with the United States". *CRS Issue Brief for Congress*. (IB94049). Washington, D.C.: Congressional Research Service, Library of Congress, 16 Oct. 2002. 18pp. 04/11/04 <http://fpc.state.gov/documents/organization/ 14836. pdf>.

Quandt, William B. *Peace Process: American Diplomacy and the Arab–Israeli Conflict since 1967*. 2nd ed. Washington, D.C.: Brookings Institution Press, 2001.

——. *Peace Process: American Diplomacy and the Arab–Israeli Conflict since 1967*. 3rd ed. Washington, D.C.: Brookings Institution Press, 2005.

Ramazani, Ruhi K. "The Emerging Arab–Iranian Rapprochement: Towards an Integrated US Policy in the Middle East". *Middle East Policy* 6.1 (1998).

——. "The Shifting Premise of Iran's Foreign Policy: Towards a Democratic Peace?". *Middle East Journal* 52.2 (1998).

Rangwala, Glen. "Blix and Elbaradei Vs Powell". *Middle East Reference* 14 Feb. 2003. 10/11/04 <http://middleeastreference.org.uk/un030214.html>.

Rather, Dan. "President Interviewed by Dan Rather". *CBS* 24 Mar. 1993. 12/07/04 <http://www.clintonfoundation.org/legacy/032493-president-interviewed-by-dan-rather.htm>.

Rhodes, Edward. "The Imperial Logic of Bush's Liberal Agenda". *Survival* 45.1 (2003).

Rice, Condoleezza. "Campaign 2000: Promoting the National Interest". *Foreign Affairs* 79.1 (2000).

——. *Rice Says Values of Islam, Democracy, Human Rights Mutually Reinforcing*. (Washington D.C.: GPO, 4 Dec. 2002) 3pp. 15/09/04 <http://tokyo.usembassy.gov/e/p/tp-soc20021206a2. html>.

Rice, Susan. "We Need a Real Iran Policy". *Washington Post* 30 Dec. 2004.

Ritter, Scott. "An Ineffective Policy toward Baghdad". *International Herald Tribune* 17 Aug. 1999.

Ross, Dennis. "The Hidden Threat in the Middle East". *Wall Street Journal* 24 Jun. 2002.

Roth, Richard A., et al. "U.S. Policy Towards Iran: Time for a Change?". *Middle East Policy* 3.1 (2001).

Rouleau, Eric. "America's Unyielding Policy Towards Iraq". *Foreign Affairs* 74.1 (1995).

Roy, Oliver. "Islamists in Power". *The Islamism Debate*. Ed. Martin Kramer. Tel Aviv: The Moshe Dayan Center for Middle Eastern and African Studies, Tel Aviv University, 1997.

Rubin, Barry. "United States and the Middle East, 1993". *Middle East Review of International Affairs* 1995. 11/12/03 <http://meria.idc.ac.il/us-policy/data1993.html>.

Rycroft, Matthew. "The Secret Downing Street Memo". *Times Online* 1 May 2005. 02/05/05 <www.timesonline.co.uk/article/0,2087-1593607,00.html>.

Sanger, David E. "Bush Looks to UN to Share Burden on Troops in Iraq". *New York Times* 3 Sept. 2003.

Sapiro, Miriam. "Iraq: Shifting Sands of Preemptive Self-Defense". *The American Journal of International Law* 97.3 (2003).

Satloff, Robert. *US Policy Towards Islamism: A Theoretical and Operational Overview.* New York: Council on Foreign Relations, 2000.

Schanzer, Johnathan. "Ansar Al-Islam: Iraq's Al-Qaida Connection". Washington, D.C., 2003. The Washington Institute for Near East Policy. <*http://www.frontpagemag.com/Articles/Printable.asp?ID=5571*>.

Schulze, Kirsten E. *The Arab–Israeli Conflict: Seminar Studies in History.* London: Longman, 1999.

Sciolino, Elaine. "Iranian Leader Says US Move on Oil Deal Wrecked Chances to Improve Ties". *New York Times* 16 May 1995.

Sharansky, Natan, and Ron Dermer. *The Case for Democracy: The Power of Freedom to Overcome Tyranny and Terror.* New York: Public Affairs, 2004.

Shlaim, Avi. *The Iron Wall: Israel and the Arab World.* London: Penguin, 2000.

Sick, Gary. "How Not to Make Iran Policy". *MEES* 38.31 (1995).

——. "The United States and Iran: Truth and Consequences". *Contention* 5.2 (1996).

——. "Rethinking Dual Containment". *Survival* 40.1 (1998).

——. "US Policy in the Gulf: Objectives and Purpose". *Managing New Developments in the Gulf.* Ed. Rosemary Hollis. London: Royal Institute for International Affairs, 2000.

Simons, Geoff. *Imposing Economic Sanctions: Legal Remedy or Genocidal Tool?* London: Pluto, 1999.

——. *Targeting Iraq: Sanctions and Bombing in US Policy.* London: Saqi Books, 2002.

Singer, J. David. "The Level of Analysis Problem in International Relations". *International Politics and Foreign Policy.* Ed. James N. Rosenau. 2nd ed. New York: Free Press, 1969.

Skidmore, David. "Understanding the Unilateralist Turn in US Foreign Policy". *Foreign Policy Analysis* 2 (2005).

Slavin, Barbara. "UNSCOM Unlikely to Return to Iraq". *USA Today* 21 Dec. 1998.

Slocombe, Walter B. "Force, Pre-Emption and Legitimacy". *Survival* 45.1 (2003).

Smith, Steve. "Perspectives on the Foreign Policy System: Bureaucratic Politics Approaches". *Understanding Foreign Policy: The Foreign Policy Systems Approach.* Eds. Michael Clarke and Brian White. Aldershot: Elgar, 1989.

Snyder, Robert. *The United States and Iran: Analysing the Structural Impediments to a Rapprochement.* The Emirates Occasional Paper. Vol. 32. Abu Dhabi: Emirates Center for Strategic Studies and Research, 2001.

——. *The United States and Iran: Analysing the Structural Impediments to a Rapprochement.* Abu Dhabi: Emirates Center for Strategic Studies and Research, 2001.

Snyder, Robert, et al. "Decision Making Approach to the Study of Foreign Policy". *International Politics and Foreign Policy.* Ed. James N. Rosenau. New York: The Free Press, 1969.

Stephanopoulos, George. *All Too Human: A Political Education*. London: Hutchinson, 1999.

Suskind, Ron. *The Price of Loyalty: George W. Bush, the White House, and the Education of Paul O'Neill*. New York: Simon & Schuster, 2004.

Taft, William H. "The Legal Basis for Preemption". Roundtable on Old Rules, New Threats. Washington, D.C.: Council on Foreign Relations. 18 Nov. 2002. 3pp. 12/11/04 <*http://www.cfr.org/pub5250/william_h_taft_iv/the_legal_basis_for_preemption.php*>.

Tanter, Raymond. *Rogue Regimes: Terrorism and Proliferation*. Basingstoke: Macmillan, 1999.

Tenet, George J. "CIA Letter to Senate on Baghdad's Intentions". *New York Times Online* 9 Oct. 2002. 10/10/02 <*www.nytimes.com/2002/10/09/international/09TTEX.html*>.

Tetlock, Philip E., and Charles B. McGuire. "Cognitive Perspectives on Foreign Policy". *American Foreign Policy: Theoretical Essays*. Ed. G. John Ikenberry. 5th ed. New York: Georgetown University, 2005.

Thomas, Ewan, et al. "How the CIA's Secret War in Iraq Turned into Utter Fiasco". *Newsweek* 23 Mar. 1998.

Tibi, Bassam. *The Challenge of Fundamentalism: Political Islam and the New World Order*. Berkeley: University of California Press, 2002.

Tuchman, Barbara W. *The Guns of August*. New York: Ballantine Books, 1994.

Tucker, David. "Combating International Terrorism". *The Terrorism Threat and US Governmental Response: Operational and Organisational Factors*. Eds. James M. Smith and William C. Thomas. Colorado: USAF Institute for National Security Studies, 2001.

Tyler, Patrick E. "Lone Superpower Plan: Ammunition for Critics". *New York Times* 10 Mar. 1992.

——. "US Strategy Plan Calls for Insuring No Rivals Develop". *New York Times* 8 Mar. 1992.

United Kingdom. Mission to the United Nations. *Explanation of Vote by Jeremy Greenstock*. (New York: United Nations, 8 Nov. 2002) 1pp. 12/07/03 <*http://www.un.org/webcast/unitedkingdom110802.htm*>.

——. 10 Downing Street. *Iraq's Weapons of Mass Destruction: The Assessment of the British Government*. (ID114567). (London: The Stationery Office, 24 Sep. 2002) 55pp. 20/10/03 <*http://www.number-10.gov.uk/output/Page271.asp*>.

——. House of Commons. *Report of the Inquiry into the Circumstances Surrounding the Death of Dr David Kelly C.M.G.* (HC247). (London: The Stationery Office, 28 Jan. 2004) 473sect. 25/10/04 <*http://www.the-hutton-inquiry.org.uk/content/report/*>.

United Nations Development Programme. *The Arab Human Development Report 2004: Towards Freedom in the Arab World*. New York: United Nations Development Programme, Regional Bureau for Arab States, 2004.

—. UNSCOM. *First Report by the Executive Chairman of the Special Commission Pursuant to the Implementation Security Council Resolution 687 (1991).* (S/23165). (New York: United Nations, 25 Oct. 1991) 29pp. 18/07/02 <*http://www.iraqwatch. org/un/UNSCOM/687/s23165.htm*>.

—. International Atomic Agency. *First Semi-Annual Report on the Implementation of UNSCR 687.* (S/23295). (Vienna: IAEA, 5 Dec. 1991) 6pp. 18/07/02 <*http:// www.iraqwatch.org/un/IAEA/s-23295.htm*>.

—. UNSCOM. *Fourth Report by the Executive Chairman of the Special Commission Pursuant to the Implementation Security Council Resolution 687 (1991).* (S/24984). (New York: United Nations, 17 Dec. 1992) 22pp. 18/07/04 <*http://www. iraqwatch. org/un/UNSCOM/687/s-24984.htm*>.

—. Secretariat. *Third Report under UNSCR 715 by the Secretary-General on the Activities of the Special Commission.* (S/25620). (New York: United Nations, 19 Apr. 1993) 8pp. 12/05/03 <*http://www.iraqwatch.org/un/UNSCOM/715/s25620. pdf*>.

—. UNSCOM and IAEA. *Interview Transcript with Hussein Kamel in Amman.* Sensitive classification note for file. (New York: United Nations, 22 Aug. 1995) 15pp. 12/07/03 <*http://www.casi.org.uk/info/unscom950822.pdf*>.

—. UNSCOM. *Ninth Report by the Executive Chairman of the Special Commission Pursuant to the Implementation Security Council Resolution 687 (1991).* (S/1995/ 494). (New York: United Nations, 20 Jun. 1995) 10pp. 18/07/03 <*http://www. iraqwatch.org/un/UNSCOM/687/s-1995-0494.htm*>.

—. Secretariat. *Seventh Report under UNSCR 715 by the Secretary-General on the Activities of the Special Commission.* (S/1995/284). (New York: United Nations, 10 Apr. 1995) 36pp. 12/08/03 <*http://www.iraqwatch.org/un/UNSCOM/715/ s-1995-284.htm*>.

—. Secretariat. *Memorandum of Understanding between the Secretariat of the United Nations and the Government of Iraq on the Implementation of Security Council Resolution 986 (1995).* (S/1996/356). (New York: United Nations, 20 May 1996) 10pp. 04/11/04 <*http://www.meij.or.jp/text/Gulf%20War/mouunirq1996. htm*>.

—. UNSCOM. *Fourth Report by the Executive Chairman of the Special Commission Pursuant to the Implementation Security Council Resolution 1051 (1996).* (S/1997/ 774). (New York: United Nations, 6 Oct. 1997) 41pp. 25/09/03 <*http://www. iraqwatch.org/un/UNSCOM/1051/sres97-774.htm*>.

—. Security Council. *United Nations Security Council Statement on Iraq.* (New York: United Nations, 29 Oct. 1997) 2pp. 25/10/03 <*http://www.fas.org/news/iraq/1997/ 10/97102904_npo.html*>.

—. UNSCOM. *UNSCOM Chairman's Letter to the Security Council.* (New York: United Nations, 15 Dec. 1998) 9pp. 12/08/03 <*http://www.iraqwatch.org/un/ UNSCOM/s-1998-1127.htm*>.

—. UNMOVIC. *Unresolved Disarmament Issues: Iraq's Proscribed Weapons Programmes.* (New York: United Nations, 6 Mar. 2003) 175pp. 13/06/04 <*http://www. un.org/Depts/unmovic/documents/6mar.pdf*>.

——. UNMOVIC. *An Update on Inspection*. (New York: United Nations, 27 Jan. 2003) 9pp. 19/06/04 *<http://www.un.org/Depts/unmovic/Bx27.htm>*.

United States. House. Foreign Affairs Committee. Subcommittee on Europe and the Middle East. *Developments in the Middle East*. 105th Cong., 2nd. Sess. (Washington, D.C.: GPO, 01 Mar. 1994)

——. Senate. *Comprehensive Iran Sanctions Act*. 104th Cong, 2nd Sess. (Washington D.C.: GPO, 25 Jan. 1995) 5pp. 12/04/04 *<http://thomas.loc.gov/cgi-bin/query/z?c104: S.277.IS:>*.

——. Department of State. "Daily Press Briefing". Conoco Oil Agreement. (Washington, D.C.: GPO. 7 Mar. 1995) 12pp. 12/09/03 *<http://dosfan.lib.uic.edu/ ERC/briefing/daily_briefings/1995/9503/950307db.html>*.

——. Senate. *Iran Oil Sanctions Act Report*. 104th Cong., 1st Sess. (Washington, D.C.: GPO, 15 Dec. 1995) 9pp. 12/03/03 *<http://thomas.loc.gov/cgi-bin/cpquery/ T?&report=sr187&dbname=cp104&>*.

——. President of the United States. *A National Security Strategy of Engagement and Enlargement*. (Washington, D.C.: GPO, Feb. 1995) 41pp. 12/06/02 *<http:// www.whitehouse.gov/>*.

——. Department of Defence. *United States Security Strategy for the Middle East*. (Washington, D.C.: GPO, 3 May 1995) 48pp. 15/06/03 *<http://www.defenselink. mil/policy/isa/nesa/mideast.html>*.

——. Senate. *Condemning Iraq's Threat to International Peace and Security*. Cong. 105, 2nd Sess., Res 711988. (Washington, D.C.: GPO, 21 Jan. 1998) 2pp. 17/12/03 *<http://weblog.theviewfromthecore.com/2004_02/ind_003148.html>*.

——. House. *Iraq Liberation Act of 1998*. H.R. 466, P.L. 105-338. (Washington, D.C.: GPO, 31 Oct. 1998) 8pp. 17/12/03 *<http://www.iraqwatch.org/government/US/ Legislation/ILA.htm>*.

——. President of the United States. *A National Security Strategy for a New Century*. (Washington, D.C.: GPO, Oct. 1998) 35pp. 15/06/03 *<http://www.whitehouse. gov/>*.

——. Congress. *Rumsfeld Commission Report*. Executive Summary of the Commission to Assess the Ballistic Missile Threat to the United States. (Washington, D.C.: Brookings, 15 Jul. 1998) 24pp. 12/01/04 *<http://www.brookings.edu/fp/research/ areas/nmd/rumsfeld98.htm>*.

——. Department of State. *Saddam Hussein's Iraq*. (Washington, D.C.: GPO, 1999)

——. House. *Foreign Operations, Export Financing, and Related Programs Appropriations Act*. H.R. 4811, P.L. 106–429. (Washington, D.C.: GPO, 19 Dec. 2000) 45pp. 17/09/03 *<http://clinton4.nara.gov/OMB/legislative/7day/12-19-00.pdf>*.

——. Department of State. *Briefing En Route to Cairo, Egypt*. 23 Feb. 2001. 3pp. 23/08/04 *<www.state.gov/secretary/rm/2001/931.html>*.

——. Department of Defence. *Quadrennial Defense Review Report*. (Washington, D.C.: GPO, 30 Sep. 2001) 79pp. 20/11/02 *<www.defenselink.mil/pubs/qdr2001.pdf>*.

——. House. Foreign Affairs Committee. Subcommittee on Europe and the Middle

East. *US Policy Towards the Palestinians.* 107th Cong., 1st Sess. (Washington, D.C.: GPO, 26 Jul. 2001) 43pp. 11/12/03 <*http://commdocs.house.gov/committees/intlrel/hfa74233.000/hfa74233_0.htm*>.

——. House. Foreign Affairs Committee. Subcommittee on Europe and the Middle East. *US Policy Towards the Palestinians, Part 2.* 107th Cong., 1st. Sess. (Washington, D.C.: GPO, 25 Sep. 2001) 43pp. 11/12/03 <*http://commdocs.house.gov/committees/intlrel/hfa74233.000/hfa74233_1.HTM*>.

——. House. *Authorization for the Use of Force against Iraq.* H.R. 114, P.L. 102–1. (Washington, D.C.: GPO, 10 Oct. 2002) 8pp. 17/12/03 <*http://www. iraqwatch. org/government/US/Legislation/ILA.htm*>.

——. Mission to the United Nations. *Explanation of Vote by Ambassador John D. Negroponte.* (New York: United States, GPO, 8 Nov. 2002) 2pp. 12 Jul 2003 <*http://www.un.int/usa/02print_187.htm*>.

——. Department of State. *Fact Sheet: Middle East Peace Process.* (Washington, D.C.: GPO, 7 Aug. 2002) 102pp. 10/01/02 <*http://dosfan.lib.uic.edu/ERC/briefing/ dispatch/1994/html/Dispatchv5Sup07.html*>.

——. President of the United States. *The National Security Strategy of the United States of America.* (Washington, D.C.: GPO, Sep. 2002) 35pp. 20/11/02 <*http://www. whitehouse.gov/response/index.html*>.

——. President of the United States. *National Security Strategy to Combat Weapons of Mass Destruction.* (Washington, D.C.: GPO, Dec. 2002) 9pp. 20/11/02 <*www. whitehouse.gov/news/ releases/2002/12/WMDStrategy.pdf*>.

United States. Department of State. *Powell Says Arafat Needs to Acknowledge Karine A Incident.* (2002: United States Mission to the European Union, 13 Apr. 2002) 6pp. 12/05/03 <*http://www.useu.be/Categories/GlobalAffairs/Jan2502PowellArafatKarine. html*>.

United States. Senate. Committee on Foreign Relations. *Threats, Responses and Regional Considerations Surrounding Iraq.* 107th Cong. 2nd Sess. (Washington, D.C.: GPO, 31 Jul. 2002) 279pp. 16/06/03 <*http://frwebgate.access.gpo.gov/ cgi-bin/getdoc.cgi?dbname=107_senate_hearings&docid=f:81697.pdf*>.

——. President of the United States. *National Strategy for Combating Terrorism.* (Washington, D.C.: GPO, Feb. 2003) 32pp. 20/11/02 <*http://www.whitehouse. gov/response/index.html*>.

——. White House. "President Bush Meets with Prime Minister Blair". (Washington, D.C.: GPO. 31 Jan. 2003) 4pp. 12/09/03 <*http://www.whitehouse.gov/news/ releases/2003/01/20030131-23.html*>.

——. National Commission on the Terrorist Attacks upon the United States. *The 9/11 Commission Report: The Full Final Report of the National Commission on Terrorist Attacks upon the United States.* (Washington, D.C.: GPO, 2004) 567pp. 12/01/05 <*http://www.9-11commission.gov/report/index.htm*>.

——. Commission on the Intelligence Capabilities of the United States Regarding Weapons of Mass Destruction. *Commission on the Intelligence Capabilities of the*

United States Regarding Weapons of Mass Destruction: Report to the President. (Washington, D.C.: GPO, 2005) 618pp. 04/04/05 <*http://www.wmd.gov/report/*>.

——. CIA. *The War on Terrorism: Frequently Asked Questions.* (Washington, D.C.: GPO, 2005) 2pp. 20/11/02 <*http://www.cia.gov/terrorism/faqs.html*>.

United States, et al. *A Performance-Based Road Map to a Permanent Two-State Solution to the Arab–Israeli Conflict.* 1 May 2003. 6pp. 25/09/03 <*http://www.mideastweb.org/quartetrm3.htm*>.

Urban, Mark. *War in Afghanistan.* London: Macmillan, 1988.

Vertzberger, Yaacov. *The World in Their Minds: Information Processing, Cognition and Perception in Foreign Policy Decisionmaking.* Stanford: Stanford University Press, 1990.

Vogler, John. "Perspectives on the Foreign Policy System: Psychological Approaches". *Understanding Foreign Policy: The Foreign Policy Systems Approach.* Eds. Michael Clarke and Brian White. Aldershot: Elgar, 1989.

Voll, John O. *Islam: Continuity and Change in the Modern World.* 2nd ed. Syracuse: Syracuse University Press, 1994.

Waltz, Kenneth N. *The Spread of Nuclear Weapons: More May Be Better.* Adelphi Papers, No. 171. London: International Institute for Strategic Studies, 1981.

——. *Man, the State, and War: A Theoretical Analysis.* New York: Columbia University Press, 2001.

——. "Anarchic Orders and Balances of Power". *American Foreign Policy: Theoretical Essays.* Ed. G. John Ikenberry. 5th ed. New York: Georgetown University, 2005.

Weisman, Steven R., and Felicity Barringer. "US Abandons Idea of Bigger UN Role in Iraq Occupation". *New York Times* 19 Aug. 2003.

Wittes, Tamara C., and Sarah Yerkes, E. "The Middle East Partnership Initiative: Progress, Problems, and Prospects". *Saban Center Middle East Memo.* (Issue 5). Washington, D.C.: Brookings Institution Press, 29 Nov. 2004. 6pp. 12/12/04 <*www.brook.edu/views/op-ed/fellows/wittes20041129.htm*>.

Woodward, Bob. *Bush at War.* New York: Simon & Schuster, 2002.

——. *Plan of Attack.* New York: Simon & Schuster, 2004.

Wright, Steven M., et al. "Briefing Paper: US and Iran on a Confrontational Course". Helsinki: Finnish Institute for International Affairs. 8th March 2005. <*http://www.upi-fiia.fi/julkaisut/muut/Briefing%20Paper%208%20March% 202005.pdf*>.

Wurmser, David. *Tyranny's Ally: America's Failure to Defeat Saddam Hussein.* Washington, D.C.: AEI Press, 1999.

Index

Note: Page numbers under US Presidents include references to their administrations.